Co-ordinating Primary Language and Literacy: The Subject Leader's Handbook

Co-ordinating Primary Language and Literacy:

The Subject Leader's Handbook

Guy Merchant and Jackie Marsh

P·C·P
Paul Chapman
Publishing Ltd

Paul Chapman Publishing Ltd
A SAGE Publications Company
6 Bonhill Street
London EC2A 4PU

British Library Cataloguing in Publication Data

Merchant, Guy
  Co-ordinating primary language and literacy: the subject
  leaders' handbook
  1. Language arts (Elementary) 2. Literacy 3. Education
  (Elementary) – Curricula
  I. Title II. Marsh, Jackie
  372.6'043

  ISBN 1 85396 370 4

Typeset by PDQ, Staffordshire
Printed and bound in Great Britain

A B C D E F G H   4 3 2 1 0 9 8

Contents

For Julie, Angela, Lesley, Hannah, Ruth and Emma

Notes on the Authors

Guy Merchant and Jackie Marsh lecture in education at Sheffield Hallam University.

Guy Merchant has worked extensively in primary schools and higher education. He has conducted research in literacy and led curriculum development projects. As Head of the Centre for English in Education, he co-ordinates the work of colleagues involved in initial and in-service education at both primary and secondary levels. He is well-known in the region as a provider of high quality training for primary English co-ordinators.

Jackie Marsh has worked for a number of years in primary schools in Sheffield where she is highly regarded as an inspiring practitioner. In 1995, she joined the Centre for English in Education where she has made a major contribution to initial and in-service training. Her research interests are the development of literacy in the early years and the uses of popular culture in the primary curriculum.

Acknowledgements

We would like to express our appreciation to all those who have contributed to this book. In particular, our thanks go to Angela Hodgson whose help and support in the early stages was invaluable. We have drawn on the hard work and goodwill of many teachers and co-ordinators in the region – especially those who have participated in our Diploma in Primary English – their help is greatly appreciated. We are also indebted to the staff and children of Sharrow Nursery and Infant School as well as Huw Thomas and his colleagues at Springfield Junior, Infant and Nursery School. Keith Adams and Maggie Lovatt of Pipworth Junior School have been enormously helpful in sharing their literacy plans with us. Jean Penchion provided us with useful insights into the inspection process. We also appreciate the hard work of Debbie Francis of Pye Bank Nursery and Infant School and the staff of Park Hill Primary School. Carol Taylor, the director of the Read On–Write Away strategy in Derbyshire, provided us with useful information on family literacy and Val Lyons of West Jesmond Primary School has kindly allowed us to use her action plans for the introduction of the literacy hour. Finally, our thanks go to Chris Plant and Do Hulse, who are literacy consultants working for the National Literacy Project in Sheffield and have helped us to keep abreast with the latest developments.

Guy Merchant and Jackie Marsh

Introduction

English occupies a central position in the primary school curriculum. It is through the medium of English that we develop children's oracy and literacy skills and these are, of course, fundamental tools for lifelong learning. As a subject in its own right, English introduces children to the enjoyment and study of texts, develops an understanding of the language system and how it works, and through a variety of forms of writing, poetry and drama helps children to experience and explore creativity. There is a long tradition of good primary practice in each of these areas and also plenty of new thinking and research. Drawing together the very best of practice in English teaching is important for all schools concerned with providing children with the opportunities of a good education. Leadership, management and co-ordination of the English curriculum are therefore crucial. This book addresses these issues by drawing on the experiences of subject co-ordinators and placing them in the wider context of curriculum development in the primary school.

We have several audiences in mind in writing this book. First and foremost are those who are already engaged in leadership roles in primary English. Language co-ordinators, literacy co-ordinators, and English subject leaders will find important background information as well as practical guidance. Our book will also be useful to those who work *with* co-ordinators – headteachers, INSET providers, consultants and advisory teams. At a time of significant development, with the adoption of the National Literacy Strategy (Literacy Task Force, 1997), we feel that it is crucially important that colleagues consider both the process and management of change as well as curriculum content and delivery. In keeping with this, we have attempted to address the difficult issues of managing real and meaningful change in the English curriculum. Becoming familiar with these issues will also be helpful to those who are planning to take on the subject leadership role. This includes students in training and practising teachers interested in career development.

Although our main focus is the development of primary English, we do not give a detailed view of the content of the curriculum, choosing instead to devote our attention to the task of co-ordination. This is because we feel that the increased demands made upon the English subject leader are such that there is now a need for a text which deals specifically with the tasks involved in co-ordinating English. However, the examples, interviews and case studies which we draw upon *are* concerned with key issues in language and literacy. Further reading on these key issues may be a necessary development for some co-ordinators. For this reason we have included an annotated bibliography at the end of the book which outlines useful texts in the field of primary oracy and literacy.

In this book, we provide a comprehensive view of the roles and responsibilities of the English co-ordinator. However, the model of development presented is not sequential. We therefore anticipate that some readers may have quite specific concerns and will wish to consult the chapters of immediate relevance first. With this in mind we have tried to ensure that chapters can stand alone and we provide easy cross-references to other sections in the book.

Terminology

Teachers with responsibility for this aspect of the primary curriculum are referred to by a variety of different terms. Most colleagues in the role describe themselves as 'language' or 'English co-ordinators', although with the implementation of the National Literacy Strategy (Literacy Task Force, 1997) schools will also need to identify 'literacy co-ordinators'. The description favoured by the Teacher Training Agency is that of 'subject leader' (TTA, 1997b). We use these terms interchangeably throughout the book whilst, at the same time, acknowledging that they may signal important differences in the way in which the role is perceived.

The term 'co-ordinator' fits well with the ethos of consensus and collegiality which we advocate in this book, whereas colleagues may find that the label 'subject leader' seems rather alien to the working practices of many primary schools. However, we feel that the roles and responsibilities are the same whatever the description and include elements of both co-ordination and leadership.

Describing the role in terms of 'English', 'language' or 'literacy' is also subject to some debate. The term 'language co-ordinator' has the longest history – being a role first advocated in the Bullock Report (1975), where the description referred to both the subject of English and the cross-curricular skills of oracy and literacy. This broad view also recognises the importance of the first or home language of bilingual children and, for this reason, teachers working in multilingual settings may still feel that the idea of a 'language co-ordinator' is more appropriate. The more subject-focused curriculum that has followed the introduction of the Education Reform Act 1988 has led to an increased recognition of English as a subject and this has resulted in a wider use of the term

'English co-ordinator'. The recent emphasis on raising standards in literacy suggests further change and the possibility of a narrowing focus for the co-ordinator working in this area. However, it must also be acknowledged that the term 'literacy' is itself difficult to define. Some writers prefer a broad description of literacy. For example, Barton suggests that literacy is 'a set of social practices associated with particular symbol systems and their related technologies' (Barton, 1994, p. 32) and Street (1997) points to the diversity of different kinds of literacy practices. The suggestion that the current National Literacy Project Framework (National Literacy Project, 1997) may be a blueprint for the next version of English in the National Curriculum has implications for how literacy may be defined within the education system. At the time of writing, it is quite difficult to predict how the roles and responsibilities of a literacy co-ordinator may evolve. However, we are confident that the approach we adopt and the advice we give will remain relevant.

We have also given careful consideration to assumptions that can be made about the gender of primary school teachers, co-ordinators and managers. We have decided to refer to the co-ordinator in the female gender on the basis that the majority of co-ordinators we work with are women. We do not wish to exclude male co-ordinators but have favoured the use of 'she' and 'her' except where this does not apply to an interviewee or a colleague in a case study. We have, rather more arbitrarily, decided to refer to the individual pupil as male.

Some underlying principles

Our ideas about the co-ordination of English teaching draw on perspectives and beliefs about the change process that are well established in the literature on curriculum development and school improvement. We make reference to this literature at various points during the text. Some of the underlying principles which inform our approach are summarised in the following section.

We believe that successful curriculum co-ordination involves an understanding of the importance of social processes in the institutional context of the school. The quality of social interaction between colleagues shows in the ways in which they work together, reflect and discuss school practice. This interpersonal context is central to policy development and curriculum change. Curriculum co-ordination will be at its most productive when it takes place in a school climate which values honest and open discussion and where the leadership style is positive and encourages development. Change needs to be owned by all the people involved in the process if it is to succeed. Therefore we advocate, throughout the book, a collegiate approach to curriculum development which builds upon the trust developed in this approach to interpersonal relationships.

Change is most likely to be sustained when it is clearly focused on the practical needs and concerns of the school. The co-ordinator will need to have a clear and informed view of primary English teaching in order to encourage teaching strategies that are appropriate to the school community. In this respect we support the approach of school-focused curriculum development. However, schools do not operate in a vacuum and are subject to increasing external pressure. We believe that effective schools will own change by interpreting external pressure in the light of their own internally agreed values and needs.

Professional dialogue about content, delivery and progression in the English curriculum is central to the process of whole-school development, but this dialogue needs to be structured by the co-ordinator if it is to result in improvements in classroom teaching. Our model of curriculum development (see Figure 1) provides you with a structure in which to work. Leading this development process is by no means an easy task, yet without it school performance and pupil achievement will suffer.

A model of curriculum development

This book is based on a simple cyclical model of curriculum development (Figure 1). The model is based on the sort of activities that co-ordinators we have worked with are engaged in. It does not assume that you will necessarily start at a given point and work through the sequence, but allows you to identify where you are within the cycle of events and which of the subsequent stages may be useful to move to next.

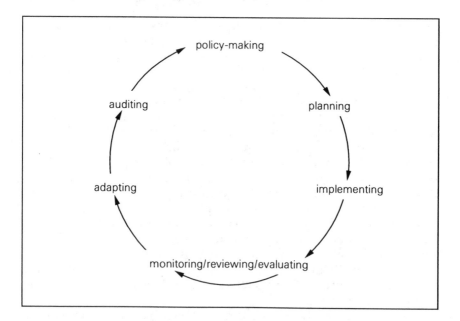

Figure 1.   Curriculum development model

Here we will provide a brief description of each phase. More detail will be found in the chapters that follow.

1. Policy-making

At this stage you are considering your philosophy of English teaching, your intentions and the classroom approaches that you support. School policy-making is shaped by the interplay of external and internal influences. The emphasis given to a dedicated hour of literacy teaching (DFEE, 1997) is an example of a currently powerful external influence. Your own school's commitment to developing the oral language skills of bilingual pupils may be a response to important local conditions and constitutes a strong internal influence on policy-making. We will be describing policy-making as a process (Chapter 4) and although we look at the design and content of school English policies we stress the importance of professional dialogue about policy.

2. Planning

This stage is important in turning your intentions into practical and achievable goals. Planning is referred to at various points in this book. Initially we address the issues of action planning and target setting. We look at various kinds of action planning including the design of a schools literacy strategy (Chapter 3). Later on we look at the processes of curriculum planning. Long-, medium- and short-term planning are addressed in Chapter 5. Here again we will be giving emphasis to the planning process as well as exploring different planning formats.

3. Implementing

This is where your plans are put into operation – it is one of the most complex elements in the change process. There would appear to be a strong element of unpredictability at this stage. Teachers and co-ordinators we have worked with often refer to this. Colleagues who were 'lukewarm' about a new approach can turn into enthusiastic advocates after trying it out; enthusiastic supporters can turn into cynics overnight! Successful implementation depends upon sensitive support. Both human and resource support are important and can be located both within the school context and externally. Again professional dialogue is important. We also suggest that there is an important distinction between initial implementation (trying out something new) and the sustained implementation that is sometimes referred to as 'adoption' (incorporating new ideas into your classroom practice).

4. Monitoring and evaluating

In most primary schools, co-ordinators have precious little non-contact time. Therefore there is limited scope for monitoring and evaluating the practice of colleagues. Recognition that this is an important part of the role has been slow to emerge. However, the Annual OFSTED Report (1995–96) underlined the fact that co-ordinators have:

> most positive impact where they are able to evaluate and feed back advice on the subject by looking at pupils' work, visiting colleagues' classes and helping with their planning.
>
> (OFSTED, 1997)

In considering monitoring and evaluation we distinguish between the two terms by referring to monitoring as an information-gathering process – finding out what is going on – and evaluation as the process of arriving at a judgement on the effectiveness of your action. From this point of view, other sources of information such as parental feedback, inspection reports and pupil assessment are considered in the evaluation process.

5. Adapting

This stage is concerned with changing your approaches, your classroom organisation or learning activities in the light of first-hand experience; in other words acting on what has been found through monitoring and evaluation. We do not enter into a detailed discussion of this process, working on the assumption that work at this stage is broadly similar to the implementation. Usually, adapting involves 'fine tuning' and does not require the level of support associated with implementation.

6. Auditing

This stage is simply a fact-finding exercise and is intended to provide the co-ordinator with an overall picture of what is going on in the English curriculum as a whole or in a certain aspect of it. Unlike monitoring, auditing is not usually tied into a specific innovation but may be the first stage in assessing the need for change in policy and practice. Therefore, in this book we look at auditing and action planning together (Chapter 3). This model is used in the National Literacy Project and we show an example of one project school's literacy strategy in the chapter.

The organisation of the book

In Chapter 1, we explore issues surrounding the role and responsibilities of the English subject leader. We begin by looking at the application process for such a post, before moving on to looking at core responsibilities. The personal skills which you will need to develop and the sort of job description that you will work to are also discussed.

Chapter 2 addresses the important topic of professional and curricular change. Here we look at the fundamental characteristics of educational change and the English co-ordinator's role in planning and managing the change process. We also look at different kinds of change and the influences that shape the primary English curriculum. This is followed by advice on the planning process. Chapter 3 concentrates on auditing and action planning and takes a step-by-step approach leading from the identification of current classroom practice to formulating priorities and targets for future action.

In Chapter 4 we look at the task of policy-making, paying attention first to the kind of developmental work with colleagues that is needed and then to formats for the design of a school language policy. Examples of policy documents are included in this chapter. We then move on in Chapter 5 to a consideration of the key issues in developing and writing a scheme of work for English. Here we include examples of planning done by teachers involved in the National Literacy Project (NLP, 1997). We also show alternative approaches to curriculum planning.

We then turn to the critical stage of turning policy and planning into classroom practice. Chapter 6 considers implementation and the subject leader's role in supporting, monitoring and evaluating new developments in the English curriculum. Chapter 7 looks at the skills needed to work with colleagues in developing more formal kinds of professional dialogue. This involves a close examination of how to plan and conduct staff meetings and training days as well as giving some consideration to liaison with external INSET providers.

The role of the co-ordinator with respect to external initiatives is considered in Chapter 8. This chapter includes an interview with a co-ordinator involved in the work of the National Literacy Project. We also consider the liaison and development work in more localised development projects.

We discuss the whole-school management of assessment, recording and reporting in Chapter 9. This chapter includes practical guidance on developing assessment in English and includes examples of formats for record-keeping. Here we also consider broader issues of accountability and comparative data on school performance. Chapter 10 addresses the issue of subject knowledge and includes an exploration of the kind of knowledge about English that newly qualified teachers are now expected to have. We go on to consider areas of subject knowledge which an English co-ordinator will wish to develop.

Chapter 11 explores the area of building partnerships with parents. Here we examine some recent initiatives and underline the importance of family involvement in children's literacy development. Chapter 12 looks at issues concerned with resourcing the English curriculum and provides practical guidance for the subject leader. Chapter 13 gives a detailed view of the inspection process from the co-ordinator's point of view. The conclusion draws together the themes of the book and gives advice to co-ordinators concerning how to set priorities and how to manage their time effectively.

Throughout the book we use practical examples that draw on case studies of curriculum development work in English. This gives the reader a sense of what other subject co-ordinators have done. However, because we concentrate on leadership and co-ordination we have decided not to provide specific detail on the subject content. At the end of the book we have included an annotated bibliography which will help guide co-ordinators to further reading in aspects of the English curriculum.

1

The Roles and Responsibilities of the Co-ordinator

The roles and responsibilities of the English co-ordinator are many and varied. Throughout the book, we address specific issues relating to each of these roles and responsibilities. In this chapter, we take a broad look at the nature of the post and suggest that a subject leader needs to be clear about which of the many potential tasks are to be included in a job description. We realise that not all of our readers will be English subject leaders already in post. We therefore begin by giving advice on how to apply for the post of English co-ordinator in school.

Applying for the post

If you are applying for a job at a new school and the post includes the responsibility of leading the English curriculum, it is a good idea to prepare yourself thoroughly. First, you will need to try and find out as much as you can about the school's current policy and practice before writing the letter of application. You can do this in a number of ways. The most useful approach is to visit the school. As you are shown around, you can then ask questions which will enable you to glean information about the school's needs, such as: What are the school's priorities in the development of English? When were the school's English policies and schemes last reviewed? What are the school's strengths in English? Are there particular staff training needs in English?

If the head is showing a large group around or looks rather harassed, you may need to ask fewer and less intensive questions. You do not want to cause unnecessary irritation before you apply. You can gather information simply from looking around in a focused way. We suggest you look at the areas listed in Figure 1.1.

Of course, if you are lucky enough to be able to visit a school during the day, you will gain much more information about how the teaching of English is approached. For example, you may be able to see the children engaged in literacy activities throughout the school and ascertain whether or not they are interested and involved in their work. You may

- Are there examples of interesting work in English on display?
- Are there a range of forms of writing on display?
- Is ICT work in English on display?
- Does the school have a developmental approach to writing?
- Are there attractive book areas in each classroom?
- Is there a range of fiction and non-fiction books on display?
- Are books attractively arranged?
- Are there any collections of books by topic, or by a particular author?
- Does the school have many big books or group reading sets?
- Are there any notices/signs around which encourage reading?
- Are there writing areas in each classroom?
- Are writing resources easily available to children?
- Are there interesting structured role-play areas? Do they incorporate literacy materials?
- Are there multilingual signs and notices around? Dual-text books?
- Are there listening centres in each classroom?
- Are there central literacy displays?
- Does the school have a library? Does it look fresh and inviting?

Figure 1.1.　　Observing a school on a visit

get a picture of how support staff are used in the literacy curriculum or whether parental involvement is widespread. Of course, it is not possible to make any hard and fast judgements about what you see in a short visit, but it can be enough to 'soak up the atmosphere' and get a broad picture of what the school would be like to work in.

A second source of information is the school's OFSTED report. OFSTED reports can be viewed on the OFSTED database on the World Wide Web. Of course, these will only provide a partial view of the school's approaches to English, but they may well provide information about key targets for improvement. Alternatively, you may be able to obtain more 'unofficial' views from colleagues on an informal basis. You will need to be cautious and discreet when using this sort of information!

Once you have formed a picture of the school's needs in English, you can draft an appropriate letter of application. The letter should, of course, address the areas you have identified as in need of development but you will also want to include a good indication of your own beliefs and values. You should not refer directly to the fact that you think the school *needs* to develop in specific areas but rather indicate what skills and experience you have in that area. For example, if on your initial visit you noticed that the school did not have very attractive book areas and that it appeared to be under-resourced in terms of books, you may write:

> I believe that, in order to raise standards in reading, schools need to ensure that they are providing a range of high quality texts that children are attracted to. I have extensive experience in choosing and ordering texts for use across the primary range and have developed a thorough knowledge of children's literature. I have worked with staff in my present post, through staff meetings, on developing stimulating and interactive book areas. Having had experience of raising extra funding for books through contacts with local businesses, I am aware of the need to be creative with limited resources.

If you do get called for interview, it is worth developing a small portfolio which provides evidence of your work in English. This could include items such as photographs of book corners and writing areas in your classroom or displays of children's work in English. You might also wish to include examples of children's work and policy documents, schemes of work, or booklets which you have been involved in producing.

During the interview, you need to emphasise both your experience and expertise in the teaching of English and your interpersonal skills – your understanding of how to work with others to achieve change. As we see throughout this book, an essential element of being a co-ordinator is managing people effectively. If you are appointed, we would recommend that you hold an audit of the language curriculum in your first term in order to develop an in-depth understanding of where the school is and what it needs. We deal with this process in Chapter 3.

It may be the case that the post of English subject leader arises in the school in which you are already working, as an internal vacancy. Perhaps the existing co-ordinator has moved to another school or has retired. You will obviously know a great deal already about the nature of the provision for English in the school. It will be fair to assume that you will have a good idea about what the school needs and how the English curriculum can be developed further. In your letter of application for the post, you need to be explicit about what you think is needed and how you plan to address those areas. You can afford to be much more upfront about this than if you were applying to another school. Of course, you do not want to go to town and detail every single area in which the English curriculum needs developing. Choose what you consider to be the priority areas. You also need to be positive about your predecessor's achievements, otherwise your letter may read as if you are critical of everything that has gone on before. We include an example of a letter of application below in order to demonstrate the way in which such applications need to meet the school's needs. A case study of the school is provided in order to contextualise the example.

Case study: Mill Street School

Mill Street School is an inner-city, multi-ethnic primary school which has 360 pupils in 12 classes. In a recent OFSTED inspection, its achievements were in line with national standards in English. However, it was felt that the writing curriculum was rather narrow, with too much emphasis on transcription at the expense of the development of compositional skills. Inspectors also commented on the limited range of writing forms used and the lack of opportunities for children to plan and draft their work, particularly at Key Stage 2. There are a number of staff who have been working in the school for many years and who take a rather formal approach to the teaching of literacy. The head is newly appointed and wants to move things on.

If you were already working in the school and wanted to apply for the post of English co-ordinator, you would need to write an application which demonstrated how you were going to approach the role. In this case, you may want to emphasise your plans for the writing curriculum.

Dear Head

I wish to apply for the role of English co-ordinator. I feel that I have a number of relevant skills which are necessary for this role. I have particular experience and expertise in English. As my CV demonstrates, I have a number of relevant qualifications, including a first degree in English Literature which ensures that my grasp of subject knowledge is sound. I have also been an active member of NATE for the last three years and have attended local conferences as well as a range of other relevant INSET. Since joining the school as an NQT, I have always been an enthusiastic member of the English working party. This has involved tasks such as devising the school's policies and schemes of work. In addition, I have been responsible for developing a series of booklets for parents on helping their child with reading and writing. In my own classroom, I strive to achieve the highest standards in the planning and delivery of the English curriculum and hope that I would have an opportunity to share good practice with colleagues. I feel that I also have a number of other skills which are needed in the post, including the ability to relate well to colleagues, a good level of organisational skills and an ability to work well under pressure.

If I were to be appointed to the post, I would introduce a number of initiatives. I would negotiate with the Senior Management Team and the rest of the staff in the production of a long-term plan for the development of the English curriculum. However, I feel that an immediate priority for the school is the review and development of the writing curriculum. I have a number of ideas for the management of this which includes:

An audit of the writing curriculum.
An audit of staff's skills and expertise in relation to the writing curriculum.

A review of evidence arising from these audits by a working party and a plan of action as a result.

The development of a series of staff meetings to develop specific areas of the writing curriculum (these would be run by myself and the LEA adviser for English).

The development of a file containing a range of ideas for stimulating writing.

The development of a paired writing project with the local secondary school.

The organisation of a 'Writer's Week' in the spring term which would provide a stimulus for a range of writing activities in school.

I feel that it is important to value the skills that all our children bring to school. Therefore another priority for me would be to raise the status of children's first languages within school. I would liaise with the language support staff in the organisation of a programme which would have the celebration of multilingualism as its aim. There has been some excellent work in this area already and I would build upon the skills and enthusiasm already in place. The recent grant for the development of family literacy workshops for bilingual parents would obviously be a major focus of work in the first year. This work has the potential to involve bilingual parents in the fabric of the school in a much more meaningful way. One of my first tasks, therefore, if I were appointed to the role of English co-ordinator, would be to set up a steering group for this project which would comprise staff, parents and LEA representatives.

I have a number of other ideas for the direction and development of the English curriculum in Mill Street School which I would be happy to discuss with you further, should I be called for interview. I feel that I have the energy, enthusiasm and vision to lead colleagues in the creation of an exciting English curriculum which enables all of our pupils to reach the highest standards.

Yours sincerely,

Chris Achebe

If you were called for interview, you would need to prepare material which would demonstrate how you planned to develop the curriculum in school. There would be no need to take a portfolio containing examples of your work – the head should be well aware of your skills in the English curriculum. Instead, you should focus on convincing the Senior Management Team that you have the necessary skills to lead the school in the review and development of the English curriculum. There are a number of ways in which you might do this.

First, you could devise a detailed action plan, using the headings suggested in Chapter 3. You could explain at the interview that it would need to be revised and developed in consultation with other staff, but it would demonstrate that you had the necessary vision for the post you were being considered for.

Second, you could take in examples of material you would use when running staff meetings on the writing curriculum. You could even present an outline of a staff meeting you would run (see Chapter 8 for advice). Or you might like to prepare a handout which outlines how you would see your role in school developing. This could take the form of a concept map which details all the roles and responsibilities you would want to take on. You could then talk to this in the interview.

At interview it is also useful to plan a number of questions which you would want to ask. It is usual practice to ask candidates if they have any questions at the end of an interview. This could be a chance to find out what support the Senior Management Team are prepared to give you in the role, in terms of both resources and non-contact time. Useful questions to ask could relate to the area of the amount of support you would be given in your role. How much non-contact time would you be provided with in order to carry out such tasks as peer observation for monitoring purposes? Would the school be prepared to fund further training in subject leadership?

If you are successful and you are offered the post, you will need to negotiate a job description with the head. It is important to ensure that roles and responsibilities are clarified from the start. In the next section, we look at the variety of roles that an English subject leader may have and make some suggestions for ways in which a job description may be negotiated.

Variations in the role of the co-ordinator

Looking at the work of English co-ordinators, we have been surprised by the wide variety of working practices, expectations and contexts that influence the role. We shall explore some of these variables here before addressing what we see as the key roles and responsibilities of the co-ordinator.

Firstly, there is the school context in which the co-ordinator works. In the case of a small school, a co-ordinator may carry several responsibilities. Alternatively, co-ordinating the English curriculum may be part of the headteacher's job. A large school may decide to have two English co-ordinators, their responsibilities being split between Key Stage 1 and Key Stage 2. This practice of sharing responsibility for English has its pitfalls. Where liaison between a Key Stage 1 English co-ordinator and a Key Stage 2 co-ordinator is good, there can be a useful division of labour. But without such liaison, or time set aside to establish liaison, problems are likely to occur. One of the biggest dangers is that a coherent view of continuity and progression between the two key stages is hard to achieve with co-ordinators' focusing their attention on their own 'patch'.

Secondly, in some schools, particularly small ones, the English subject leader will be responsible for a number of different curriculum areas. Given the importance of English as a core curriculum subject, we feel that this practice of allowing teaching staff to carry multiple responsibilities is problematic. As we outline the tasks of the co-ordinator in this book it will become clear that it is too much to expect from a teacher with a normal teaching load to co-ordinate several areas of the curriculum effectively. The workload will be unreasonable and keeping up to date in two (or more) subject areas difficult to achieve. In the case of small schools, it will be impossible to avoid this multiplicity of roles. In these cases, we would urge headteachers to be aware of the central importance of literacy co-ordinators and to ensure that they do not have other responsibilities which carry an equally difficult workload – special needs co-ordination, for example.

Thirdly, the expectations of the co-ordinator may differ. Since there is no standard role specification or recognised source of advice on job functions, the kinds of activity that co-ordinators become involved in are subject to considerable variation. In some cases there are issues concerning the division of labour between senior management and co-ordinator. It may, for instance, be expected that the English co-ordinator takes full responsibility for work in the subject area and is left to her own devices. If this is the case, she needs to know that she has the backing of senior management when it is needed. There is nothing worse than putting all your energy into curriculum development only to have your well-planned initiatives stifled by your seniors. In a similar way, the 'autonomous' co-ordinator needs quite practical support if she is to be effective. For instance, if monitoring work is required, or if staff training is identified as a need, senior management need to make the resources available.

In other situations, co-ordinators may have relatively little autonomy. They may feel that they have nothing else to do than to 'look after the library', whilst the headteacher takes control of the English curriculum. Co-ordinators in this situation often find that they are required to do the 'donkey work'. They have to write the policy, produce medium-term plans, organise a book week and so on. These important activities can seem like chores if they are not a result of your own efforts and collaborative decision-making.

Finally, there is the issue of overlapping roles. We have already looked at this from the point of view of school organisation – where there is a division of responsibility between key stages. However, many co-ordinators experience difficulties if another colleague has control over an aspect of the English curriculum. In cases where a colleague is the designated link person for a literacy initiative or another member of staff has responsibility for the early years, conflicts of interest are always possible. Such issues are not insurmountable and in some situations it is useful to have an ally, someone on the staff who shares the same vision as you. However, clarity in role and responsibility is always important even in situations where conflict is unlikely.

We have used our own experience of working with co-ordinators in exploring these variations in roles and responsibilities. It is inevitable that there will be many more differences – differences resulting from local factors, school organisation and management styles. Although we have identified problematic areas, we are keen to point out that we are not in favour of a single model or role description. However, we are emphasising the importance of negotiating your role with the headteacher and see advantages in having a role description in writing.

General roles and responsibilities

Although we have argued against a single, standard role description for the subject leader or co-ordinator, we do feel that at a more general level there should be some common ground in terms of responsibilities. The work of the Teacher Training Agency in drafting National Standards for Subject Leaders (TTA, 1997b) provides us with a useful starting point here. The following points are based on the TTAs view of the core purpose of subject leadership:

- to provide leadership and direction for the subject
- to ensure that the subject is managed and organised to meet school and subject aims and objectives
- to encourage high standards of teaching and learning in the subject
- to play a major role in school policy development
- to ensure that the subject meets the needs and aspirations of pupils and raises standards of achievement
- to support, guide and motivate colleagues and other adults
- to evaluate the effectiveness of teaching and learning in the subject
- to set priorities and targets to improve provision
- to contribute to the monitoring process
- to identify needs in the subject in relation to the needs of the school.

We feel that these statements provide a good starting point for negotiating a job description that is relevant to the particular needs and situations of individual primary schools.

To fulfil these tasks, a co-ordinator will need to develop certain skills. Some of these will be specific to the subject itself and some will be more general leadership skills. This book focuses on subject-specific issues whilst acknowledging the importance of other skills. Generic subject leadership skills include an ability to encourage others to work together effectively in a professional setting through an understanding of interpersonal relationships; an ability to provide the necessary vision and direction for policy, planning and target setting; and an ability to organise the distribution and effective use of human and material resources. As well as this, the co-ordinator will need to be able to manage her time efficiently and provide an appropriate level of professional support. She will need good planning skills and be able

	Tasks of the English subject leader
Support staff	Need to fully involve them in the planning, delivery, monitoring and evaluation process.
	Need to include them in staff development audits and training.
	May need specific guidance if they are working on a particular area, e.g. supporting children with literacy difficulties.
	Need to work with bilingual support staff in planning appropriately for bilingual children across the school.
New staff	Need to be introduced to the school's policies and schemes of work for English.
	Need to be introduced to monitoring and assessment of children's progress in English.
	Need an initial audit of needs in terms of the English curriculum and appropriate support given.
	They will have had previous experience of teaching English in schools and may have many ideas to contribute. Need opportunities to do so.
	Need to be inducted into the school's approach to the teaching of English which includes policies, schemes of work, monitoring and assessment arrangements.
NQTs	Need appropriate support in English in relation to the strengths and weaknesses indicated in the Career Entry Profile.
	May need support with such issues as reporting to parents on attainment in English.
	Need a programme of appropriate support throughout the initial year of teaching. This will include support given by the English subject leader.
Student teachers	Mentors and class teachers with whom the students are working will have responsibility for inducting students into the school's approaches to the teaching and learning of English. However, students may have particular questions relating to the English curriculum which would be best directed to the English subject leader.
Student teachers whose subject specialism is English	If a student's specialism is English, it would be very useful if the English subject leader could give them an overview of the roles and responsibilities of her post. This could be done in the form of a brief interview during the time the student is on placement.

Figure 1.2. Tasks in relation to staffing

to plan for meetings and to follow up on decisions taken.

Working with other adults is an important dimension to the role of the co-ordinator. Figure 1.2 outlines the nature of the tasks relating to the support of new staff, Newly Qualified Teachers, support staff and students on placement.

In addition to this, the English subject leader will often be involved in working with parents. This sort of work is described in more detail in Chapter 11.

Current work on the National Professional Qualification for Subject Leaders is an indication that training to provide co-ordinators with some of these generic skills is recognised as a priority (TTA, 1997b). However, it is our feeling that subject knowledge as well as the specific needs of English co-ordination are necessary complements to this proposed qualification.

Role negotiation

Your role description is important in defining the scope of your responsibilities as an English co-ordinator. Clearly, the school's expectations and your own perception of the role need to be given careful thought. It is becoming more common for co-ordinators to have written role descriptions, although as we shall see a document of this kind does not necessarily clarify every aspect of your work. OFSTED inspections have forced schools to think more carefully about what is put on paper about leadership roles. Staff role descriptions are regularly used as evidence of the effectiveness of leadership and management in school inspections. Such documentation can be used to demonstrate how 'In a well-managed school, responsibilities are clearly defined and there is effective delegation' (OFSTED, 1995).

Negotiating your role is important in clarifying expectations, identifying the kind of support you can expect and ensuring that you are not asked to do too much. Coles and Banks (1990) draw our attention to the importance of negotiating with the headteacher.

> It is extremely important that senior colleagues, especially the headteacher, are aware of how you perceive your role. The degree of support that you enlist will significantly influence the effectiveness of the strategies you use.
>
> (Coles and Banks, 1990, p. 23)

Clearly then, a written role description will help in narrowing the scope for misunderstanding and making sure that you are not asked to do the impossible. However, we do feel that the process of negotiation is equally as important as any piece of paper. It is part of a more open approach to leadership and helps to clarify aspects of the job that may be quite difficult to describe in writing.

Even if you have been in post as a co-ordinator for some time, it may be worth reconsidering your job description and renegotiating your role.

Over time your role may well have expanded. Often expectations that the English co-ordinator will do certain things (e.g. organise the library, make arrangements for book week, etc.) become part of the culture of the school. It may be the case that you would like others to take responsibility for some routine tasks to enable you to focus on a new innovation. This process may occur quite naturally during appraisal. On other occasions *you* may need to take the initiative.

We realise that the issue of non-contact time is one which needs to take into account the specific circumstances in which co-ordinators work. However, non-contact time is essential if the English subject leader is to be effective. There needs to be a whole-school policy on such a matter. Some schools work on the principle that non-contact time needs to be allocated to tasks, not people. Therefore if a particular subject area is the focus of attention, that co-ordinator will need extra non-contact time in order to carry out the necessary tasks. Given the centrality of English within the curriculum, we would argue that the English co-ordinator needs a regular amount of non-contact time in order to keep up with developments. Then if English was a particular priority for any specific year, the co-ordinator could be allocated a little more non-contact time. It is not sensible to be prescriptive about these matters. Some headteachers argue that, because of the difficulties of allocating non-contact time, they should take on the role of the monitoring and evaluation of the curriculum. They need to ensure that they feed back key information to the relevant co-ordinators if this is to be an effective method. In some cases, headteachers may be willing to teach the class of the English subject leader whilst she carries out peer observation. This would obviously lead to a more cohesive approach to the monitoring and evaluation of the English curriculum. We deal with issues relating to monitoring and evaluation in Chapter 7.

Chapter summary

The roles and responsibilities of the English subject leader cover a large range of areas and should be matched to the needs of the school. It is inevitable that the co-ordinator will also bring her particular strengths and interests to the job. For example, if the co-ordinator has a particular passion for drama, that will no doubt be reflected in the curriculum of the school. As long as this takes place within a framework which encompasses all the essential areas of the English curriculum, we see this as a welcome feature of the nature of the post. Life would be very dull if all co-ordinators brought exactly the same skills and strengths to the role! This is one of the reasons why it is important that English co-ordinators regularly make contact with other co-ordinators in the area. In such forums, skills can be shared and ideas exchanged. We feel that LEAs should encourage such a practice in a systematic and organised fashion, with co-ordinators across a particular geographical area being encouraged to take it in turns to lead sessions for other co-ordinators on an area of interest or expertise. Of course, co-ordinators could be proactive and organise such sessions for themselves. Networks are vital to the task of keeping oneself informed and in touch with new developments in the teaching and learning of English.

English subject leaders who are new to the post could use such a forum in order to find a 'mentor', an experienced language co-ordinator, who would be willing to provide advice and support in the first year of this onerous responsibility. In the next chapter, we move on to the first task that a new co-ordinator may want to carry out: an audit of the language curriculum.

2

The Process of Change

This chapter is concerned with some of the larger issues of institutional change and school improvement that provide a context for the work of the subject co-ordinator in a primary school. We will begin by looking at some of the fundamental characteristics of educational change. We continue by looking at different kinds of change, the English curriculum itself, and the recent influences that are shaping its development. This leads us on to a discussion of the relationship between curriculum development and professional development. We then look at the co-ordinator's role in planning and managing the change process.

Change in schools

Schools, like any other organisation, are part of a changing world. The rapid economic, social and technological changes of recent years exert an influence on the education system in its totality as well as the life of individual schools. But often it may appear that schools are in some sense isolated from this world of change. After all, there has been no change in the age at which children start compulsory schooling; only minor alterations have been made to the length of the school day; school holidays follow the traditional pattern and many of the routines and formalities of the school day remain the same. This view of stability and familiarity is, of course, only partially true. Talk to practising primary school teachers about this and they will quickly remind you of the large-scale changes in curriculum content, assessment of pupil performance and school accountability that have been introduced in the last ten years or so. Change, they will tell you, has been imposed upon them.

In thinking about educational change, it is all too easy to overlook the ways in which schools are continually adapting to meet the demands of new circumstances. A fresh intake of pupils, staff turnover, and changes within the school's catchment area are just some of the more fundamental issues that schools routinely respond to. Put these with the demands of the daily activity of teaching, part of which, by necessity, involves adapting our work to the various needs of children, and it is clear why there is sometimes resistance to change in schools.

There have also been many changes with regard to the English curriculum over the years. Just as new initiatives are introduced and adapted, another approach appears which schools are encouraged to adopt. On the one hand, this constant evolution of the English curriculum means that, at times, teachers are introduced to a range of new ideas which improve practice; on the other hand, it also means that we miss the opportunity to conduct thorough longitudinal evaluations of each innovation. In the following section, we provide a brief overview of the changes in the English curriculum over the last thirty years in order to provide a context for the discussion of ways of managing change in schools.

Change and the English curriculum

If we look at developments in the primary school English curriculum over the last thirty years, we can see how the tension between external and internal pressure has changed. From the post-Plowden era of the late 1960s up until the introduction of the National Curriculum (1988), the power to change lay in individual schools and with individual teachers guided by the advice of the local authority, central government departments and HMI. Change at this time was typified by the gradual modification of professional thinking and practice with the introduction of new initiatives, curriculum materials, as well as local and national guidance. Stoll and Fink (1996) describe this as 'additive change'.

Despite this rather unstructured approach to development, some significant work was undertaken in the English curriculum. Mostly as a result of the pioneering work of Douglas Barnes and his colleagues (1971), teachers became far more aware of the role that language plays in the learning of different curriculum subjects. The concept of 'language across the curriculum' was popularised and received official recognition in the Bullock Report, *A Language for Life* (1975). The report of the Bullock Committee has been particularly influential and is still referred to by co-ordinators. Amongst the recommendations of this committee were that every school should have a language policy and a designated member of staff – a language co-ordinator – to develop that policy and turn it into practice. The report also raised professional awareness of many other language issues including the education of bilingual pupils. The committee produced a clear justification for the recognition and use of community languages in the school setting and contributed to the development of practice in second language learning.

The project work of the Schools' Council was also influential in the 1970s. This work was based on a research and development model and typically involved schools in piloting new approaches which would later be disseminated through conferences and publications. Again, this could be seen as additive change, but nevertheless it was influential. From these Schools' Council projects, work on the development of reading skills (Lunzer and Gardner, 1976) was particularly influential in promoting the use of DARTS activities to encourage children to read beyond sentence level.

Recognition of the multilingual nature of British society and the necessity to rethink educational policy and practice was explored by the Swan Committee. The Swan Report (1986) addressed wider issues but gave a thorough exploration of the language debate. The work of the Schools' Council Mother Tongue Project developed useful curriculum materials aimed at giving value to community languages and promoting their use in the school setting (Houlton, 1985).

Important contributions to our understanding of children as writers were also made by another project funded by the Schools' Council: the National Writing Project. Work done by the project has been influential in shaping how primary teachers work to develop children's writing skills and has informed the current Programme of Study for writing in the National Curriculum. References for the useful and practical materials generated by teachers working in this project are included in the annotated bibliography at the end of this book.

The writing project was followed by another national initiative, this time focusing on oracy. Although useful classroom work was developed under the auspices of the National Oracy Project, the demise of the Schools' Council and the massive, transformational change brought in by the Education Reform Act 1988 weakened the impact of the oracy project.

In 1987, the then Secretary of State for Education and Science (Kenneth Baker) set up the Kingman Committee to give advice to the profession on the teaching of English language. The report, published in 1988, was controversial. As Brian Cox, who served on that committee, has since commented:

> The Kingman Report was not well received by right-wing Conservatives because they wanted a return to the traditional teaching of Latinate grammar, and the Report came out firmly against this. Many politicians and journalists were ignorant about problems in the teaching of grammar and about the status of Standard English, and simply wished to reinstate the disciplines of study typical of schoolrooms in the 1930s.
>
> (Cox, 1991, p. 4)

Continuing concerns about the teaching of English language led to the establishment of another national project. The LINC project produced materials to develop teachers' subject knowledge and provided extensive in-service training. However, the view of language study embodied in the LINC materials was strongly criticised in some quarters and although much of the work of the project has been influential, the government decided not to publish the training materials.

We can now clearly see the increase of external pressure as the legislative force of the National Curriculum began to transform English teaching. However, it must be recognised that English as a subject has continued to be contentious. The work of the National Curriculum English Working Party, which was later published by the NCC (1989) and is popularly referred to as the Cox Report, was also the subject of intense political pressure. For an informed account of this we refer you to the committee chair's own account of events (Cox, 1991). This committee's hard work led to the publication of the first version of English in the National Curriculum. Since 1989, the curriculum has been revised and simplified. This curriculum will be reviewed by the QCA, along with the other subjects, in the year 2000.

Concerns about the level of children's literacy skills have tended to dominate recent discussion about education. Although evidence of a decline in standards is not entirely convincing, it is clearly the case that any improvement in pupils' performance at school will be largely dependent upon successful literacy teaching. It would be impossible to provide a summary of such a broad topic here. Instead we will focus on current trends in literacy work.

Important influences come from practical teaching approaches embodied in programmes like Reading Recovery and from initiatives with wider aims such as Family Literacy. Reading Recovery (see Clay, 1979), originally designed in New Zealand, is an intervention programme of one-to-one teaching which aims to help children in the initial stages of literacy before they fall too far behind their peer group. Family Literacy describes a variety of schemes which aim to provide literacy support for both parents and children. These schemes aim to break the cycle of inter-generational illiteracy and also to provide educational success for both parents and their children.

The National Literacy Project, which began in September 1997, is introducing an approach to literacy teaching that is far more structured than what has previously taken place in most primary schools. Although the project includes some of the features of existing good practice, these have been drawn together to form a timetabled literacy hour and a termly plan. The net result of this may be more systematic and confident teaching of literacy skills. However, the time constraints of a daily literacy hour could well result in a narrowing of the English curriculum. We discuss issues relating to the literacy hour more fully in Chapter 5.

Kinds of change

As we can see, change is an inevitable part of educational life. It is important that the English co-ordinator understands the nature of change in order to utilise the processes to their best effect. Various categories of change have been proposed by curriculum development and management theorists. Here we select some perspectives which will help to inform your view of the changing English curriculum.

Hargreaves and Hopkins (1991) examine the factors that lead to school improvement. They distinguish between the external and internal forces that provide pressure or support for change. New practices that have emerged as a result of the Education Reform Act 1988 and its subsequent Statutory Orders constitute a response to external pressure on schools. A particular example of *external pressure* that has a direct bearing on the English curriculum is the introduction of a 'literacy hour' in the primary school curriculum. Here the external pressure constitutes strong advice and even recommendation but does not as yet have the force of legislative requirement.

On the other hand, school governors and the school's own management structure have the potential for *internal pressure* for change. Part of this pressure may arise through the school's own self-review and development planning processes. A school that identifies that there is a need for a more coherent approach to the development of children's handwriting is creating this kind of internal pressure. Alternatively, changes in the school's catchment area may lead the school to recognise that its curriculum practices should reflect the various needs of bilingual children.

These kinds of pressure to change are not always complemented with sufficient resources for support. However, central government, the LEAs and a variety of other funding bodies continue to provide *external support* in terms of specialist professional help, training and funding for material resources. Again, if we look at the National Literacy Project, the level of external support includes training, advice from literacy consultants, planning documentation and a small budget for classroom resources. For primary schools, the scope for *internal support* is usually limited. Although resources are available, it is more likely to be the moral support of colleagues and the creative use of time that is going to be most helpful.

Curriculum and professional development

A central function of the English co-ordinator is to ensure that all pupils realise their full potential in this core curriculum subject. In order to achieve this, it will be important to look at how all aspects of oracy and literacy are developed within the school. Inevitably, as you move through the auditing, policy-making and planning sequence, the particular teaching strengths and weaknesses of colleagues will become apparent. To deliver the curriculum that you have agreed, some degree of change will be required. One central means of ensuring lasting change in curricular practices is through staff development. It is undisputedly true that 'there is no curriculum development without professional development'. As Fullan explains:

> Since the essence of educational change consists in learning new ways of thinking and doing, new skills, attitudes, etc., it follows that staff development is one of the most important factors related to change in practice.
>
> (Fullan, 1982, p. 66)

So what exactly is professional development? We tend to jump to the conclusion that it involves signing up on a course – but we need to remind ourselves that professional development is much broader than this. Even if it does involve course attendance, there are often different types of courses to choose from. And surely, it is what colleagues do in their classrooms after and as a result of training that is of central importance.

Professional development happens as a result of a dialogue about our working practices. It is certainly possible to engage in professional dialogue without actually changing; it is unlikely, however, that we will change without this sort of dialogue. So if professional development is central to the process of change in schools and classrooms, it is important for us to identify the different contexts in which this dialogue can take place. Some of these different contexts will now be explored.

The critical friend

In its simplest form, professional development involves talking about what you do or might do in the classroom. This may be through informal discussion with a 'critical friend' or in a more structured and formal setting. Discussion may result from a common interest: for example, you may work with a colleague who shares your passion for children's literature. In the course of trading ideas about ways of working with particular books or around the work of a favourite author, you will be generating new ideas that may well be mutually enriching. This sort of professional relationship can contribute to evolutionary change.

Mentoring and coaching

Dialogue of a more formal nature takes place within the context of a mentoring or coaching relationship. Stoll and Fink (1996) suggest that a coaching relationship is likely to involve activities like lesson planning, observation of teaching, joint problem-solving or the evaluation of teaching materials. So, an English co-ordinator might wish to work collaboratively with a new member of staff in developing the teaching of a timetabled literacy lesson. The co-ordinator will initiate this by establishing a 'coaching' relationship which could begin with a discussion of the lesson format, its advantages and disadvantages. Arrangements would be made for both the co-ordinator and the new member of staff to observe each other's literacy sessions. Reflection and discussion resulting from these observations will lead to further work. For instance, this could involve agreeing targets for improving literacy teaching or collaborative work looking at a problematic area of lesson organisation. This sort of coaching could, of course, be part of a more general programme of peer observation which we will be looking at in more depth in Chapter 3.

Reading and study

Reading and study also have an important role to play in professional development. The recent literature on the school as a 'learning organisation' underscores this point (Barth, 1990; Garratt, 1987). Activity of this kind can happen on a number of different levels. Reading an article in a professional publication, such as *Primary English*, may provide you and your colleagues with practical guidance on a particular topic. The academic study of books and research articles, characteristic of award-bearing courses offered by HE institutions, may contribute to new ways of thinking about the English curriculum. As we have already observed, the process of talking about new ideas with colleagues will help to make ideas relevant to your classrooms. The basic process of discussion, trialling and reflection helps in turning ideas into practice and then refining them.

Attending courses

INSET provision may well involve colleagues in similar processes to those we have just described. However, as we suggested at the beginning of this section, there is more to professional development than simply attending courses. This is not to suggest that course attendance is a 'bad investment', but merely to encourage us to think more clearly about how the sorts of learning that take place at such an event can be used to inform and develop practice. For the co-ordinator, this means trying to ensure that colleagues attend in-service courses that are appropriate to their needs and that follow-up systems are in place. By this we mean that a colleague who attends a course on new developments in early reading should be asked to report back to relevant staff and to take some sort of action in the classroom to trial or implement new approaches. At a later date, the co-ordinator would need to work with this colleague or team in order to evaluate the effectiveness of the new approaches. How we manage the follow-up to INSET work is of crucial importance. As Fullan observes:

> most forms of in-service training are not designed to provide the ongoing, interactive, cumulative learning necessary to develop new conceptions, skills and behaviours.
>
> (Fullan, 1982, p. 66)

In-service which involves the whole school staff clearly has some advantages which we now need to consider. Not only does it allow staff to learn and discuss new ideas together, it also makes it easier for the co-ordinator to plan for on-going support and follow-up. In order for this to happen effectively, school-focused training needs to be part of a concerted effort to review and develop the English curriculum, to have the full support of management and to be a specific focus on the schools development plan. (See Chapter 7 for a fuller treatment of in-service.)

Research

Professional development also takes place through various forms of research. This category includes the fundamental activity of 'finding out what happens in the school' (see auditing in Chapter 3) as well as the more formalised systems of enquiry that constitute educational research. An English co-ordinator or a colleague may be involved in such research as part of an award-bearing course. Alternatively, some or all of the school staff may collaborate with an external agency with a research interest. For example, academics from HE may be interested in the impact of a family literacy programme on the school community. The process of setting up a project, working with colleagues in HE and evaluating different aspects of the programme will involve the school in an extended debate about home–school partnerships and literacy development in different contexts. This sort of relationship can be particularly beneficial for the school, not only in the sort of professional dialogue that it develops but also in the ways in which it can raise the profile of the school and build on the skills of individual members of staff.

In this section we have focused on five important aspects of professional development. In dealing with them separately, it has not been our intention to suggest that they work in isolation. After all, they share the common thread of focused professional dialogue. As we will see in the following chapters, this dialogue is a central part of the process of policy-making and scheme planning.

Nevertheless, there is a professional obligation to critically evaluate new ideas, approaches and resources, and most teachers see this as an integral part of their work. It is from this point of view that teaching defines itself as a profession, reaching beyond the essential tasks and routines of daily classroom life. By far the most challenging aspect of this professionalism is that of initiating and evaluating changes in classroom practice, whether those changes are to take place in one's own classroom or in the classrooms of colleagues. Real changes in classroom practice are difficult to achieve. Change, after all, is hard work and may be perceived as a threat since it:

> can involve the loss of firmly held beliefs and ideas, of comfortable habits, of established patterns of behaviours and of confidence and self-esteem.
>
> (Day *et al.*, 1993, p. 55)

As a curriculum co-ordinator it is important to understand the process of change. It is all too easy to be fired-up with good ideas and intentions, only to have your enthusiasm dampened by a negative or defensive reactions from colleagues. So, planning for innovative development must take into account both the possibility of resistance and the potential for systematic improvement in the curriculum. In the next section, we look at some of the reactions colleagues may have to proposed changes and suggest ways in which the subject leader may respond to these.

Change and the teaching staff

As we have seen, change depends upon colleagues trying out new ideas and approaches, critically evaluating their effectiveness and changing or adapting their practices as a result. This, of course, assumes that we are open to new ideas in the first place and willing to keep our own practice under review. We feel that this sort of openness is an essential part of teacher professionalism, although we do recognise that some colleagues may be resistant to change. In reality, partly because classroom life is complex and demanding, we are not always as receptive to new ideas and practices as we would like to be. For that matter, we may feel that we just do not have the necessary time or energy at our disposal.

As an English co-ordinator you may, for example, have learnt about the use of 'big books', whether through INSET, your own reading or talking with colleagues in other schools. You feel that the sort of direct teaching of reading that using a big book can offer falls in line with new requirements for literacy teaching and is just what the school needs. In talking informally with school staff, all you seem to encounter is negativity. Some typical responses are:

- 'When am I going to have time?'
- 'Where are we going to get the resources?'
- 'Is this the latest bandwagon?'
- 'Why put in all this effort now, when they're going to tell us how to do it soon?'
- 'What's wrong with what we do now?'

The comments of your colleagues may be quite habitual reactions to change. You may feel that they are common obstacles that you encounter in your role as a co-ordinator. In Chapter 7 we look at ways of working with these sorts of reactions in the context of a staff meeting or INSET session. Here, we focus on what may lie behind these statements.

Rather than despair at the general lack of enthusiasm, let's look at each in turn. The first two reactions are important. Considerations about time and resources are actually quite fundamental. They are questioning the *practicality* of a proposed change and need to be taken into account when planning for development. The third and fourth comments capture characteristic reactions to the recent climate of change. They give us insight into the professional *context* in which we are working. The idea of 'bandwagons' and 'changing fashions' suggests that too much has changed too quickly – this reaction is sometimes referred to as *innovation fatigue.*

The fourth comment also refers to the context in which we are working. There is a commonly held belief that the profession has become *disempowered* by successive central direction. Again we need to take this into account as we plan for change by encouraging colleagues to take ownership of new ideas, to adapt and experiment with them and to take credit for what they have done. Finally, 'What's wrong with what we do now?' may seem like a defensive reaction; but it is also an important comment. It suggests that colleagues need a reason to change. Before 'jumping on the bandwagon' they must first identify the *need to change.* When this process has been worked through it's usually the case that change ceases to become a bandwagon and becomes an innovation.

So far, we have been able to identify three important factors in the change process. These are practicality, the overall context and the need to change. However, in addition to these, we need to take into account the ways in which colleagues work together as a school staff, because if change is going to be influential, it will alter the working practices of the school as a whole. The professional relationships between staff, their potential to engage in critical discussion about the curriculum and their skill at challenging each others' beliefs and practices as well as their capacity to work together and to support one another constitute the interpersonal context that we are part of as a curriculum co-ordinator. Taking this view, school development is about *working together* to find out about ways to improve practice and become more effective. Day *et al.* (1993) identify five principles that are necessary for a staff to work together in this way:

> a climate of trust and openness; plan and work together to improve teaching; reflect on practice and experiment with new ways of teaching (without feeling that mistakes will be frowned upon); those affected by decisions should be involved in making them; high expectations for teachers (teaching quality).
>
> (Day *et al.*, 1993, p. 50)

A subject co-ordinator cannot change the school climate or culture single-handedly. The principles of collaborative working outlined by Day and his colleagues may or may not be present in your school. However, we feel that they are sound working practices worth striving for – even if they are not the established way of working in the school.

Planning and managing change

When we look at change in schools, it becomes quite clear that success is achieved through careful management and planning. However, because change is based upon personal and interpersonal development, it demands an approach that is characterised by flexibility. Striking the right balance between planning, management and flexibility is an art in itself. School developments that lack clear direction are likely to founder. On the other hand, development that does not allow for the modification of plans and subsequent changes in direction is likely to exclude and disempower colleagues.

A starting point for the English co-ordinator will be to work out where and when change is possible. As Fullan (1982) observes, we need to influence those factors which we can change and reduce the powers of those which we cannot. One technique often used for identifying opportunities and obstacles in institutional change is referred to as force-field analysis. Following this technique, the co-ordinator uses a simple diagram to identify the key elements of the proposed developments and the factors likely to facilitate or inhibit change. Figure 2.1 is an example of a force-field analysis drawn up by a primary school English co-ordinator. The numbers on the left-hand side of each row represent the perceived strength of each factor or force. After completing the force-field analysis, the co-ordinator can work out how to harness or strengthen the positives and how minimise or deal with the negative forces.

We conclude this section on planning and managing change with a look at some of the skills which you will develop as a curriculum co-ordinator. All of these are generic skills which apply to all types of

---

Facilitating forces

+ 5   The LEA advisory service strongly support the idea of blocked work on children's literature
+ 4   Some colleagues are already doing excellent work on literature
+ 3   Staff are concerned about the way the literacy hour inhibits extended work in English
+ 2   There is some excellent short course provision at the local HE institution
+ 1   There is a possibility of some financial support through an SRB project

-1   A few members of staff are still having difficulty getting to grips with the literacy hour
-2   Some study of literature is already done in the context of the literacy hour
-3   More resources and training are needed if the staff are to realise the benefits
-4   Other subject leaders are concerned about the amount of time that is being allocated to English
-5   The headteacher is not convinced of the value of extended work on literature

Inhibiting forces

Figure 2.1   An example of an English co-ordinator's force-field analysis

change, and you will most probably be continuing to develop them throughout your career. They are as follows:

- *Motivation* – your role as co-ordinator is dependent on your being able to motivate your colleagues as well as to maintain your own motivation.

- *Communication* – you need to be able to communicate your decisions clearly to colleagues and to management – but you also need to be able to listen to them.

- *Working with others* – you need to be able to collaborate, to delegate and to support the work of your colleagues.

- *Working with conflict* – often change can provoke argument, disagreement or defensive emotional reactions and you need to be able to work diplomatically with these.

- *Goal-setting* – you need to be able to set priorities and targets as part of your action plan.

- *Monitoring and evaluating* – you need to be able to keep a track of what is going on and at times to gauge its effectiveness.

- *Resources* – you may also be responsible for auditing, organising and providing human and material resources.

Finally, you need to be adaptable by not assuming 'that your version of what the change should be is the one that could or should be implemented' (Fullan, 1982).

Chapter summary

We have considered a range of issues in relation to change and the English curriculum. A recurrent theme in the chapter is the need for the language co-ordinator to understand the nature of change in order to ensure that the process of developing the English curriculum in school is as smooth as possible. We have stressed that change is a dynamic process and as such it can never occur without ensuing difficulties. There will always be problems, the need to back-pedal, the need to pause and re-evaluate the way things are progressing. As long as the co-ordinator can approach these difficulties with a calm understanding of the inevitability of them and have at hand a range of strategies for dealing with them, she will be able to move the school on in fundamental ways. Policies and practices will be introduced in ways which enable staff to embrace them, not shun them. In the next chapter, we consider the processes involved in developing a language policy.

3

Language Audits and Action Plans

Organisational change, even in small primary schools, can be quite a challenge. As we observed in the previous chapter, changing and developing the curriculum will involve us in thinking about what we teach, how we teach it and how our schools and classrooms are resourced. Planned change needs to take into account the starting point, and the stages of development through which we hope to move to achieve our desired outcome.

In this chapter, we begin by looking at ways of establishing an informed view of current school practice. This is referred to as the auditing process and simply aims to show 'where we are at' as a school and what constitutes current policy and practice in English. We then look at peer observation as an aspect of auditing and explore some of the complex issues that this raises.

Relatively small-scale changes often generate further work. So, it is important for the co-ordinator to invest time in the planning process. In the third section we make some general observations about this planning process using illustrations from the work of language co-ordinators. We conclude by offering guidance on the preparation of action plans.

The auditing process

An audit is the first stage in the development process. It helps you to establish your starting point and will inform your future planning. The scale and focus of the audit will largely depend on the school's current priorities. On some occasions you may just wish to focus on a relatively small area. For instance, following a staff meeting, you may have come to the conclusion that approaches to the teaching of handwriting vary somewhat from class to class. There is general agreement that a more coherent approach to handwriting would ensure progression. As co-ordinator you want to find out about the current practice in school before looking into staff development, in-service provision and resources. This process of finding out would constitute a small-scale audit.

If English has been chosen as a major area for development then you will almost certainly need to conduct a thorough audit which looks at all the major aspects of the subject. Here an audit will give you a picture of current strengths and weaknesses in your school's English provision and it will also help you to identify priorities for development (DES, 1989).

A more substantial audit will also be necessary on other occasions. If you are newly appointed as a co-ordinator for English, you will want to find out the state of the school's practice as soon as you have established yourself with your new class. Similarly, a more thorough audit may be necessary as your school prepares for inspection.

An audit should be a fairly straightforward fact-finding exercise. Often, as a staff you may think you know what you're doing, but you can, of course, be wrong! The audit does not involve organising a thorough research study, but attempts to find out what's going on in an impartial or objective way. So gathering information for your audit does not require any particularly sophisticated techniques – just time and tact.

Even though auditing is only information gathering, it is worth recognising that it can sometimes provoke some rather defensive reactions. For instance, staff may feel that their choice of resources and the ways in which they use them will be criticised. They may feel that change is in the air and react to protect or defend themselves. Curriculum evaluation and development can, as we saw in the previous chapter, be seen as a threat.

It is not always possible to avoid this sort of reaction, but you can take some steps to minimise negative feelings. First, it is important that you yourself have the support of the head and where appropriate the management team. Second, you should try to get the agreement of colleagues. Making clear your purposes and intentions at a staff meeting is a useful way of doing this. It may well be worth pointing out, even at this stage, that changes may be necessary. It is better to be clear about the role of the audit in the change process than work by stealth. Finally, external support from advisory teachers, advisers and LEA inspectors may also be useful.

Planning your audit

It is important to give some thought to your audit before you begin. Sometimes you have a clear idea of what you want to focus on, but at other times, discussion with a senior member of staff or a trusted colleague may help you to develop more precision in your thinking. Having decided what you want to find out from the audit, you need to go on to look at the most appropriate way or ways of gathering your information. Figure 3.1 gives some suggestions of how certain approaches can be matched to different kinds of audit.

What do I want to know?	How can I find out?	How shall I present it?
How do colleagues teach poetry?	Individual discussion. Year group discussion. Observe lesson. Children's work.	Brief written summary and verbal report at next staff meeting.
How do colleagues teach reading and writing?	Individual discussion. Questionnaire. Structured observation of lessons. Children's work.	Written report including factual evidence of what colleagues do at various stages.
Who uses the school library and when?	Ask colleagues. Observe library use. Involve children in observation or self-monitoring. Keep a journal of practice in own class.	Use observations to produce a statistical table showing how and when the library is used.
What texts do colleagues use for literature work?	Discussion. Circulate list. Colleagues monitor own use of literature.	Type up list of titles used with questions to prompt further discussion at staff meeting.
Which reading schemes are used at Key Stage 1?	Look in classrooms and shared areas. Talk to colleagues. Arrange a time to help out hearing readers. Ask to look at colleagues' reading records.	Produce a list of the most frequently used schemes in each age group and circulate for future discussion.

Figure 3.1.   Planning for an audit

Conducting a large scale audit

As we have already seen, there will be some occasions when a fuller audit is required because of either internal or external factors. In this section, we will use examples of a reading audit used by North Lincolnshire LEA as part of a development project involving a network of primary schools. This audit explicitly aims to help the co-ordinator to address the question 'Where are we now in our teaching of reading?'

We will begin with an overview of the structure of the audit, before going on to look in a more detailed way at each section. The audit itself is sub-divided into six sections which ask for both quantitative and qualitative information. Section 1 focuses on the overall school context; Section 2 on the school policy and the structures that support its implementation; Section 3 on the deployment and expertise of the school's human resources; Section 4 involves a review of the material resources; Section 5 looks at teaching approaches and Section 6 addresses the children's experience of reading.

The school context

The first section aims to gather basic information about the school, its pupils and how they are organised for the purposes of teaching. Questions about the number of pupils on roll, the gender balance, the proportion of ethnic minority pupils, class sizes, the number of pupils with special needs and under-fives provision are included. Further questions look more specifically at the area of reading. Staff familiarity with the school's policy on reading and the ways in which the school measures pupil attainment are included in this section. This basic information-gathering process will raise questions about how the school approaches the teaching of reading.

Policy and implementation

Here, the school's beliefs and practices concerning the teaching of reading are examined in more depth. This looks beyond the school's statements of intent as represented by its 'policy-on-paper' and attempts to get an impression of what actually goes on in classrooms. First, the co-ordinator needs to build a picture of her colleagues' aims in this curriculum area and then look at how far these match up with any official policy statement. With respect to this statement, the co-ordinator then needs to find out when and how it was developed and how it is implemented and reviewed. This section will help the co-ordinator to identify needs with respect to policy development.

Human resources

In this section the co-ordinator is collating information about the level of teacher expertise and the involvement of other adults in the teaching of reading. Finding out colleagues' level of confidence in this curriculum area is a starting point. How expertise is shared between colleagues, and how new ideas and approaches are disseminated is the next stage. Questions about staff participation in in-service work are included. When was the last time they attended a course on reading? What sort of in-service work on reading would they like? Also, the co-ordinator's own training needs are addressed.

With reading, the use of other adults is an important element to consider. So the degree of parental involvement needs to be considered as well as the nature of the work they are engaged in. Similarly, the ways in which the school uses ancillary staff and voluntary helpers is monitored. This will help in identifying training needs and areas in which communication can be improved.

Material resources

Although this is a reasonably straightforward task, it is important to gain an accurate view of the material resources in the school and how they are used by staff and pupils. First, consideration is given to resource storage and distribution – this includes audio-visual material as well as ICT hardware and software. The quantity, quality and appropriateness of reading material is then considered. Is the full range of resources used by all staff, and how are they used? And are the materials appropriate in meeting the needs of all children? This section will help in informing decisions about the location and organisation of resources and to set priorities for expenditure.

Teaching approaches

This section looks at the methods that teachers use in developing children's reading skills and experience. Through interview and peer observation the co-ordinator builds up a picture of how her colleagues interpret the programmes of study and the school scheme of work for their particular age group. This will help to identify areas of strength and weakness for further staff development work.

Pupil experience

The final section attempts to gauge wider influences on the child's experience of reading. So the quality and possible variation in their pre-school experience is considered as well as the degree to which a whole-school ethos has been established. Parental and staff attitudes to reading are seen as important and children's level of motivation and their self-image as readers are considered.

Techniques for gathering information for an audit

In our discussion on planning for an audit, we looked at the need to identify appropriate tools for gathering information. Our suggestions included discussion with individual members of staff or teams; observation, focusing on the use of resources, the working patterns of pupils or the teaching approaches of staff; lists or inventories of resources; self-monitoring such as the use of journals; and the analysis of samples of pupils' work or teachers' records. Another popular approach is the use of a questionnaire for colleagues. These techniques will be used to complement the information provided by the school's policy statements, planning documents and record-keeping systems.

For a small-scale audit the co-ordinators' task is simply to find the most appropriate technique. However, a larger audit, such as the one outlined above, will inevitably draw on a range of sources. Rather than giving a detailed view of the full range of techniques, this section looks closely at the use of questionnaires and the role of peer observation, and concludes with a more general look at other sources of information.

Questionnaire

A particularly useful technique for conducting an audit is to use a questionnaire. The main advantage of this technique is that it does not depend upon non-contact time. Also it is fairly 'safe' for colleagues because they can reply in their own time and can, of course, choose to remain anonymous. The disadvantage, as we all know, is that our questionnaire responses, even with the best will in the world, may not be entirely accurate. As suggested above, we may think we know what we do, but we can be wrong!

Questionnaire design is a complex topic in its own right. Here we will give some simple advice. Some basic principles of questionnaire design are listed in Figure 3.2.

- Keep it as short as you can (two sides of A4).

- Consider layout (if it looks good it seems worth doing).

- Use a covering note thanking colleagues and reminding them of the purpose.

- Use simple questions (either open-ended, yes/no or both).

- Test it out on a friend first (are the questions clear/answerable?).

- Think about how you will analyse (yes/no are easier to use).

- Work out distribution, time-scale and arrangements for return.

Figure 3.2   Some principles of questionnaire design

Peer observation

If using a questionnaire is non-threatening and economical in terms of time, then the technique of peer observation can be just the reverse. For many people, the idea of being watched by another adult as they teach is unnerving and may evoke unpleasant memories. It is also costly to the school in that it involves releasing a member of staff to conduct the observation. Despite this, it is a very useful way of finding out what happens in classrooms and, if it is careful managed, can be a very powerful aspect of professional development. In the context of the auditing process, observing colleagues can help us to find out exactly how English is taught, whereas other techniques merely give an indication. However, it will be important for you to stress to colleagues that this sort of observation is not related to the appraisal process.

As a co-ordinator, it is important for you to establish a clear purpose for the observation of colleagues at work. If the audit has been carefully planned, observation will give you insight into an aspect of the English curriculum in action. However, staff must agree about the value of observation and the particular approach that is to be adopted. Where peer observation is already established as a way of working, there will not be the need for too much preparatory work. Nevertheless, a general acceptance of the principle of classroom observation in your subject area and support from senior management is a basic minimum.

Given the general climate of resistance to observation, it may be useful for you to clarify the intentions of this approach. The questions below will help you to do this.

- Is the observation about finding out what colleagues do in the classroom?
- Is the observation to check on whether they are following school policy?
- Who will be conducting the observations?
- What preparatory work will be done before the observation?
- When will observations be done?
- What criteria will be used to guide the observations?
- How will feedback be given to individuals?
- What will happen to the findings?

A problem-solving approach to the English curriculum audit may help colleagues to develop a sense of commitment to the process of observation. For instance, a school staff may be reviewing the reading curriculum and need to examine the organisation of reading time and the skills that teachers use in hearing children read. Although discussion may give the co-ordinator a fair impression of current practice, most staff will agree that their own reports on matters like the length of time given to hearing readers, the frequency of interruptions and the kinds of support that they offer to children may not be particularly accurate. In this situation, the idea of working collaboratively to find out what staff do, using peer observation as a tool, will be particularly fruitful. If time permits, colleagues may wish to design their own criteria and develop a system of reciprocal or paired observation.

Successful peer observation depends on a climate of mutual trust and shared sense of purpose. Whether you intend to operate a system of reciprocal observation (as described above) or whether you, as co-ordinator, intend to be the sole observer, careful thought needs to be given to how trust and purpose will be kept to the fore. This means that the three stages of negotiation, observation and feedback must be given time and status. We will deal with each stage in turn.

Even though the principle of observation will have been agreed beforehand, it is important that the negotiation stage is conducted in a thorough and professional manner. First, the colleague you are observing will need to be reminded of the purpose of the observational visit. You will also need to negotiate a suitable time and date and agree upon the duration of the observation. If you are using specific criteria, or an observational grid or checklist, this needs to be talked through with your colleague. There may also be information you need before the visit and those being observed should be offered the opportunity of providing any further material that they think may be helpful. Finally, you will need to discuss the arrangements for giving feedback. Usually, this is best done fairly soon after the observation.

As we have already suggested, some colleagues may find peer observation uncomfortable and so every effort should be made to minimise these anxieties. However, it is also difficult to be an observer. You will find it helpful to stick to your brief and follow the criteria you have already agreed upon. Avoid the temptation of being drawn into classroom life or distracted by children. This can be particularly difficult with young children, but a clear instruction not to disturb the observer is likely to minimise interruptions. It will also help the colleague you are observing if you arrive and leave at the agreed times.

The feedback you give to those you have observed will be extremely useful if it is conducted in the spirit of an honest, professional discussion. A good starting point may be to check how your colleague felt that the session went. Allow time for them to explain the context, and to account for the way things turned out. You will then need to summarise your observations. It is helpful to begin by focusing on the positives. Phrases such as: 'I liked the way you did ...' and 'I was impressed by the way your class ...' can be effective when said with some conviction, but remember that your honesty and enthusiasm are as important as the words you use. If you are less happy with aspects of what you have observed, it is worthwhile at the audit stage simply to turn your observations into questions. You will also need to share any written observations you have made, check their accuracy and invite further discussion. Colleagues you have observed may then wish to make changes or record their own perceptions depending on the agreed level of confidentiality and the arrangements for more formal reporting. In the context of an audit, it is most likely that observational notes will remain confidential and that your findings will take the form of a summary which does not comment on the practice of individual teachers. If peer observation is new to the school or to the colleague you have been working with, it will be worthwhile to conclude the feedback discussion with some reflective evaluation of the process itself (for instance, 'Did you find that useful?').

In one Sheffield school, Pye Bank Nursery Infant, the co-ordinator found that peer observation needed to be introduced sensitively. Debbie says:

> At first, the staff were a bit wary and so I had to reassure them that I was not looking for faults but trying to find out about particular things. I always tell them what I am looking for and give feedback when I have finished. I then write up what I have found and make it totally anonymous. I report this back to the head in the half-termly co-ordinator meetings and we decide then what action to take about anything that might come up. I also let her know what is going well in school. Staff have got used to it now and it works really well.

Other sources of information

Questionnaires and classroom observations tend to focus on the views and practices of the teaching and support staff. In auditing the English curriculum it may also be worth looking at the views and practices of other adults such as non-teaching staff and parents. For instance, a focus on early literacy will inevitably need to incorporate issues of home–school partnership and communication with parents about school policy. At the stage of conducting an audit some preliminary work in gauging the extent of involvement and the level of satisfaction of parents with aspects of the English curriculum may well prove useful.

Children's own attitudes and performance will also inform the auditing process. In talking with pupils and looking at samples of their work we can learn a lot about the value, appropriateness and effectiveness of our curricular provision. This sort of scrutiny will also provide us with an impression of standards and progression within and across key stages. On a more formal level it may be useful to look at teacher assessments and test scores.

As a co-ordinator you need to know how your pupils' performance in English compares with available data on local and national standards. As part of your on-going monitoring role you should also know how pupil performance compares with previous years, and how it varies between different subjects and different age groups. It will also help to look at the performance of the different sub-groups in the school population. For example, the differences in attainment in English between girls and boys has been identified as a concern (SCAA, 1996a). Similarly, schools working in a multicultural community need to be aware of the achievements of different minority groups if their curricular provision is to redress any imbalance. Later in this chapter, in the section on action planning, we look at using information gained from SATs.

Reporting back

The final stage of the audit process is concerned with reporting back to the staff group as a whole. What you should be aiming for here is the presentation of a summary of your findings. If your audit has been carefully planned, your colleagues will appreciate that this summary is derived from more detailed information and where appropriate this can be made available to them on request. The real challenge, however, is that of moving on from the audit to planning for specific developments. Often, co-ordinators choose to present a draft action plan with the summary of their findings. If you have plenty of time it may be better to involve colleagues in discussion about points for development that seem to them to arise from the audit.

Whether the audit summary is in the form of a document that is circulated for comment or a more formal verbal report to the school staff, it is useful to observe the following principles:

- Thank colleagues for their time and support.

- Draw attention to the features of current practice that you value.

- Avoid specific reference to colleagues with 'In some classrooms...'.

- Raise questions: 'Is x always the best way?'

- Invite comments on your summary and suggestions for follow-up.

The planning process

A language audit will inevitably highlight areas that the school can improve upon. With a large-scale audit, it will be necessary to agree priorities. It is best to do this with colleagues – either as a whole staff or with a smaller group (for example, all Key Stage 1 teachers). Combining this priority-setting with feedback from your audit has clear advantages, in that areas for action can be closely tied to specific school needs.

Agreeing priorities is an important step from the familiarity of existing practice into the uncertain realm of change. Careful work at this stage in identifying clear and achievable targets may help to minimise the feelings of threat or uncertainty that may be associated with change. Sometimes, deciding on priorities can be difficult. We have found it useful to look at different categories of action as a preparatory stage. This model considers **imperatives**, **preferences** and **possibilities**.

By starting with the question, 'what has *got* to be done?', we address **imperatives**. These are usually the most important issues. More often than not, imperatives are the result of external pressure (such as new curriculum orders, or inspection) but they may also result from a realisation that current practice in a particular area is unacceptable by our own professional standards. An imperative for change is based on the recognition that current practice must be developed.

Preferences relate to the question, 'what would we *like* to do?'. These are important issues to consider because colleagues will feel motivated to work in this sort of area and already have some commitment to change. Ideally we would like to spend time with colleagues, after the audit, trying to establish a vision of what children's experience of the English curriculum should be like. Indeed in some situations, this may be possible and should always be an option. Unfortunately, the pressures of centrally driven curricular change have tended to push most curriculum co-ordinators towards a consideration of imperatives. However, it is worth recognising that there may well be some areas in which what colleagues would 'like to do' coincides with what they 'have to do'.

The question, 'what is it *possible* to do?' addresses **possibilities**, or how practical or achievable the targets are. Here we need to consider constraints such as the time and resources available to us. We may have agreed some admirable priorities, but on reflection we discover that they are unrealistic. For instance, colleagues may strongly feel that a well-resourced library needs to be established within the school, but when refurbishment, storage facilities and book purchases are costed out, the plan may be unworkable.

The model of setting priorities based upon imperatives, preferences and possibilities provides guidance for the co-ordinator's work with colleagues. However, the practicalities concerned with turning plans into action, keeping the momentum going, monitoring and evaluating progress are more specifically the concern of the co-ordinator. These issues are addressed in subsequent chapters.

A final point to be made about the planning process concerns the relationship between the priorities that you agree as a staff and your own personal priorities as an English co-ordinator. Inevitably, as a subject specialist you will have developed your own thinking and practice with respect to English. You will be familiar with new ideas, teaching approaches and resources both from training and from your previous experience. It would be too simplistic to suggest that there will always be agreement between your personal priorities and those agreed with your colleagues. After all, the curriculum co-ordinator has a leadership role in the school and will have an informed view of what constitutes good practice in English. This vision will inevitably be wider than some of the specific concerns we have already referred to. There may be occasions when it is necessary for the co-ordinator to insist that something is carried out if she can see that it will be beneficial in the long run. Hopefully, the need for this event may never arise.

Co-ordinators need to make the most of opportunities to develop their own subject knowledge. Some in-service courses provide opportunities for both building subject knowledge and setting personal priorities for your role in school. Even if such provision is not available to you, it is still worth considering your own priorities. Working on your personal priorities will be time well spent. The long-term planner in Figure 3.3 can be used to help develop your own personal priorities as a co-ordinator.

LONG-TERM PLANNER

1. What would I like to have in place in three years time?

    •

    •

    •

    •

2. What stages do we need to go through?

    •

    •

    •

    •

3. What advice and support do I need?

    •

    •

    •

    •

4. What are the strengths to build on?

    •

    •

    •

    •

Figure 3.3   Co-ordinator's personal long-term plan

Drawing up an action plan

An action plan enables you to formalise the priorities you have agreed upon as a school staff and to identify the practical steps you will need to take. There is no single agreed format for an action plan; essentially, a good action plan merely indicates the stages of change, identifies specific targets which will help to achieve that change, names those who are to carry out tasks and sets out a timescale in which these tasks are to be carried out. (For an example of an action plan, see Figure 4.2 in

Chapter 4.) Some guidance on each of the sections of an action plan is provided below.

- **Aims**. This refers to the broad intentions that inform the action you are proposing.

- **Success criteria**. This refers to the tangible, observable and in some cases measurable results that you hope to achieve. Ideally outcomes will reflect some of the areas for concern that your audit has identified.

- **Tasks**. This refers to the separate actions which need to be taken in order to achieve your aims and outcomes. Tasks, of course, vary enormously. They may include training, assessment and recording procedures, resource management, teaching approaches – in fact all aspects of our professional work. So it is important to be specific here.

- **Timescale**. This refers to the time frame during which each specific task should be undertaken. This enables you to sequence the action which you initiate, and to phase in change over a period of time. If you are trialling a new approach, it is helpful to specify a timescale and then evaluate its effectiveness afterwards. If you are adopting a new approach, set a reasonable timescale for implementation.

- **Action by**. This specifies who is responsible for carrying out each specific task. It is worth giving this careful consideration. Try to make sure that your own initials aren't set against every single action! After all, important developments are everyone's responsibilities. In some cases it may be important to feature the headteacher, key stage co-ordinators or year group teams.

- **Evaluation**. This is about monitoring the action plan itself and refers back to the success criteria, tasks, timescale and 'action by' sections. How will you know that the outcomes have been achieved? How will you monitor and evaluate the tasks? How will you check on the appropriateness of the timescale? How can you ensure that those named in the plan actually take the intended action?

Agreeing an action plan

After completing the action plan, it is the co-ordinator's responsibility to have it formally agreed. This will involve making sure that the school management supports your proposals and then arranging for time to present your action plan to the staff. Where others are specified in the 'action by' section, it will be useful to discuss this with them beforehand to ensure that they are agreeable to the task.

If your action plan is the result of wider discussion and results from the sorts of processes described in this chapter, it will not need extensive discussion. During the meeting you will simply need to invite comments and then agree as a staff to accept this as an action plan. Clearly all those involved will need a copy of the final version and it may well be useful to display a further copy on the staff noticeboard.

The action plan for English can then be fed into the School Development Plan. Because of the need to cover all the curriculum areas in the SDP, the senior management team may not want to incorporate every aspect of the English action plan. It will be important, therefore, to decide upon which areas are the priority and need to go into the SDP.

Setting whole-school literacy targets

The Literacy Task Force have stated that all schools need 'to make a commitment to...set literacy targets agreed with their LEA and in line with the LEAs targets for schools' (Literacy Task Force, 1997, p. 23). These literacy targets need to be set in conjunction with the development of an action plan for English, as the two are interrelated. What information should a school use when developing literacy targets?

The results of formal assessment would be one place to start. The subject leader should analyse the scores for English and see if any patterns emerge. SATs results could be analysed over a period of years in order to see if there were any perceptible patterns such as a gradual rise in the number of children achieving a particular level in reading, or a lack of progression in any area. Lawley (1997) suggests that analyses of test results can be made:

- between one year's cohort and the next, or several previous years' cohorts

- between the way the same cohort performs in one year and in later years

- by gender of pupils

- between the school and other schools in the LEA or area

- between the school and national results

- between the school and similar schools in the LEA or anywhere in the country (e.g. similar type of catchment area)

- between what is predicted to be achieved and what is actually achieved

(Lawley, 1997, p. 20)

To this list, we would also like to add that schools should analyse results according to ethnicity, date of birth and free school meals. Whilst using free school meals is a crude indicator, it can provide a picture of attainment amongst pupils who may come from families of low socio-economic status. We would also like to problematise the task of comparing like school with like. In our experience, no two schools are the same. Similarity in catchment area is no guarantee of similarity of children and teachers need to use such comparisons with an awareness of the crude nature of the measurement. Another factor to take into account when examining SATs results is their unreliability as a means of assessing standards over a number of years. The English SATs have changed each year since their introduction, with a clear pattern of inconsistency in the way in which the levels are assigned each year.

Once the SATs results have been analysed, schools can then set targets. These must be realistic targets. For example, if, after careful consideration of the assessment results, there is a large discrepancy between the teacher assessment and the SATs, this would indicate that the staff need further training on the assessment of English and so would form an important future target.

Other targets could be set using the outcomes of other procedures such as language audits or monitoring and evaluation procedures. For example, if the language audit identified the development of information retrieval strategies as an area that needed further attention, then one target could be to ensure that all staff have had sufficient training in developing these skills in children. A further target would be to ensure that each teacher has planned for the introduction of these skills in a manner appropriate for the age group taught.

Another source for devising literacy targets would be an OFSTED inspection report. Any areas identified in a report as in need of attention would be included in a post-OFSTED inspection action plan. However, there may be a key area which is in need of more urgent attention than any other and could be included in whole-school literacy targets. The main point to remember is that whole-school literacy targets should be:

- achievable

- related to the raising of standards in literacy

- measurable

- arrived at through a process of careful consideration of evidence.

Targets need to be specific to each individual school. In terms of what may be expected, we would suggest that a few carefully chosen and achievable targets would be better than a large number of vague or over-ambitious ones. It is essential that they are linked to the School Development Plan and any action plan that English may have. In Figures 3.4 and 3.5, we see an example of the literacy targets set by West Jesmond Primary School. Along with these specific targets, the school has outlined how it will introduce and develop the use of a literacy hour. This type of action plan is required by schools who are involved in the National Literacy Project. The first stage involves curriculum organisation and class management of the hour. The second stage involves staff training and development time and the third defines monitoring procedures.

FORM C: SCHOOL ACHIEVEMENT TARGETS KEY STAGE 1

SCHOOL West Jesmond Primary	LEA Newcastle	DATE 9·6·97

STANDARDS AT SUMMER 1997	PROJECTED TARGET SUMMER 1999	SUCCESS CRITERIA: KEY NLP OBJECTIVES TO BE ACHIEVED	PROGRESS AT SUMMER 1998	STANDARDS ACHIEVED SUMMER 1999
Reading 9% pupils achieved Level 1	Eliminate all L1s by the end of KS1 except for state-mented pupils or those at Stage 4, or E2L or newcomers	• to read on sight high frequency words (list) • to read familiar texts aloud with pace and expression appropriate to the grammar. • to use phonic and word recognition knowledge as a cue (and to tackle unfamiliar words)		
Writing 10% pupils achieved Level 1	as above	• to use capitals and full stops to mark sentences in writing. • identify and compare basic story elements (beginnings, middles, ends) and collect examples.		
12% pupils achieved level 3	increase by 15% (5% in first year, 10% following year)	• to investigate how extended stories are broken up (paras, chapters etc.) and map how each section is related to sections of stories • to re-read own writing to check for grammatical sense (coherence) and accuracy (agreement). Identify errors and suggest alternative constructions		

HEADTEACHER'S SIGNATURE.................

Figure 3.4   West Jesmond Primary School Literacy Targets

FORM E: NATIONAL LITERACY PROJECT SCHOOL ACTION PLAN 1997 - 8

	SCHOOL: West Jesmond Primary	LEA: Newcastle	DATE: 9.6.97		
	ACTION TO BE TAKEN	START & FINISH DATES	BY WHOM	SUCCESS CRITERIA	COSTS	OUTCOME AT JUNE 1998
---	---	---	---	---	---	---
programme of NLP implementation	Follow N.L.P timetable / Year group planning meetings / Advice from co-ordinators / Agree timing of literacy hour / Agree mixed ability — or sets	Sept 97 / June 97 onwards ; July 97		All classes implementing literacy hour		highly motivated staff and pupils working the NLP ; literacy hour well established - well planned organised and delivered
staff training and release time	staff meetings - / plan training programme following course in June. / ½ day per week non combat time - co-ordinators (shared) Thurs.	June		training delivered to full staff in all aspects of NLP	£2400	all staff confident in delivering literacy hour ; positive attitude to teaching of literacy
monitoring arrangements e.g. for teachers' planning, quality of teaching, assessment arrangements, pupils progress	KS1 and reception plans to M.M / KS2 plans to J.D / classroom observation R.KS1 M.M KS2 J.D R-Y6 V.L. / half termly review meetings - senior staff	Sept 97		monitoring arrangement in place ; review meetings timetabled		mid project targets reached. ; all pupils progress tracked.

Figure 3.5. West Jesmond Primary School Literacy Targets – action plan

Chapter summary

The process of conducting language audits and devising action plans is made easier if the co-ordinator is organised and focused. This chapter has suggested a number of ways in which the language co-ordinator can develop an effective level of organisation. We have outlined the processes involved in devising action plans and setting whole-school literacy targets and emphasised the need to be realistic, taking into account the nature and needs of the school. There can be nothing more demoralising than failing to reach targets which are obviously set too high. Given the stressful circumstances that most teachers operate in, target setting needs to be done with sensitivity and care. All schools should be concerned with raising standards of literacy; none should be involved with undermining the confidence and self-esteem of teachers.

4

Developing and Writing a Language Policy

This chapter looks at the subject leader's role in developing whole-school policy. We begin by looking at the significance that has been given to language policies since the late 1960s. We then go on to ask the question, 'What is a language policy?' This is followed by advice on devising a language policy and guidance on the form that it should take. Excerpts from a reading policy are included in order to illustrate the points made in this section. We conclude by considering the implications of the dynamic nature of the policy-making process.

Language policies

The role of a language policy in defining and framing the English curriculum has been an important development in recent years. The 1944 Education Act was not prescriptive about curriculum content or methodology and schools were free to decide themselves what to teach and how to teach it. There was little parity of provision between schools and what there was occurred more through coincidence than cohesive planning. However, as we saw in Chapter 2, the 1960s and 1970s saw many new initiatives and developments in the teaching of English. There were suggestions from some academics working in the field of language and literacy that schools needed to work towards formulating whole-school policies. Harold Rosen (1969) asserted that:

> A more intractable problem has been that some schools are not in the habit of organizing discussions about anything. They have neither the tradition nor the organization for formulating policies agreed on by the staff.
>
> (Rosen, 1969, p. 149)

He and other members of LATE (London Association for the Teaching of English), recognised the importance of language in all learning, proposed that schools should adopt language policies.

> Arising from discussion and investigation it should be possible for some schools to put into operation a language policy which would act as a guide to all their

teachers. Such a policy would, of course, be developed and modified in the light of experience gathered from its formulation and application and would, therefore, be shaped to meet the needs of specific schools.

(Rosen, 1969, p. 168)

The need for language policies was given official recognition by the Bullock Committee which had been set up because of the concern for standards in English. The Bullock Committee's report, *A Language for Life* (1975), proposed that schools devise a policy for language across the curriculum as well as 'a systematic policy for the development of reading competence in pupils of all ages and ability levels'.

This led to a somewhat greater consistency between schools in terms of what was expected in the form of policy documents. Nevertheless, it was still a rather *ad hoc* affair and schools were often given little guidance as to what a policy was or should include. This was also true of curriculum content. In November 1985, the Senior Chief Inspector, Eric Bolton, said:

> It is difficult to identify sufficient common ground, or at least sufficient common language, to begin to discuss the primary curriculum nationally, let alone carry out the kind of scrutiny and development required to develop a primary curriculum framework and agreed objectives.

(Bolton, 1985)

Changes brought in through the Education Reform Act (1988) have led to the establishment of a more cohesive framework for curriculum development and policy-making in the form of the National Curriculum.

What is a language policy?

A language policy is a document which provides a cohesive framework for the delivery of the English curriculum (Ashworth, 1988). A language policy is essentially a statement of the principles and practices which underpin the content and delivery of the English curriculum. As such, a policy is a central way of communicating to a range of audiences, as Figure 4.1 indicates.

It is clear that because the policy has audiences which are both internal and external to the school, the document itself needs to be clearly written, without ambiguity or the inclusion of irrelevant details. Although the policy should be accessible to parents, it is questionable whether the format of policy documents is the best way to communicate the school's philosophy on the teaching of literacy and oracy. We return to this issue in Chapter 11 when we explore the most effective ways in which policies can be outlined for parents.

A major function of the policy is to articulate the approaches staff take to the teaching of English in the school. The policy needs to communicate these key ideas in a clear and accessible manner in order

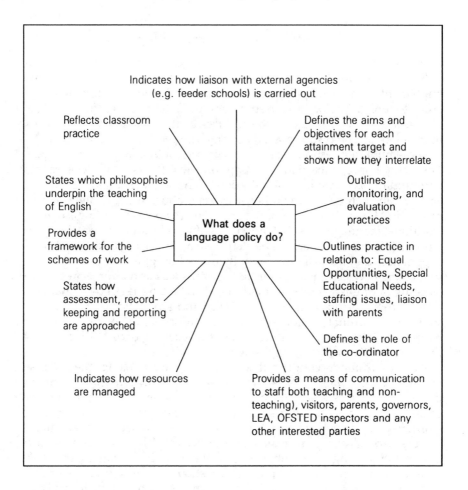

Indicates how liaison with external agencies
(e.g. feeder schools) is carried out

Reflects classroom
practice

Defines the aims and
objectives for each
attainment target and
shows how they interrelate

States which philosophies
underpin the teaching
of English

Outlines
monitoring, and
evaluation
practices

**What does a
language policy do?**

Provides a
framework for the
schemes of work

Outlines practice in
relation to: Equal
Opportunities, Special
Educational Needs,
staffing issues, liaison
with parents

States how
assessment, record-
keeping and reporting
are approached

Defines the role of
the co-ordinator

Indicates how resources
are managed

Provides a means of communication
to staff both teaching and non-
teaching), visitors, parents, governors,
LEA, OFSTED inspectors and any
other interested parties

Figure 4.1. A language policy

to provide information for new or temporary staff, or students undertaking a school placement. The policy will also have a role to play in terms of external accountability. A curriculum policy document allows external agencies (such as OFSTED) to assess how far the school is meeting its stated aims and intentions with regard to a particular subject. It is therefore essential that the policy reflects what is happening in the school. This is only possible if the whole school has some involvement with the devising of the policy. If staff do not feel any sense of 'ownership' of the document, it will be unlikely to be used effectively (Day, Whitaker and Wren, 1987; Corson, 1990). With these principles in mind, we will now examine the processes by which the most successful policies can be created.

Devising a language policy

Corson (1990) suggests that there are four stages to the development of a policy. These are fact-gathering, decision-making by policy-makers, implementation of the policy and evaluation. We will use this model in order to look at the process used by one particular school. In using this case study, we will focus on the features of the policy-making process that can be adapted to the needs of any school.

The school in question is an inner-city school in a large northern city. The school is a Victorian building on two floors, with classrooms surrounding a central hall on both floors. The school serves a catchment area which includes council, housing association and privately owned properties. Over 85 per cent of the children are speakers of English as an additional language. The first languages of the children include Punjabi, Urdu, Bengali and Gujerati. The staff have a variety of backgrounds and experiences and a small number of them are bilingual. Because of recent staff changes which meant an influx of new ideas and approaches to the teaching of English, it was decided to appoint a language co-ordinator to oversee the development of a new policy and scheme of work. The first step the co-ordinator took was to gain information about what was happening in the school with regard to the teaching of English. This was the start of the 'fact-gathering' stage.

The co-ordinator conducted a language audit, using the process outlined in Chapter 3. There was a wealth of information gathered through this process which needed examining and analysing. The co-ordinator did not feel that she could do this alone and so set up a working party which consisted of a number of staff who between them represented all the year teams of the school. The co-ordinator also ensured that bilingual members of staff were on the working party. (We outline the important principles which should underpin any working party in Chapter 7.) The working party met weekly at first in order to assess all the information gathered and draw up a picture of where the school was at the present time. This analysis was then formed into an action plan which provided a basic framework and timetable for future work. Figure 4.2 outlines an action plan.

From this action plan, the working party could enter the 'decision-making' process (Corson, 1990). At all stages, the working party consulted the staff, taking the work in progress to them at staff meetings for feedback and comment. Keating *et al.* (1996) conducted a survey of schools in three counties in relation to their development of English policies. They found that everyone taking part in the research:

> confirmed the importance of ownership, usually high as a result of the collaborative nature of the process and of the need to return to the documents on a regular basis, to reflect and evaluate. Thus the process becomes on-going.
>
> (Keating *et al.*, 1996, p. 38)

Aims	Success criteria	Tasks	Timescale	Action by
To develop a set of overall aims and objectives to inform our curriculum development	Agreed aims and objectives inform our language policy	Staff meeting to discuss the basic aims and objectives in our teaching of English	September 1995	S.J. (Co-ordinator) to organise it; all staff to attend
To develop staff knowledge and expertise in teaching English	Areas identified for staff development across the school	Programme of staff development devised and immediate needs for INSET identified	September 1995 to July 1996	S.J.; LEA adviser; language consultant
To develop a language policy	Language policy written and disseminated	Set up working party to write policy in consultation with staff	October 1995 to July 1996	S.J. to set up working party
To develop a resource base for teaching of English	Resources purchased and distributed; use monitored	Resources identified for development and purchased	October 1995 to March 1996	Head and S.J.
To develop a scheme of work for writing	Scheme of work for writing in place and carried out	Devise scheme of work for writing	September to November 1996	S.J. and working party
To develop a scheme of work for reading	Scheme of work for reading in place and carried out	Devise scheme of work for reading	December 1996 to February 1997	S.J. and working party
To develop a scheme of work for speaking and listening	Scheme of work for speaking and listening in place and carried out	Devise scheme of work for speaking and listening	March to May 1997	S.J. and working party
To inform parents about policies and practice	Parents aware of policy and practice in school	Policies and schemes disseminated to parents through leaflets and open evenings	June 1997	Whole staff; S.J. to co-ordinate
To monitor curriculum developments	Clear picture of practice and outcomes	Monitoring of delivery of English curriculum	January 1997 to June 1998	S.J.; whole staff
To evaluate curriculum developments	Policy and practice evaluated and areas for future development identified	Evaluation of policies and schemes; areas for further development identified	June 1998	S.J, working party; consult with whole staff

Figure 4.2. Action plan arising from a language audit

The development of policies and schemes of work also went hand-in-hand with staff development in the case study school. As Ashworth (1988) suggests is possible, policy-making presented this school with 'a major opportunity for reviewing and developing' the language policy. Lasting changes and school improvement is most often accomplished through staff development (Alexander, 1992). It may be the case that the devising of a policy would not need this extensive review of practice if a school merely wanted to reflect in the policy a curriculum that they felt satisfied with. However, curriculum development should be a continuous process (Campbell, 1985) and so some degree of development should feature in any policy-making process.

Format of language policies

We want now to turn to the format of a policy. Local education authorities differ widely in the advice they give to schools on the structure of policies. There is no single preferred format; the document should meet the needs of the particular school. It is important that the policy document is concise and succinct as schools need to have numerous policies on curriculum areas and other aspects of school life. The policies we have seen in our work with teachers from numerous authorities vary from being two to ten or more sides of A4. There is no perfect length; the policy will be as long as it needs to be for an individual school's needs. The language policy should refer to the following areas:

Philosophy	Resources
Aims	Planning, monitoring and evaluation
Organisation and methodology	Assessment and record-keeping
Equal Opportunities	Staffing and the role of the co-ordinator
Special Educational Needs	
Policy review	Parental and community involvement
	Cross-curricular issues

There may be other areas that individual schools may wish to include. For example, if the school serves children who speak English as an additional language, the policy may contain information regarding the approaches to teaching bilingual children, although often this is a separate document. We will now look at each of these areas in turn and explore what questions need to be asked at each stage in order to inform the policy. Within each section, we include an example of the type of statement that might be contained in a reading policy under each of the headings. These sections are in italics.

Philosophy

This section of the policy outlines what the school feels the subject is about and what value is to be gained from teaching it to children. It provides a working definition of the subject. It can also define how the school feels the subject should be taught. The statement of philosophy is then used to inform the approach to the subject taken in the rest of the policy.

Questions a school might ask in order to develop their philosophy include:

- What is this subject about?

- Why is this subject important?

- How best do children learn this subject?

Philosophy

Reading should be a source of pleasure, enjoyment and richness as well as provide a means of partaking in a range of activities in public, cultural and working life. We need to equip children with the skills necessary to become fluent readers as well as ensuring that they participate as 'active meaning makers' in the process. Children bring with them to school a wide range of attitudes towards, understanding of and experiences with reading. We need to recognise this diversity of children's experiences, skills and understanding and work with them and their families to develop each individual as an able and enthusiastic reader.

Aims

This section outlines what the school wants the children to achieve in that particular subject. It is a statement of what the school is aiming towards in terms of learning outcomes and confidence in and enjoyment of the subject. There is only one question which needs to be asked in this particular section, which is:

- What do we want children to achieve and experience in this subject and how best can we enable them to do it?

Aims

- *To develop children's confidence in themselves as readers.*

- *To develop children's key skills in order for them to read with fluency, accuracy, understanding and enjoyment.*

- *To develop children's knowledge of and familiarity with a wide range of children's literature, both narrative and non-narrative.*

- *To encourage children to respond to the texts they read in a thoughtful and imaginative way, using all language modes.*

- *To develop children's ability to use information texts and locate, extract and use relevant information.*

Organisation and methodology (teaching and learning strategies)

This is where the school can start to outline how the aims identified above can be achieved. This section outlines how the children's learning experiences are organised for that particular subject. This will include references to the methodologies used in teaching the subject and relevant features of class management and organisation. Of particular importance is the range of opportunities and experiences offered for that particular subject. It will also include a reference to the time allocation allowed for the subject.

Questions a school might ask in order to outline their organisation of the subject:

• How are the children organised for learning in this particular subject?

• What are the teaching and learning methods employed?

• Why are these methods used?

• What opportunities and experiences will children have in this subject?

• What is the time allocation for this subject?

• What teaching support is there for the class teacher in this subject?

• How are the learning experiences for this subject integrated?

Organisation and methodology (teaching and learning strategies)

Children are taught as individuals, in groups and as a class. We feel that all three methods are important as they develop particular skills, outlined in the grid. (See Figure 4.3.)

The key skills are approached in varied and systematic ways in order to ensure that children have a wide range of strategies at their disposal. Various approaches to the teaching of reading are adapted and integrated to meet individual needs. A flexible approach is taken in the use of different methodologies and materials. Reading is integrated with writing and speaking and listening in meaningful contexts for specific work with texts. Ability and mixed ability groups are used for different purposes and planned to meet specific objectives.

The quality of the texts provided in order to facilitate children's reading development are of paramount importance. We therefore use a wide range of both scheme and non-scheme books which allows for a flexible but structured approach. Children make their own books and these are also used as general reading material.

Children have access to a wide range of both narrative and non-narrative texts in each classroom, which are situated in the reading areas. Children's reading skills are also developed through the use of IT in the form of television, computers and listening centres. Reading is incorporated into all aspects of the classroom, including the socio-dramatic role play area. A print-rich environment is provided in order to stimulate children's reading.

Type of reading	Provides opportunities to:
Reading individually to teacher	Develop knowledge/familiarity with a range of fiction and non-fiction Relate world of texts to own experiences Develop key reading skills – use of phonic/graphic/syntactic/semantic/bibliographic cues Consider the characteristics and features of different kinds of texts Develop skills in reading aloud Develop the ability to talk about characters, events and language in texts Evaluate the texts read and refer to relevant passages to support opinions Discuss their own reading development in terms of skills, knowledge, understanding, attitude
Whole class reading using big book	Develop knowledge/familiarity with a range of fiction and non-fiction Relate world of texts to own experiences Develop key reading skills – use of phonic/graphic/syntactic/semantic/bibliographic cues Consider the characteristics and features of different kinds of texts Develop the ability to talk about characters, events and language in texts
Group and guided reading	Develop knowledge/familiarity with a range of fiction and non-fiction Relate world of texts to own experiences Develop co-operative skills Develop key reading skills – use of phonic/graphic/syntactic/semantic/bibliographic cues Consider the characteristics and features of different kinds of texts Develop skills in reading aloud Develop the ability to talk about characters, events and language in texts Evaluate the texts read and refer to relevant passages to support opinions Attempt texts which may be too difficult to read independently

Figure 4.3. Organisation of reading

Children are encouraged to read for a range of purposes and audiences. This includes reading with:

- *the teacher*
- *other adults*
- *parents/carers*
- *each other*

- *younger children*
- *older children.*

Planning, monitoring and evaluation

This section delineates the methods of planning for the subject. It should include reference to whole-school, year-group and individual-class planning. It also demonstrates how the school monitors the delivery of the planned work and evaluates how far the plans have been achieved. It is only by reflecting on the outcome of the plans that schools can assess where they have got to and where they need to go next. The three aspects of this section, then, are inextricably linked. This section also outlines how the key areas of progression and continuity will be managed. It should be clear how work will be differentiated to meet individual children's needs.

Questions a school might ask in order to outline their planning, monitoring and evaluation of a subject include:

- How do we plan for this subject at the whole-school level?
- How do we plan for this subject at the year-group and class level?
- What is the subject leader's role in this process?
- How do teachers know if they have successfully carried out those plans?
- How is that knowledge disseminated?
- How is that knowledge acted upon?
- What is the time allocation for this subject?
- How is progression and continuity in this subject ensured?
- How do we ensure work matches children's abilities?
- How are the learning experiences for this subject integrated?
- How is the subject monitored and evaluated throughout the school?
- How are the results of the monitoring and evaluation process fed back to staff?

Planning, monitoring and evaluation

A. Planning

Planning for reading is done at three levels: whole-school planning (long-term); year-group planning (medium-term); individual teacher's planning (short-term). Planning is done within the framework of the National Curriculum. Schemes of work for each year group have been devised and year teams and teachers link their planning in with these. Medium- and short-term plans are monitored by the subject leader; long-term plans are monitored by the subject leader and head teacher.

The model of planning used for schemes of work is based on the SCAA document *Planning the Curriculum at Key Stages 1 and 2 (1995)*. This involves the development of Continuing, Linked and Blocked work. We see this model relating to reading in the following way:

- *Continuing work: Work on key skills, responses to texts, experience of a variety of purposes and audiences for reading; reading a range of narrative and non-narrative texts including both print and screen-based texts. The work includes text level, sentence level and word level work.*

- *Blocked work: An opportunity to focus on a particular skill in depth, e.g. work based on a particular text.*

- *Linked work: Reading work which relates to another subject or subjects as part of a topic.*

Planning shows progression and continuity which is an integral part of the schemes of work.

The time allocation for English is six hours per week.

This system of planning is constantly monitored and regularly evaluated by all staff and the subject leader in order to ensure that it meets the needs of the children, is efficient and manageable and adapts to any changes in curricular requirements.

B. Monitoring and evaluation

The subject leader co-ordinates a programme of monitoring and evaluation of the teaching and learning of reading in school. Evidence used to inform such evaluations includes:

- *teacher's plans*

- *children's reading records*

- *peer observations*

- *interviews with staff and children*

- *sampling of readers*

- *teacher assessments and SATs results*

- *whole-school moderation meetings held once a year in order to ensure consistency in monitoring and assessment.*

Assessment and record-keeping

This section outlines how individual children's work in this particular subject area is monitored and assessed. It will include reference to forms of record-keeping.

Questions a school might ask in order to develop a policy for assessment and record-keeping in a particular subject:

- What are we assessing in this subject?

- How do we assess the children's learning in this subject?

- How do we record our assessments?

- How often do we update our records?

- What do we use as evidence of children's learning?

- What is the nature of our formal assessment?

- How do we ensure that our assessment is consistent across the school?

- How do we incorporate pupil's self-assessment?

- How do we use the results of standardised assessments?

Assessment and record-keeping.

Children's reading development is constantly monitored and assessed in order to inform further planning, teaching and reporting. A variety of modes of assessment are used in order to provide a broad and balanced picture of a child's reading skills. A variety of record-keeping methods are used as records are suited to the purposes of assessment.

Children's reading development is monitored and assessed in the following ways:

- *Children's reading behaviour (attitude to reading, range of texts chosen, etc.) is observed and noted in their reading records.*

- *Children's progression in reading is assessed informally through listening to them read regularly. Comments are made each time they read in their reading record book. This includes comments on individual, paired and group reading.*

- *Running records are used regularly (at least once every half term) in order to provide specific evidence about children's reading strategies.*

- *A reading conference is conducted with each child once a term in order to provide a fully rounded picture of their attainment in reading. This includes a section which notes the children's self-assessment of their reading development.*

- *A checklist of key skills attained (e.g. phonological awareness, phonic and graphic knowledge) is kept for each child. This forms part of the reading assessment portfolio.*

- *Formal assessment of reading occurs through reading SATs in Year 2. These are monitored yearly in order to inform our targets for the subsequent year.*

> *Assessment is used to inform future planning for teaching and to set targets for individual children. The assessment process is reviewed regularly in order to ensure that it is effective and manageable for teachers.*

Resources

This section should not merely consist of a list of resources used for that particular subject. It should state how those resources are managed and deployed.

Questions a school might ask in order to develop a system for organising resources include:

- What is the teaching and learning environment like for this subject?

- How is the budget for resources allocated?

- How are resources chosen for this area?

- How are they managed?

- How do we develop children's independence in using these resources?

Resources

The subject leader controls the budget for resourcing English. The amount allocated to the subject is decided on a yearly basis and is dependent upon the priorities noted in the School Development Plan. The subject leader meets with the staff and whole-school needs for English are decided upon. The subject leader then orders and distributes the resources. A yearly audit is taken by the co-ordinator prior to the relevant staff meeting.

Each class has a clearly identified reading area which has a wide range of reading material, e.g. fiction, non-fiction, information books, poetry, recipe books, comics, books made by children in the class. In addition, each classroom contains a range of purchased and teacher-made materials to support reading development – games, jigsaws, tactile letters, etc. Regular loans are made from the School Library Service to supplement the resources in school.

Each class has a listening centre and a stock of story tapes/language games. There is a computer in each base and a range of software which develops reading skills. Relevant television programmes are selected for use with the appropriate age groups, e.g. 'Storytime' and 'Words and Pictures'.

Each class has a range of scheme and non-scheme books which are taken home regularly in reading folders. There is also a stock of 'storypacks' and story tapes and accompanying books which are available for the home–school reading initiative.

Each class has access to the school library through timetabled sessions. These sessions are structured to facilitate the development of library and information-retrieval skills as well as provide an opportunity for the children to browse.

Each class has the opportunity to visit the local public library once a fortnight. Children are encouraged to borrow books for home use.

Equal Opportunities

This section of the policy outlines how the school will ensure that it enables all children to have equal access to the curriculum. In particular, it will outline strategies used to enable the school to approach the subject in an anti-racist and anti-sexist manner.

Questions a school might ask in order to ensure it is promoting Equal Opportunities in a particular subject include:

- What does research have to say about how 'race', gender or class affect the teaching and learning of this subject?

- What are we doing to ensure that children have equality of opportunity in this subject?

- How is this monitored?

Equal Opportunities

All reading resources are checked for race, class, gender or ability stereotypes in terms of illustrations or text. We ensure that girls and boys have equal access to the reading curriculum. We encourage boys to read a range of fiction texts by providing titles which appeal to their interests, and we ensure that girls are introduced to a range of non-fiction texts and have equal access to computers. Dual-texts books are included in all the classroom collections as a way of valuing children's first languages and encouraging family involvement in reading.

Cross-curricular issues

This is an opportunity for schools to outline how the subject is applied across the curriculum. This is particularly important in a subject such as English as it is the means through which other curriculum subjects are taught.

Questions a school might ask in relation to cross-curricular issues include:

- How does this subject apply to other curriculum subjects?

- How is this detailed in planning?

- How do we knit the various strands of this connection together?

Cross-curricular issues

It is obvious that English is linked to other subjects in an integral way. English is the medium through which children learn. We draw extensively upon the English curriculum in other subjects, e.g. in group discussions, using writing frames for non-narrative writing across the curriculum, reading instructions, etc. and study skills in research work, amongst many others. Where a topic in

> *one subject lends itself to extensive English work, we plan this using the linked medium-term planner.*

Parental and community involvement

As we outline in Chapter 11, we take a wide view of the concept of parenting. We include in this category: birth parents, step-parents, foster parents, adoptive parents, co-parents and any other carers who may be responsible for a child on a day-to-day basis. This section outlines how parental involvement in the particular subject area is encouraged. It also states how the school communicates with parents about the particular subject. In this section, the method of reporting children's achievements to parents can be included. It is also important to outline how the wider community might be involved in a particular subject, if relevant.

Questions a school might ask about parental and community involvement include:

- How are parents involved in this subject?

- Do we do anything which encourages the involvement of parents in this subject?

- How can parents make their views known about the teaching of this subject?

- How do we report children's achievements to parents in this subject?

- What links with the community does this subject promote?

Parental and community involvement

We have a series of events and structures which are designed to encourage the involvement of parents in their child's reading development. When children first enter the school or nursery, we give parents copies of a leaflet designed for them which explains our reading policy and shows how they can help their child. We offer all parents the opportunity to take part in a three-session course on 'Helping your child with reading and writing'. The course is offered in most of the community languages spoken by our parents. A yearly open evening is devoted to the English curriculum and provides us with an opportunity to develop particular themes. Parents are encouraged to come to school early with their children and share a book in the reading area with them before they go. They are also welcomed into school to take part in reading activities in the classroom. This is not organised on a workshop basis but is flexible to meet individual parents' needs. A parent library operates in the Nursery. This is limited because of lack of funds, but parents are allowed to borrow up to two texts a week.

The wider community is invited into school during literacy-related events, e.g. Book Week. A weekly English class for Asian women is held in the school and occasionally takes part in classroom activities.

Special Educational Needs

This section outlines what support children with Special Educational Needs are given in this particular subject area. It need only be brief as the school should have a separate policy on meeting the needs of children with Special Educational Needs.

Questions a school might ask about children with Special Educational Needs include:

- How are children with Special Educational Needs in this subject identified?
- What action is taken to meet their needs?
- How does the co-ordinator work with the SENCO?

Special Educational Needs

Children with Special Educational Needs are integrated into the classroom and classroom materials/curriculum are adapted to meet individual needs. Systematic and regular assessment is made and from this Individual Education Plans are designed for each individual. The Special Needs Co-ordinator and staff ensure that each child has clear identifiable targets which are communicated to parents. The Special Needs Co-ordinator meets regularly with the English subject leader to discuss relevant strategies and materials for children with reading difficulties. Children with reading difficulties are supported in a variety of ways:

- *Reading support is given by a teacher who has been trained in Reading Recovery techniques and who has adapted some of these techniques for group work. Children targeted as needing extra support are involved in small group reading sessions twice a week.*

- *Families of children on individual education plans for reading are visited at home and strategies for working with their child are explored. They are also invited to join the Family Literacy programme when places are available.*

- *It is important that children with difficulties are not presented with a narrow reading diet and so care is taken to provide a rich, stimulating reading curriculum which encourages meaningful interaction with texts.*

Staff development needs and the role of the co-ordinator

This section provides an opportunity to outline how staff development needs in relation to the subject are identified, prioritised and met. The role of the subject leader in the development of the subject throughout the school can also be outlined in order to make the role clear to everyone.

Questions a school might ask about staff development needs and the role of the co-ordinator include:

- How are staff development needs in this subject identified?
- How are these needs collated and prioritised?
- How are these needs met?
- How is staff development in the subject monitored?
- What is the role of the subject leader in this process?
- What other responsibilities does the subject leader have?

Staff development needs

The subject leader will conduct regular discussions with staff on their development needs in reading. Issues that occur as a whole-school issue will be targeted for development through staff meetings and whole-school curriculum days. These will take place in a negotiated programme alongside other curriculum priorities. Individual staff will, of course, have particular needs. The subject leader will provide support using a range of possible methods:

- *working alongside the teacher in the classroom on the particular area of need*

- *suggesting relevant INSET courses*

- *providing a list of books, articles, etc. which the teacher could consult*

- *providing informal support through discussions, etc.*

The needs of NQTs in English will be assessed by the subject leader in the first term of the new appointee's post. The NQT will then be provided with appropriate support by the subject leader. As part of the NQT's induction (see Induction Policy), the English subject leader will introduce the NQT to the English policies, schemes of work and assessment and recording systems.

Support staff will be given guidance by the English subject leader in the teaching and assessment of reading. The support staff will attend relevant INSET and staff meetings when necessary.

Student teachers will have an initial meeting with the English subject leader in which they will be introduced to the English policies and schemes of work. Thereafter, the student's development will be supported and monitored by the class teacher with whom she/he is placed and the mentor. If a student's specialist subject is English, the subject leader will provide them with additional information regarding the role of the English subject leader.

Additional roles of the subject leader with regard to reading

- *To monitor school curriculum planning, delivery and achievement in reading in the variety of ways noted above.*

- *To develop appropriate assessment arrangements including records. To oversee end of key stage assessment arrangements.*

- *To set whole-school literacy targets. To keep up to date with recent curriculum innovations and relevant research and advise colleagues appropriately.*

- *To oversee parental liaison in the area of reading, e.g. booklets, workshops.*

- *To co-ordinate the purchase of reading resources and be responsible for their organisation.*

- *To organise displays around school relating to reading; organise special book events, e.g Book Week.*

Review and evaluation of the policy

This section outlines what the process is for the review and evaluation of the policy. It will also place this review in a timescale, although how specific this is depends on the needs of the school. It will differ from subject to subject, according to the priorities detailed in the School Development Plan.

Questions a school might ask about review and evaluation of the policy include:

- What is the process for the review and evaluation of the policy?

- What is the timescale for this?

- Are there any factors we need to take into account (for example, is subject a high priority in the School Development Plan)?

Review and evaluation

The policy statement for reading will be reviewed and evaluated by staff on a yearly basis to ensure relevance, effectiveness and practicality. Any major changes will be undertaken by a working party for English. The working party will consist of five members of staff to represent the range of year groups. The working party will include staff from the Bilingual Support team.

Further considerations

As we have already seen, there are many different models for language policies. Some local education authorities advocate the inclusion of sections we have not mentioned; for example, liaison with outside agencies and links with the community. Other authorities keep the headings to a bare minimum and stress the need for brevity and clarity. It is entirely the individual school's choice; schools need to develop a policy that meets their particular needs. We strongly believe that it is the way in which policies are formed that is the most important factor in the whole process. There is little point in having a clear, succinct and detailed policy if that policy is not reflected in the classrooms.

We feel that it is valuable for schools to have separate policies on reading, writing, and speaking and listening. Of course all three areas are interlinked and this needs to be acknowledged in a preface, but there are specific aspects of each area which need to be explained. In addition you may wish to attach to the policy any other material the school finds useful. In some cases, this will take the form of additional policies. Here are some examples of different sorts of documents which could be attached to policies:

Reading

- Use of library policy
- Ideas for resourcing a reading area
- Range of types of texts, purposes, audiences for reading
- Criteria for selecting books
- List of reading schemes used by school
- List of relevant ITC resources and software

Writing

- Marking policy
- Spelling policy
- Example of script the school uses
- Ideas for resourcing a writing area
- Range of forms, purposes and audiences for writing
- Diagram of the stages in the process of writing
- List of relevant ITC resources and software
- Alphabets of different scripts that represent the languages spoken by children in school

Speaking and listening

- Drama policy
- Range of purposes and audiences for speaking and listening
- List of relevant ICT resources and software

Once the language policies are in place, they should be regularly updated to ensure that they are reflecting the best of new practice, if that practice is based on sound research. There is little point incorporating the latest 'trend' or bandwagon unless it is an improvement on current practice. The policies should also be disseminated widely. The staff should be familiar with the content if the school has used the processes suggested in this book. This should avoid the unfortunate scenario of, 'We've got an inspection looming – familiarise yourself with the English policy!'

The English subject leader should ensure that the policies are reviewed on a yearly basis and that any changes are agreed by the whole staff. We believe that the policy documents should have a thorough review every three years or so in order to ensure that they are living documents. As Browne (1996) states:

> An effective language policy is not static. It will change in response to classroom practice, teachers' experience, discussion with colleagues and continuing staff development. As teachers implement the policy they will be learning and redefining its guidelines for themselves. As the staff become familiar with the policy and experience for themselves its implications for their role and their management of the children's learning, new needs will be identified.
>
> (Browne, 1996, p. 263)

Chapter summary

In this chapter, we have explored the issues involved in developing language policies. The function and nature of policies has been considered and it has been stressed that the policy needs to be a true reflection of practice in the classroom if it is to be a useful working document. The format of a language policy has been outlined and the questions that need to be asked in order to inform the document have been identified. Finally, we remind the co-ordinator that if the language policy is going to be a living, breathing document which communicates practice to a range of different people for a variety of purposes, it needs to be regularly reviewed and updated. This is also the case for schemes of work, and in the next chapter we turn our attention to the development of what may be considered to be the cornerstone of the curriculum.

5

Developing and Writing a Scheme of Work

In this chapter, we address some of the key issues involved in developing and writing a scheme of work for language. We begin by looking at what a scheme of work is and how it fits into whole-school curriculum planning. The principles put forward for the development of a scheme of work are based on the model for managing change outlined in Chapter 2. We move on to examine a scheme of work which is currently being adopted by many schools: the National Literacy Project's *Framework for Teaching*. We provide examples of the project's planning process. Although widespread adoption of this particular scheme is likely, there will still be a need for many co-ordinators to write schemes of work which are appropriate for their particular circumstances. Therefore we move on to look at what needs to be considered in the process of devising a scheme of work and provide examples from a range of sources. The chapter concludes with a discussion of the key issues facing co-ordinators as we look forward to the millennium and the challenge of further curriculum changes that it will bring.

What is a scheme of work?

The centrality of a scheme of work to the teaching and learning of a subject is widely recognised (Dean, 1995; Bell and Rhodes, 1996). A scheme of work is based on the philosophy and aims outlined in the language policy and maps out exactly what activities the children will be undertaking to achieve those aims. It records the teaching and learning methods used by the school in order to deliver an effective curriculum. It provides a sequential picture of the skills and knowledge children will acquire. These are set out in the order that they are expected to achieve them.

In the English curriculum the idea of a learning sequence is problematic in two ways. First, skills and knowledge are not necessarily acquired in a linear or sequential fashion. For example, the ability to respond to a poem begins in the early years and continues beyond Key Stage 2. The depth and quality of response as well as the level of analysis do, of course, develop, but it is ridiculous to think in terms of children having 'done poetry' and now being ready to move on to scripted drama. Second, prior knowledge is a major factor in language learning and children will have different levels of prior knowledge in different areas of English (Stevenson and Palmer, 1994). In addition to this, each individual child learns at his own pace. What one child achieves in his reception year may take another child a further year to accomplish. Nevertheless, it is generally accepted that teachers need guidelines which set out what is expected of each year group. This ensures continuity and progression across the school.

It is also essential that parallel classes are working within the same framework in terms of expectations and curriculum content. A scheme of work is an important mechanism for ensuring parity between classes of the same year group. However, although schemes of work provide a framework for teaching, it is important that teachers interpret them with some flexibility. The individual teacher must retain sufficient autonomy to enable her to provide appropriate experiences that match the learning needs of the children in her class. An effective school will have confidence in teachers' professional judgements in terms of what is suitable for each child and therefore will expect curriculum guidelines to be interpreted with flexibility.

Curriculum guidelines also need to provide much more than content; they need to ensure that the processes through which children learn are central (Day *et al.*, 1993). This means that the emphasis should not only be on *what* is taught and learnt, but also *how* English is taught and learnt. Therefore, we can see that carefully structured schemes of work which plan for continuity and progression, whilst allowing for flexibility in order to meet individual needs, provide a means for ensuring that children are taught by teachers who are actively thinking about *what* they are teaching as well as *how* they are teaching it. It is also clear that any scheme of work which is not built upon a strong understanding of the key principles of how children acquire skills, knowledge and understanding in a subject has little chance of providing a durable framework for teaching.

How do schemes of work fit into whole-school planning?

Your school will need to have schemes of work for all subject areas that fit together to provide a broad and balanced curriculum. The process of developing this provision is complex and dynamic. A huge balancing act is required; not only do we have the statutory requirements for curricular provision (the National Curriculum and religious education) but there are also other curriculum areas which some schools will want to include (health education; personal, social and moral education) as well as considerations such as providing an appropriate curriculum for bilingual children or children with special educational needs. In addition to this, guidelines have been provided for the overall structure of the curriculum in terms of the amount of time which should be spent on each subject (Dearing, 1994).

Time allocation continues to raise problems in curriculum planning. The Literacy Task Force's *National Literacy Strategy* (1997) requires all primary schools to adopt a literacy hour. This inevitably has repercussions for other areas of the curriculum as schools are finding that they need extra time if they are to address all aspects of the English curriculum. We discuss the implications of any further changes in the final section of the chapter.

What proportion of the timetable should be allocated to English?

Different schools will have different priorities with regard to the amount of time spent on English. It is also likely that the emphasis given to different aspects of the subject will vary from school to school. For instance, if you are working with bilingual children, they will benefit from a greater proportion of time spent on language-based activities. Children who have specific language learning difficulties will also need more input in this area. In addition to this, different children's needs will change as they move through the key stages. Schools need to analyse their situation carefully in order to achieve the right balance. As schools begin to adopt a literacy hour, it is clear that a minimum of five hours a week will be spent on English. How much more time they spend on the subject will depend on the school's approach to language across the curriculum and also how the school addresses the areas of English that are not fully encompassed by the National Literacy Project's curriculum framework.

How should the curriculum be structured?

The School Curriculum and Assessment Authority (1995) recommend that schools adopt a three-tiered model of curriculum planning: long-, medium- and short-term. Figure 5.1 gives an overview of this structure.

Long-term planning

Long-term planning is a process 'through which the various elements of the school's curriculum can be matched with the overall time available for teaching' (SCAA, 1995). It encompasses continuity and progression in all subjects across the key stages and ensures balance and cohesion within and across these subjects. The schemes of work for each subject and for each year group need to be organised into 'manageable and coherent units of work' (SCAA, 1995). This work then needs to be organised so that it is spread across three terms. So, for each year group, there will be a year-long plan of the subject content of each aspect of the

---

Long-term planning

Done by headteacher, subject co-ordinators and staff.
(Or, in the case of the National Literacy Project's Framework for Teaching,
is already provided.) Consists of schemes of work for each subject,
sequenced into year groups across the key stages.

↓

Medium-term planning

Done by class teachers and support staff in teams across year groups.
Contents of termly schemes in each subject are sequenced into weeks
in order to ensure continuity and progression.

↓

Short-term planning

Done by class teachers and support staff. Weekly and daily plans which
outline a balance of different subject areas over the week.
Based on schemes of work and the termly overview.
Can be modified according to needs.

Figure 5.1.   Long-, medium- and short-term planning

curriculum which is based on the time allocated for that subject overall. Usually, each subject co-ordinator is responsible for developing schemes in their subject. Once the long-term plan is in place, the school will have a framework for each year group for three terms. We are not concerned at this point with the content of that framework; we will first deal with the overall structure of the curriculum.

Medium-term planning

Medium-term planning is concerned with developing termly or half-termly plans for each year group. This is usually done by year group teams, or an individual teacher in a small school. If the yearly schemes of work have been planned properly then this stage should simply consist of ensuring a balanced sequence of work over the term and breaking the work down into weekly units in a progressive and cohesive sequence. This is not always straightforward. What a team assumed would take a week may extend to two weeks, or may be completed in days. There needs to be flexibility to suit changing needs.

Medium-term planning is usually done in teams across parallel year groups. This process is more complex in schools with vertically grouped classes. Here, teachers must ensure that they are planning work for the specific age groups within one class. Given that children's abilities differ greatly, there may be children who, for certain activities, are working at the same level as children from a lower or higher year group. It is impossible to prescribe a formula that will match every situation but it is nevertheless important to have a framework. Within that framework, teachers can adapt work to meet the needs of the children in their class.

Curriculum areas may be linked together through topic work. Schools generally have cycles of topics for each year group in order to ensure that work is not repeated unnecessarily. There has been much discussion about the suitability of topic work to the demands of the National Curriculum (Clemson and Clemson, 1989; Alexander, Rose and Woodhead, 1992). However, it appears that some topics provide a useful way of drawing together areas of the curriculum in a cohesive manner providing that they are planned effectively. Webb and Vulliamy (1996) assert that their research indicates that 'topic work continues to remain popular'. Schools need to ensure that topic work is used alongside subject teaching in a thoroughly planned and creative way.

Short-term planning

Short-term planning refers to the weekly and daily plans that teachers make. These are drawn from the schemes of work and termly or half-termly plans of the year group. This planning is made much easier by having a framework which provides clear goals but also allows teachers enough flexibility to change plans if necessary. As we shall see, the weekly planning sheets produced by the National Literacy Project are one approach to short-term planning.

This analysis shows how curriculum planning can be organised. In this model it is clear that schemes of work are the cornerstone of whole-school curriculum planning. Once comprehensive schemes of work have been developed for all subject areas, planning becomes a matter of working from these schemes in such a way as to ensure cohesion and progression. We believe that the more detailed that schemes of work are at the year-group level, the easier medium- and short-term planning will become.

A framework for the teaching of English

Many schools are now adopting the National Literacy Project's *Framework for Teaching* (1997) as their scheme of work for English. We now go on to explore the issues that this raises for the planning of the English curriculum. The rest of this chapter is divided into three main parts. The first part looks at this framework and outlines how one school uses the framework to inform their medium- and short-term planning. We also consider the framework's main strengths and pose some key questions regarding its adoption in schools. The second section provides guidelines for schools who want to devise their own schemes of work, based on the SCAA framework (1995). The final section considers how the *Framework for Teaching* (1997) can be adapted to incorporate the best features of the SCAA (1995) model.

Using the National Literacy Project's *Framework for Teaching*

The National Literacy Project recommends that each primary class is timetabled for an hour of literacy teaching each day. The hour is structured so that it contains a balance of whole-class and group teaching. The programme is designed to ensure that children, over the course of a week, spend about 60 per cent of their time working with the teacher and the other 40 per cent working independently, and that the teacher spends 100 per cent of her or his time involved in direct teaching. The structure of the hour is shown in Figure 5.2.

The first 10–15 minutes	This should involve a whole-class writing or reading session with a shared text. This could include a big book, a passage from a text which is photocopied for the whole class and/or placed on an overhead projector transparency, or a collaborative writing task which is linked to reading in some way.
Next 10–15 minutes	For KS1, this should consist of a whole-class session on word level work (phonological awareness, phonics, word recognition, spelling, vocabulary extension). At KS2, the work could be at word or sentence level (grammar and punctuation).
Next 20–25 minutes	This should consist of directed group activities. The teacher should spend two sessions of (approximately) 15 minutes with each group in the class over the duration of a week.
Final 10 minutes	The hour should conclude with a session in which the class share what they have done during the session or draw together key points, etc.

Figure 5.2.   The structure of the literacy hour

The framework has been carefully designed in order to develop children's skills, knowledge and understanding in English on three levels:

text level, which focuses on comprehension and composition

sentence level, which is concerned with grammar and punctuation

word level, which deals with phonics, spelling and vocabulary.

The framework as a whole is based on National Curriculum requirements. It includes the reading of a wide range of texts, narrative and non-narrative writing, and a systematic approach to the teaching of phonics, grammar, punctuation and spelling. From this framework (or long-term plan), the teaching staff have to devise their medium- and short-term plans. Here, a teacher from Pipworth Junior School in Sheffield, Maggie Lovatt, describes how this process occurs:

> We begin by placing the NLP's teaching objectives into the specified half-term planner for the year group, then transferring them on to our medium-term planner. The NLP has teaching objectives and we need to make sure that we have learning objectives. Also, the NLP provides key points for what to do rather than how you should be doing it and I find it very difficult to teach solely from the NLP plan. I have to process my ideas. We had already established our own way of doing medium-term plans and I prefer it. I know exactly what I am doing and what I need from our planner as it has assessment and resources columns on it.

Maggie and the year team use the NLP's medium-term planning grid to decide what they are going to cover over the half term. The example provided in Figure 5.3 is a plan for Year 5 classes. The texts which are used as a basis for the English work are outlined in the left-hand column. Activities are then planned working on whole-text, sentence and word level in the remaining columns. These activities are taken from the appropriate section of the *Framework for Teaching*.

From this, the team uses the school's medium-term planner (Figure 5.4) to flesh out the activities and add learning objectives.

The work planned included using information texts to research the topic of 'Space and the Planets'. This related to the science topic for that half term.

Once the medium-term planning is in place, the teachers plan their weeks using whatever structure they find most useful. Maggie uses the weekly planner recommended by the NLP. The first two sections detail what she is doing in the shared reading session and the whole-class teaching session at the beginning of the hour. In each of the next five columns, she outlines group activities based on the medium-term planner. The groups rotate around these activities during the course of the week. The activities are differentiated for each of the ability groups. Maggie always spends her time with the last column, the guided reading group, as the NLP specifies that teachers should do this. Each group gets to read with her once a week. The final column outlines who is reporting back in the plenary session. She explains:

> I like the weekly planner as it enables me to see at a glance what each group is doing over the week. I always put the most difficult group activity in the first column and my most able group do it on Monday. They then show what they have done in the plenary. By the time the least able group get to do it, at the end of the week, they have a good idea what to do. I always differentiate activities for each group.

Maggie's weekly plan based on week 3 of the medium-term planner is shown in Figure 5.5.

PIPWORTH JUNIOR SCHOOL
National Literacy Project – Half Term Planner (2nd Half Term)

CLASS: Y5L/W   WEEK BEG: TERM: Spring 2   TEACHER: Maggie Lovatt   YEAR GROUP: 5

WK	Range (Texts)	Comprehension and composition	Grammar and punctuation	Phonics, spelling and vocabulary
6	(Non-Fiction) Save Our Earth	Ongoing through first three weeks: **NON-FICTION READ** **RANGE:** Information books on same or similar themes to use titles, headings, layout, contents, index, etc. to predict structure and content of book prior to reading, e.g. what can you expect it to tell you? Where might you find particular information? Which of several books might be the more useful. Etc. ● to make a simple presentation of information from a variety of sources, e.g. in a class encyclopaedia chart, etc. ● to select theme to investigate (perhaps linked to work in other subjects) – prepare reading, i.e. note what pupils already know, frame questions to be answered and means of recording information, select which books/sections, etc.	● to understand and use the terms 'noun' and 'adjective' appropriately	● to make word banks, class glossaries, dictionaries, etc. or key words linked to particular topics or themes. Use own experience, reading, word searches in information books, dictionaries, etc. to locate words – re-read, use and learn to spell
7	The First Lunar Landing		● to investigate words and phrases that signal: time (when, meanwhile, during, etc.); place/position (here, there, over, under, etc.); cause (because, if, then, when, makes, results in, etc.)	
8	The First Lunar Landing	● to learn how to 'scan' text to locate key words, phrases quickly – use extracts, mark text or make notes. Use 'writing frames' to write notes as connected text. **WRITE** ● to use note-taking to capture key ideas in a few words – use notes to create connected text using 'writing frames' to structure descriptions, reports and explanations	● to identify 'paragraphs' in reading and investigate how they are used to organise ideas. Understand and use the term 'paragraph'	● to learn spellings of irregular or unusual words linked to personal interests, class topics, etc. and high frequency irregulars, from lists 1 and 2, e.g. because, come, people, piece, friend, school, their, water, eyes, money, watch, world, young, etc. ● to experiment with ways of remembering irregular or unusual spellings though creating own mnemonics, word plays, jingles, etc.
9	Poems Not to be Missed 'Macavity'	Ongoing through fourth and fifth week: ● to write own examples of descriptive, expressive language based on those read and collected from stories and poems. Link to grammatical work on adjectives ● to identify and collect examples from poems. Link to work on expressive language in stories – compare poetic with narrative/descriptive examples – compare the	● to explore use of adjectives through reading and writing; link to figurative language in poetry and fiction reading	● to proofread to identify mis-spelt words in own writing; keep individual lists (e.g. spelling logs) to note, practise and learn to spell them. Use these words as a basis for investigating others with similar patterns and meaning
10	Poems Not to be Missed 'Dream of a Bird'	voice, style and forms in stories and poems ● to write own poems based on themes, ideas and structures in those read. Use poem texts to support and structure writing.	● to investigate how words and phrases can be predicted from grammar, e.g. through oral/written cloze, making deletions and considering consequences, etc. Experiment with ordering and reordering sentences to retain or change meaning	● to introduce alternative, more interesting, descriptive, accurate, etc. words in own writing; words for 'then', 'and', 'got', 'nice', 'good', etc.

ONGOING:
HANDWRITING: ● to practise handwriting in conjunction with spelling. Ensure correct orientation and formation in a legible joined style.
WRITING: ● regularly practise new spelling by 'LOOK, SAY, COVER, WRITE, CHECK' strategy; ● to secure recognition and correct spelling at 200 high frequency words from list 2 ● to make organisation and sequence of writing clear using paragraphs, numbering, headings, etc. – use structures as models: We will cover this in topic work through books on space.

Figure 5.3   NLP medium-term planner

PIPWORTH JUNIOR SCHOOL – MEDIUM-TERM PLANNING

Topic Focus: Earth and Space   Curriculum Area: English; Non-Fiction   Term: Spring 2   Teacher Maggie Lovatt

P.O.S.	Learning Objectives	Activity/Organisation/Methodology	Evaluation + Assessment	Resources
S&L 1ai,ii, iii, iv, 2a, 3b, I, ii Covered throughout R1a, b, ci, iv, 2a, ci, ii3 W1c	Children will use reference books to create specific information	**Week One** Shared reading: Save our Earth. Pay particular attention to: titles, headings, layout, contents, index. Use these to predict the structure and content of the book prior to reading, e.g. what can you expect the book to tell you? Focus on the following two sections – 'Our Home Earth' and 'Earth is at Risk'. List any new or topical words for use in later activities. Identify high frequency words from list 2 Identify nouns, adjectives and verbs Group tasks: 1. Children to create own Earth and Space glossary. Provide children with cards with the words already printed on and space for definition and diagram if necessary. Words allocated accordingly to difficulty. Children to find out meanings using glossaries of other books, dictionaries, previous knowledge. Display in classroom under 'Earth and Space glossary'. Encourage children to refer to it.	Our Earth: evaluation and assessment through interaction and marking will take place during each session (T.A.)	Big book: Save our Earth Blackboard Spelling List 2 Cards with words Topic books, dictionaries Suggested words: earth, axis, spin, orbit, shadow, equator, hemisphere, day, night, hour, dark, light
R2cvi		2. Using bank of words where the different parts of speech (verbs, nouns, adjectives, adverbs) are colour coded. Children to create sentences and then identify the function of different coloured words. Children to work in pairs. 3. Use the layout of guided reading book to acquire specified information, e.g. 'On what page would I find facts about the sun?' 'Find the section about DDT' 'List the illustrations in this section, etc'.	During guided reading, focus on the way children: Locate information in order to ascertain whether or not they are able to use reference books effectively When marking work, focus on the manner/style 'info' has been written, i.e. whether it has just been copied rather than aspects selected.	Bank of words, colour coded, A5 paper, pencils Appropriate guided reading books, A5 paper, pencil
R2Civ		4. Using a writing frame children to read through an extract from the shared reading text and make condensed notes. 5. Guided reading.		Text extract Writing frames Appropriate guided reading books

P.O.S.	Learning Objectives	Activity/Organisation/Methodology	Evaluation + Assessment	Resources
S&L 1a i, ii, iii, iv. 2a, 3b	Children will use reference books to locate specific information	**Week Two** Shared reading: The First Lunar Landing. Continue to pay attention to layout, use 'small' books too. Focus on scanning text to locate key words and phrases quickly. Note any words which signal time. Identify high frequency words from list 2. Group tasks:	Ask children to show me how to find specific information. Ask children to identify specific words – can they do it quickly which therefore suggests that they are scanning or is it slow and therefore suggests that they are reading carefully?	Big book: The First Lunar Landing. Selection of small books.
R2Cvi		1. Continue with glossary from week 1.		Spelling list 2.
R2c ii, iv	Children will organise information in a clear and accessible manner	2 and 3. Use topical books to gather information on the moon. According to group ability, guidance will be given, e.g. Group A – points to cover. Group E – specific questions to answer. 4. Children to investigate words which signal time, e.g. when, meanwhile, during. Look through previous weeks guided reading text and list. 5. Guided reading.		Selection of earth and space books; paper; appropriate guidance. Previous wks guided reading text. Appropriate guided reading books.
S&L 1a i, ii, iii, iv. 2a, 3b		**Week Three** Shared reading: The First Lunar Landing. Pay particular attention to headings, organisation of information and paragraphs. Identify high frequency words as previous 2 weeks. Identify any unusual or normal words which are difficult to spell, e.g. necessary, astronaut. List on blackboard. Group tasks:		Big book: The First Lunar Landing List 2 Blackboard
W2d v, vi		1. Children to learn to spell unusual or irregular words from list 2 and topical words. Experiment with ways of remembering through creating own mnemonics. •2 and 3. Same approach as week 2 but children will focus on particular planets and/or the sun in our solar system. •4. Children to organise factual information (sentences about a topic which can be organised under various sub-headings into paragraphs). 5. Guided reading.	When viewing finished products: how is the info organised – clearly and logically, or slapdash? Have children included indexes, headings? Are their facts accessible?	List 2 and blackboard words Factual 'info' of varying degrees of difficulty, A5 paper. Appropriate guided reading books.

* These particular activities are linked to science work on earth and space, where the children will use the information gathered to make their own reference/non-fiction books.

Curriculum Area: English; Non-Fiction/Poetry

P.O.S.	Learning Objectives	Activity/Organisation/Methodology	Evaluation + Assessment	Resources
S&L 1a I, ii, iii, iv. 2a, 3b covered throughout R1ciii, d iii, iv plus those covered in N-F R1a, b, ci, iv 2a, ci, ii, 3.	Children will distinguish between figurative and narrative poetry	**Week Four** Shared reading: 'Poems Not to be Missed'. Pay particular attention to descriptive and figurative language in 'Macavity'. Note how each verse refers to a different aspect of Macavity's life/character. Think about how each verse refers to a different aspect of Macavity's life/character. Identify high frequency words from list 2. Compare Macavity the Mystery Cat to more expressive poems: note the differences in language.	Evaluation and assessment through interaction and marking will take place during each session (T.A.) Through questioning, are the children able to note differences in language. Are they able to offer examples?	Big book: Poems Not to be Missed
W1 a, b W3 b		**Group tasks:** 1. Using big book, children to collect descriptions of Macavity. 2. Identify the adjectives in the above descriptions. 3. Choose own cat or other animals. Brainstorm the descriptions which could be used for it.		Big book, A5 paper, pencils Previous work on descriptions A4 paper, thesaurus
W1 a, b, 3c W2 d		4. Introduce personal word books for children, identify any words mis-spelt in animal descriptions and put correct spellings in word book. 5. Guided reading, poems.	During guided reading, are the children able to identify narrative and/or figurative poems?	Word books, descriptions, dictionaries, pencils Appropriate guided reading books
S&L 1a, ii, iii, iv. 2a 3b		**Week five** Shared reading: 'Poems Not to be Missed'. Pay particular attention to feeling and mood of 'Dream of a bird'. Discus what it would feel like to be away from familiar territory, e.g. moving house, school. Identify high frequency words from list 2. What phrases and words can we use to express these feelings? E.g. lost, lonely, empty like a shell.		Big book: Poems Not to be Missed.

P.O.S.	Learning Objectives	Activity/Organisation/Methodology	Evaluation + Assessment	Resources
W1b, 2bi, ii, iii, iv, v		**Week Five continued** Group tasks: 1. Experiment with ordering and reordering sentences to retain or change the meaning. 2 and 3. Children to try writing their own narrative poem: subject to be their journey to school. Structural guidance and pointers given according to ability of group. 4. List feelings when falling out with a friend. 5. Guided reading, poems. Ongoing: secure recognition and correct spelling of 200 high frequency words from List 2 though LSCWC. This will be done outside of the literacy hour (10 mins before assembly).	Are the finished poems telling a story? If they are, then have they taken on board the idea of narrative poetry?	Selection of sentences to reorder. Structural guidance. A5 paper, pencils. Appropriate guided reading books.

Figure 5.4   Pipworth's medium-term planner

The school has tried to alleviate the heavy planning load for teachers by allowing teachers in the same year group to plan a few weeks and rotate their plans around. This means that teachers only have to plan two or three weeks work rather than the whole of a seven-week half term. Maggie asserts:

> I would rather plan for two-week chunks and rotate those because then you can build up on work done in the first week. We have found that single week rotation doesn't allow this. It does cut the workload. This half term I've only had to plan for three weeks rather than seven.

It is inevitable that each school and teacher will adapt the literacy hour to meet their needs. Maggie says:

> I didn't like the children doing handwriting as a group activity away from me as I can't check letter formation and so now on Thursdays we do 15 minutes handwriting as a whole class. By Thursday I have done a lot of my teaching and we are whizzing through the texts so I can fit it in. I also do a 10-minute spelling test weekly. Sometimes on Fridays I have extra help. If I do, I give them the guided reading group and it allows me to go and work with another group. I make sure I focus on the special needs children and make sure they are getting their IEPs done but I also want to get the balance so that they are not missing out. A lot of them haven't got the concentration span to sustain things for 25 minutes but they have got the enthusiasm when they are doing the shared reading. They are enjoying the book and want to do the activities so it is getting the balance and fitting it into their level. I'm still working on this.

Maggie's excellent planning skills have adjusted to the NLP over time to a point where she is obviously in control and using the framework to plan a range of interesting work based on a variety of texts. She asserts that teachers have to try things out and be prepared to adapt and change things if necessary:

> You've just got to go in there, do it and see how things happen. We all want to get it right first time and you can't. You have to let it evolve. It's having the patience to think, 'Right, well just see how this goes'.

It can be argued that the *Framework for Teaching* (1997) provides a carefully structured scheme of work for English. It is obvious, from the examples provided by Pipworth Junior School, that it is enabling some schools to plan for a variety of work based on a broad range of texts. This book is not the place to enter into a debate about these recent developments in planning and teaching literacy. However, we have certain general questions which the subject leader will need to address when considering if this scheme of work is to fulfil its function in meeting the needs of all children (see Figure 5.6).

We envisage the *Framework for Teaching* being adopted by a great many schools during the next few years. It will also, no doubt, be adapted to

CLASS: Y5L/W
YEAR GROUP: Y5
TERM: Spring 2
WEEK BEG: 3.3.97
TEACHER: Maggie Lovatt

	Whole-class work: shared reading	Whole-class work: phonics, spelling, vocabulary	GROUP TASKS — Mnemonics	GROUPS TASKS — Researching planets in solar system	GROUP TASKS — Research used to make reference books in topic time	GROUP TASKS — Organise factual information into paragraphs and under sub-headings	GROUP TASKS — Guided reading	Plenary
Mon	The First Lunar Landing. Identify paragraphs and words difficult to spell	Review Look-Say-Cover-Write-Check (LSCW) words	A Folens WS p. 25 — choices of words from blackboard list. Make up — T OA I	B Pointers to cover. Outer plants Uranus, Neptune, Pluto — T OA I	C Boxes to record specific info – Jupiter and Saturn — T OA I	D Sentences to organise under various sub-headings — T OA I	E Planets in the solar system. 'The Moon and Stars' — T OA I	Share mnemonics (A)
Tues	Discuss how information is organised into paragraphs	Continue to identify difficult words, suggest mnemonics	B As A – own mnemonics — T OA I	C As Monday – boxes to record specific info. – Jupiter and Saturn — T OA I	D Questions in boxes: Mars (L) Earth (W) — T OA I	E As D, but easier sentences — T OA I	A 'The Solar system and the Sun' pp. 6–7 pp. 24–25 'Incredible universe' — T OA I	Share facts about Mars/Earth (D)
Weds	Recap on taking notes	Use mnemonics to spell difficult words	C 3 words: lunar, astronaut and equator – make up mnemonics — T OA I	D As Tuesday – questions in boxes: Mars (L) Earth (W) — T OA I	E General information about planets in solar system. Specific questions to answer. — T OA I	A Identify number of paragraphs in various newspaper articles — T OA I	B 'The Solar system and the Sun' 'Atlas of space' — T OA I	Share info about solar system (E)
Thurs	Discuss use of sub-headings	Scan text to locate spelling (LSCWC) words	D 3 words: lunar, orbit and equator – make up mnemonics — T OA I	E General info. about sun: again, specific questions to answer on guided reading book — T OA I	A Pointers to cover – The Sun — T OA I	B As A — T OA I	C 'Earth and Space' pp. 22–23 — T OA I	Organisation of paragraphs (B)
Fri	Evaluation of big book	Block letters in LSCWC words – children to identify missing letters	E Above words but with guidance from adult who will also be the scribe, work as a group — T OA I	A As Thurs – pointers to cover – The Sun — T OA I	B As Monday — T OA I	C As D — T OA I	D As C but pp. 20–21 focus — T OA I	Evaluation of The First Lunar Landing work

Key: T = Teacher   OA = Other Adult   I - Independent

Figure 5.5 **Pipworth's weekly planner**

- How far can the framework be adapted to meet the needs of specific schools?

- How do children in the early stages of acquiring English as an additional language manage the rigid structure of the literacy hour?

- What are the implications for the writing and oracy curriculum if teachers spend *all* of their time with groups on guided reading?

- What are the implications for hearing individual children read? (This is not part of the hour.)

- Given the time constraints of the curriculum, how can extended reading and writing activities be incorporated into the framework?

- What are the implications for extended literature-based work?

- Some schools are using the same big book for five days. Do all the texts used have the depth and versatility to sustain this treatment without them becoming tedious for children?

- How can the *teaching objectives*, as outlined in the NLP, be matched to what children need to *learn* rather than what we would like to teach?

- What happens if children do not acquire the necessary skills, knowledge and understanding to move through the scheme at the rate which is outlined? What happens if the variation within the class is very great?

- How are the National Curriculum requirements for speaking and listening addressed, as oracy plays a fairly restricted part in the *Framework for Teaching*?

- Related to the last point, how much time will schools have for such essential activities as structured role play areas and drama? Will the time be taken from the rest of the curriculum? What implications does this have, given that schools are already recommended to continue with other English practices, such as USSR and class reading of stories, outside the literacy hour?

Figure 5.6. Questions relating to the NLP *Framework for Teaching*

meet individual schools' needs and the co-ordinators of the National Literacy Project in Sheffield emphasise that this process of adaptation and modification is already occurring. However, we also believe that even though OFSTED inspections will measure schools' schemes of work against the framework, there will still be some schools which will want to devise a scheme of work that is particular to their needs and circumstances. For that reason, we are also including an alternative model for developing a curriculum framework.

Developing and writing your own scheme of work

Because of the wide-ranging nature of the English curriculum, it can be overwhelming for a co-ordinator to be faced with the prospect of developing a scheme of work. It is important that, where possible, the task is not undertaken by the co-ordinator alone. As we outlined in Chapter 1, it is essential that the whole staff are involved with developing a scheme of work. In a large school, a working party can develop the scheme and report regularly to the whole staff. The scheme can then be revised and amended in the light of feedback from the whole school. In a small school, the co-ordinator may well have to produce the scheme alone. The support of colleagues working in similar settings and of the LEA's advisory service are important here. However, the co-ordinator will still need to discuss drafts with other staff in order to ensure that they are happy with the scheme.

It is essential that the scheme of work is based upon actual classroom practice. There is no point in developing schemes which look good on paper but which have no basis in reality. However, writing a scheme of work can, and should, go hand in hand with curriculum development. Negotiating the scheme may well provide the co-ordinator with a useful tool for identifying and developing areas of good practice and prioritising areas which need immediate attention. For example, if as a co-ordinator you identified the teaching of information skills as an important aspect of your scheme of work, but found through discussion that there was little classroom expertise in this area, then you would need to organise professional development work to raise staff awareness and develop practice. We look at ways of organising such staff meetings in Chapter 7.

By adopting this view of policy-making we need to accept that progress will be slow. It will mean that a school has to set priorities whilst developing its scheme of work. These priorities will include the kinds of staff development that are necessary to turn policy into practice and so a certain number of staff meetings will need to be allocated to the process. As we pointed out in Chapter 1, the school needs to co-ordinate curriculum development so that sufficient staff development time is given to each subject area. This should be outlined in the School Development Plan (Dean, 1995; Bell and Rhodes, 1996). Figure 5.7 provides an overview of this developmental process of devising schemes of work.

Taking into account the factors discussed already concerning the nature of the development of schemes of work, we now want to focus on the process of writing a scheme for English. Let us assume that you are using the developmental model outlined in Figure 5.7. You now need to set the schemes of work out using a format that is useful and easy to

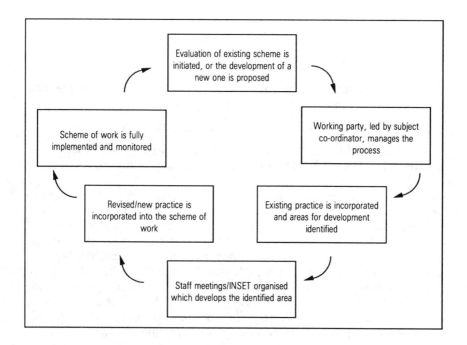

Figure 5.7 The process of developing schemes of work

handle. The schemes of work are intended to be working documents and so should be both useful and accessible to a class teacher. Teachers should be able to draw out their weekly and daily plans from the formats (see Figure 5.8).

Having organised the framework for the content of the scheme of work, what is the next step? We use the model for curriculum planning outlined in the SCAA document, *Planning the Curriculum at Key Stages 1 and 2* (SCAA, 1995). This involves the breaking down of the curriculum into units of work, identified as **continuing, blocked** and **linked**. These units can be defined in the following way:

Continuing	**Blocked**	**Linked/topic**
Aspects of English which require regular and frequent teaching	Aspects of English which can be taught as cohesive and separate blocks	Aspects of English which can be linked to work in other subjects areas

We will now deal with each area in turn and outline how they can be applied to the language curriculum and form the basis of a cohesive scheme of work.

Continuing work

SCAA (1995) defines continuing work as that which:

- requires regular and frequent teaching and assessment to be planned across a year or key stage to ensure progression;
- contains a progressive sequence of learning objectives;
- requires time for the systematic and gradual acquisition, practice and consolidation of skills, knowledge and understanding.

We interpret this as referring to the daily work that teachers plan in order to develop children's literacy and oracy skills. It is impossible to plan for *every* instance of language development in the classroom and we would not want to advocate such a sterile route to language acquisition. However, it is important to plan a comprehensive and systematic range of activities which will develop skills, knowledge and understanding in the three attainment targets. Continuing work, then, consists of those aspects of the English curriculum that need regular teaching and practice in order for children to progress adequately through the programmes of study. The National Literacy Project framework provides a structured approach to teaching continuing work in literacy.

We advocate a systematic approach to this method of planning. Looking at the programmes of study for each of the three attainment targets, they are organised into 'Range', 'Key Skills' and 'Standard English and Language Study' (National Curriculum, 1995). It would seem appropriate, therefore, to plan for these three areas specifically when developing schemes of work. Of course, it is inevitable that some activities will encompass more than one of these areas. Reading nursery rhymes to children, for example, is both extending the range of children's experience of written text and developing a key skill (phonological awareness). However, the learning intention which is the priority in that particular activity should be identified and the activity recorded accordingly. Despite these complications, the attempt to map out a language curriculum will be made easier by a systematic approach and so working through the areas of 'Range', 'Key Skills' and 'Standard English and Language Study' will provide a solid framework for curriculum content. Of course, schools will also want to expand upon the National Curriculum and ensure that their scheme of work answers questions that are relevant to their needs, for example:

- Are the children introduced to the scripts and writing systems of other languages?
- If children are bi-literate, are they given opportunities to use their skills in the classroom?

• Are children given opportunities to use ICT in writing tasks?

A consideration of these questions will enable a working party to establish what experiences the children should have in order to develop their skills, knowledge and understanding in these areas and a solid programme for continuing work in writing can be devised. The activities should be sequenced into year groups. Figure 5.8 contains an excerpt from a continuing scheme of work for writing. It sets out the learning experiences for the reception year group at Sharrow Nursery Infant School in Sheffield.

Blocked work

SCAA (1995) defines blocked work as that which is drawn from a single subject or aspect of the curriculum. It:

• can be taught within a specific amount of time, not exceeding a term

• focuses on a distinct and cohesive body of knowledge, understanding and skills

• can be taught alone or have the potential for linking with units of work in other subjects or aspects of the curriculum.

In terms of work in English, we see this as an opportunity to plan units of work aimed at developing particular skills or knowledge in each of the three attainment targets. These blocks of work may be very short (lasting for a couple of sessions in one week), or they may develop over several weeks. Obviously, the amount of time spent on blocked work will vary according to the nature of the tasks. The time spent on blocked work will also affect the amount of continuing work which is planned.

Figure 5.9 sets out the areas that are particularly suitable to being taught through blocks of work. The list is not exhaustive. Although the three attainment targets are separated, we acknowledge that they are interlinked. Language work often involves a mixture of talking, reading and writing.

It is important that blocked work is planned so that it builds upon skills and knowledge the children already have. A block on writing different forms of poetry, for example, needs to take account of what the children have done already in this area instead of repeating work they have already done. To illustrate this, we have devised a developmental programme for the introduction of different forms of poetry. These are based on the ideas of Sandy Brownjohn (1994) and if you are interested in finding out more about these forms, we recommend her books as further reading.

We are not advocating spending one or two weeks a year on writing poetry and then not encouraging the children to write poetry during the rest of the year. All forms of narrative and non-narrative writing should

Scheme of work for English   Continuing work in writing   Year group – Reception

Links to POS	Learning purposes	Experiences/activities	Organisation	Assessment	Resources
AT3, 2a.	Be able to differentiate between writing and pictures. Recognise the connections between speech and writing. Understand that writing is a means of communicating ideas. Understand that writing can take many forms – there are a variety of scripts.	Discussions over a period of time – use a picture book as a starting point. Where are the pictures? What is this (pointing to writing)? How is it different from the pictures? When I read the story, how do I know what to say? Where is the writing here (using a dual-text book)? Does anyone in your family write using this script?	Whole-class discussions.	Are children able to recognise the differences between pictures and writing? Do they recognise the connection between writing and speech?	Range of picture books including dual-text books.
AT3, 1a.	Understand the purposes and value of writing as a means of communicating, remembering, organising ideas, etc.	Brainstorm – what do we use writing for? Why do we need to write? Take in a variety of forms of writing as a prompt, e.g. forms, letters, cards, shopping list, notices. Variety of scripts.	Whole-class and small group discussions.	Are children aware of the range of purposes there are for writing and the different forms writing can take?	Range of forms of writing, e.g. shopping list, forms, notices, cards.
AT3, 1a, 2a.	Develop confidence in themselves as writers and encourage independence in writing.	Independent mark-making and writing encouraged in a variety of situations, e.g. role-play areas, writing table.	Provide resources and set occasional tasks in role-play/writing areas for individuals/groups.	Do children take the opportunity to undertake writing in the classroom, independently of the teacher? Do they enjoy writing?	Well-stocked writing area – see enclosed stock list. Provision for literacy in the role-play areas.
AT3, 1b, 1c.	Have opportunities to write in response to a variety of stimuli, using difference forms and for a range of purposes and audiences.	Set writing tasks in response to a variety of stimuli which will encourage writing in a range of forms, for different purposes and for a variety of audiences. Forms include: stories, diaries, lists, notes, instructions, letters, messages, invitations, etc. Purposes include: to inform, to entertain, to communicate ideas, as a reminder, etc. Audiences include: peers, teacher, parents, other classes, etc.	Whole-class, group and individual tasks. Teacher acting as scribe where appropriate.	Are children familiar with a range of forms of writing? Are children aware that writing can have different purposes? Are children able to adapt their writing to the perceived needs of the audience?	Examples of different forms of writing in various scripts.

Figure 5.8   Continuing scheme of work for writing

Speaking and listening

Role-play area which focuses upon specific skills, e.g. complaining
    about faulty goods to a shop
Storytelling week – invite storytellers into school
Narrating stories/poems to different audiences
Making story tapes for specific audiences
Taping instructions for games/activities the children have devised
Videoing the children giving news broadcasts/weather reports/
    advertising
Drama work based on a particular text/theme
Puppet theatres
Making radio programmes involving a range of skills, e.g. interviewing,
    explaining, persuading

Reading

Reading and responding to poetry
Myths, fairy tales and legends
Using features of information books, e.g. contents pages, indexes,
    glossaries
Reading works by a key author
Work on particular genres
Reading versions of the same story and comparing
Book Week
Using libraries
Reading to particular audiences

Writing

Pop-up books, lift-the-flap books
Writing poetry
Instructions
Scripts
Comics
Writers week – invite local authors in, run parent/child writing
    workshops, ask children to write profiles of themselves as authors,
    etc.
Particular features of style, e.g. paragraphing/punctuation.

Figure 5.9.   Suggestions for blocked work

be part of the continuing scheme of work for writing. Rather, blocked work presents us with an opportunity to build up particular skills, knowledge and understanding in a more focused way. In our example we focus on the skills involved in composing specific forms of poetry. Figure 5.10 shows what this programme of blocked work might look like throughout the primary school.

Year	Forms of poetry focused upon in blocked units of work
Reception	Rhyming names Tongue twisters Group poems, teacher as scribe Children dictate statements about a particular theme, then rearrange statements to compose poem
Y1	Acrostics Advertising jingles Limericks Kennings
Y2	Haiku Tanka Cinquains
Y3	Epitaphs More work on haiku, tanka, cinquains Short form extensions
Y4	Counting syllables (e.g. ten syllable lines) Iambics Rondolets
Y5	Narrative poems Ballads
Y6	Pantouns Sonnets

Figure 5.10 Poetry in blocked units

Through these particular periods of blocked work, children will be introduced to various forms of poetry. Their features will be examined and discussed before the children attempt to write their own. Once the children have been introduced to these formats in this intense, focused way, they will feel more confident about using different forms when writing poetry at other times.

The format used for the continuing scheme of work should also be used for the blocked scheme of work. Figure 5.11 gives, as an example,

Scheme of work for English.   Blocked work: A critical look at newspapers.   Year group - Y6

Links to PoS	Learning objectives	Experiences/ activities	Organisation	Assessment	Resources
AT1, 1a.	To understand the purpose of newspapers in society.	Discussion about what purposes newspapers serve in our society. Teacher lists the comments made.	Whole class.	Do the children understand the role/ uses of newspapers?	Large sheet of paper, marker.
AT1, 1c. AT2, 2c.	To develop skimming and scanning skills. Identify relevant information.	Children analyse the contents of a newspaper. Make a list of all the features found e.g. news stories, T.V. guide, etc..	Group work.	Can the children use skimming and scanning skills to identify appropriate information?	Variety of newspapers.
AT1, 1a.	To develop understanding of the role of newspapers.	Return to list made as a class about the function of newspapers - does anyone want to add anything to that list? Why?	Whole class.	Do the children understand the role/ uses of newspapers?	List made in first activity.
AT2, 1b, 2b, AT3, 1a.	To develop an understanding of the concept of 'news'.	What sort of news does a tabloid newspaper report? Children make a list of the types of stories that one edition contains e.g. stories about famous people, disasters.	Group work.	Do children understand the concept of 'news'?	Tabloid newspapers.
AT1, 1a, 1b, 1c, 2a. AT3, 1b, 2b.	To develop the ability to organise speeches and present arguments to a large audience. To develop inferential and deductive skills.	Analysis of order of importance given to news. Children compare the front-page story with articles in the rest of the paper. Have to decide why that particular story is on the front page and whether they agree with that decision. Relate their findings in a presentation to the rest of the class.	Group and whole class work.	Can the children use inferential and deductive skills when reading? Can they construct cohesive arguments in a speech?	Collection of newspapers.
AT1, 1a, 1c, 2a.	To develop the ability to ask relevant questions.	Brainstorm questions for an interview with a local newspaper editor to find out how they prioritise news. Conduct the interview.	Group work.	Can children identify relevant questions?	Invite local editor to school. Tape recorder.
AT3, 1a, 1c,2a.	To use the report genre appropriately.	Write a report on the interview. Children state how far they agree with the editor's strategy.	Individual work.	Can children use the report genre appropriately?	

Figure 5.11 Extract from blocked scheme of work

an excerpt from a school's blocked work on newspapers. The work has been planned for a Year 6 class. This block of work is intended to be taught over a two-week period.

Linked work

In the SCAA (1995) model for planning the curriculum, linked work describes how two or three subject areas can interrelate. They state that units of work from different subjects can be linked when:

- they contain common or complementary knowledge, understanding and skills, e.g. developing reading and writing skills through work in history

- the skills acquired in one subject or aspect of the curriculum can be applied or consolidated in the context of another, e.g. work on co-ordinates in mathematics applied to work in geography on four-figure grid references

- the work in one subject or aspect of the curriculum provides a useful stimulus for work in another, e.g. creating music from a poem or a pictures.

It would seem sensible to use this model of planning for topic work. Given that topic work is still widely used in primary schools (Dean, 1995), it would appear that systematically planned linked work retains the best features of topic work whilst eradicating some of the difficulties identified by various researchers (Campbell, 1993).

For example, it may be that a topic on 'Weather' is needed in order to cover the relevant attainment targets in science and geography. The links to English could consist of writing reports of experiments, writing and videoing weather reports, making information books about aspects of the weather. There would also be links to other subject areas such as maths, technology, art and music. Figure 5.12 is an extract from a school's linked scheme of work on 'Our bodies'. The work has been planned for a Year 1 class and is intended to take place over a term.

Using continuing, blocked and linked work in short-term planning

So, how does this method of planning affect the short-term planning of the class teacher? The teacher will sequence the activities contained in the continuing scheme of work over the term. The blocked and linked work will then be fitted in around this. A typical week's work for a Year 2 class, planned in this manner, may take the format shown in Figure 5.13. The blocked work is drama work based on the text *Where the Wild Things Are* and the linked work is connected to the topic of 'Weather'. The time allocated for English is 6.7 hours per week.

Linked work - English, Science, Design and Technology. Topic - Our bodies. Year group - Y3

Links to PoS	Learning objectives	Experiences/ activities	Organisation	Assessment	Resources
Science - AT2, 2f. Eng. AT1. 1a, 2a.	To understand that humans have skeletons and muscles to support our bodies and help us move.	Discussion about what we can feel under our skin. Find a part of yourself where you can feel bone. Describe it. Feel the muscles in your arms and legs. Describe them. What purpose do they serve?	Whole class.	Do children understand that humans have skeletons and muscles to support our bodies and help us move?	
Sci. AT2, 2f. Eng. AT2, 1b, 2c.	To develop the ability to locate relevant information in books and computers.	Children investigate the function of the skeleton and muscles using information books and the computer. Put information found onto a database.	Individual/ group work.	Can children locate relevant information in books and computers?	Information books, computers.
Sci. AT2, 2f. Eng. AT3, 1a.	To become familiar with the structure of a skeleton.	Draw and label the parts of the skeleton, using information books for labelling.	Individual work.	Are children familiar with the structure of a skeleton?	Information books.
Sci. AT2, 2f. Eng. AT2, 1b, 2c.	To investigate the differences between hinge joints and ball and socket joints.	Find out which of your joints move like hinges. Which joints swivel? Make two lists and compare them with a partner. Use information books/ computers to check your investigation.	Individual and paired work.	Do children understand the differences between hinge joints and ball and socket joints?	Information books, computers.
Sci - AT2, 2f. D & T - AT 1a, b,c, 2a, 3a, 3c, 1 Eng. AT3, 1a,1c.	To become familiar with the structure of a skeleton and the nature of joints.	Design and make a skeleton which has joints that move. Write a description of the process of designing and making the final product.	Individual work.	Are children familiar with the structure of a skeleton and the nature of joints?	Card, paper fasteners., cotton reels, string etc.
Sci. AT2, 2b, f. Eng. - AT2, 1a, 2a AT3, 1a, c, 2a.	To discover which foods are calcium-rich for growing bones.	Discuss the need for calcium. Use information books to find out which foods are rich in calcium. Make a leaflet about the need to eat calcium and provide information about relevant foods. Include a calcium-rich recipe.	Paired work.	Do children know which foods are calcium-rich for growing bones and can they relay that information effectively?.	Information books.
Sci - AT1, 1a, d,e, 2a,b, 3a. AT2, 2f. Eng - AT3 1a, 1c	To understand why bones are strong. To devise and carry out a fair test.	Make cylinders out of card to represent the long cylindrical bones in our body. Design a fair test which will compare their strength to a flat piece of card. Write a report of the experiment.	Paired/ group work.	Do children understand why bones are strong? Can they devise and carry out a fair test?	Card, sellotape, weights, rulers etc.

Figure 5.12 Extract form linked scheme of work

Continuing work	Blocked work	Linked work
Reading – individual, group and paired reading activities using a range of fiction and non-fiction books. (1 hour) Reading aloud to an adult in a group reading situation (15 minutes) Listening to an adult read a range of fiction and non-fiction material (45 minutes) Work on key skills: Phonic games and activities (40 minutes) Key word/spelling games and activities (45 minutes) Class discussion about punctuation, using big books (15 mins) Writing a letter to parents, inviting them to video showing of weather forecasts (20 minutes) Working on specific letter formation, based on individual needs (10 minutes)	*In previous week, the blocked work had consisted of: Read through the text as a class. Discuss. (20 minutes) Assign groups a scene from the book in order to make a still picture of it (30 minutes)* This week: Hot seat children as Max and Max's mother (15 mins) Telephone conversations between Max and his mother (15 mins) *Next week, the blocked work will be:* *In groups, improvise a scene between Max and his mother on his return. There can be other family members present. (30 minutes)* *In groups, write script based on improvisation (1 hour)*	Reading a range of weather forecasts from a variety of newspapers in groups. Noting down the features (20 minutes) Writing own weather reports in pairs (20 minutes) Reading a variety of information texts about a particular aspect of the weather. Using a chart to collate information (30 minutes) Writing an evaluative report on a technology activity – making a weather vane (20 minutes)

Figure 5.13. A week of continuing, blocked and linked work

If schemes of work are developed at the whole-school level for the continuing and blocked work, teachers medium-term planning will become much easier. All that would be required would be to:

- highlight the continuing scheme of work for the year to show which activities were happening that term
- use the blocked schemes of work where they fitted in
- develop a linked/topic scheme of work, drawing together work in all the different areas that fit into a particular topic.

The role of the English co-ordinator is to oversee the process in the school and to ensure that each year group has an appropriate balance of continuing, blocked and linked work. Effective monitoring systems will need to be in place to ensure that the schemes of work are successful across the range of year groups and flexible enough to allow for individual classes' needs.

Merging SCAA's model and the National Literacy Project's model

So far, we have presented two different ways of planning the English curriculum. The first used the National Literacy Project's framework; the second used the SCAA planning model as a way of interpreting the programmes of study. Both approaches emphasise the systematic acquisition of skills, knowledge and understanding. Both ensure that the scheme of work plans for continuity and progression. So, can they be combined in any way?

One way is to match the content derived from the SCAA model against the NLP objectives. As we have already seen, continuing work is likely to contain much of the work which is detailed in the *Framework for Teaching*. The blocked scheme could then run alongside a literacy hour by focusing on a particular topic (see Figure 5.9). This will, of course, increase the total amount of time spent on English, but may be seen as an important way in which a school defines its curriculum priorities.

Linked work offers some interesting possibilities. We have already seen the potential for developing some aspects of language as part of teaching and learning in other subjects (see Figure 5.12).

The *Framework for Teaching* could be enriched by the cohesive approach taken by the SCAA model. Including blocked work alongside a literacy hour could provide opportunities for planning a range of exciting, focused work which synthesises work on word, sentence and whole-text level in an interesting way. This could lead to the literacy hour developing from a model in which children undertake a sequence of tenuously related activities to an hour in which there is integration and overlap. We feel that this model presents a more meaningful teaching and learning experience than that presented by the framework in its present format.

The role of the subject leader

There is obviously a key role for the co-ordinator in overseeing the planning process once the schemes of work are in place. Whatever model for scheme of work that the school is using, the subject leader will need to oversee the process of transferring long-term plans to medium-term plans. One co-ordinator describes how he does this:

> The year teams plan the half term's English and then they all give their plans to me. I then take them all home and look over them to make sure that they are

cohesive across the school. I look back at last term's plans to see if they are building upon them. If I feel that something needs tweaking or changing a little, I let the team know and they act upon it. For example, I noticed that the Year 6 team, in their work on plays, had introduced work on Shakespeare's *Romeo and Juliet*. I knew that the local Theatre in Education were planning to stage a production of *The Tempest* later on in the term and so I persuaded the Year 6 team to change their plans. It needs someone to oversee the whole process to ensure that things are cohesive.

It is important, of course, to let staff know when their plans are looking good as well as pointing out how they could be improved. We all need some positive feedback now and again in order to remain positive about our work. It is essential that the English co-ordinator celebrates the English work in school. Raising standards in English will not happen without raising teachers' self-esteem.

The subject leader will also have a role in adapting national projects to meet the needs of the school. We discuss this more fully in Chapter 8. In terms of schemes of work, this process of matching and adjusting will occur with initiatives such as the National Literacy Project. A co-ordinator at Springfield Primary School in Sheffield describes how the school adapted the framework to meet their needs:

> We already had developed some good plans in relation to a variety of topics which were focused on Key Stage 2 texts. When we implemented the Literacy Project, we thought that it was important to keep all of that good work. And so what we did was match our original schemes to the literacy framework. So, for example, we already had an excellent range of work developed for the Tudor topic and so we fitted that into the NLP requirements for studying playscripts and did a Shakespeare play in that half term. The next term, the NLP required us to work on fantasy texts, imagined worlds, and so we used a scheme of work already developed on *Through the Dragon's Eye*. We had also done a lot of work on using writing frames and so that went in as well. That way, we had the best of both worlds.

We include an example of Springfield's overview of the match between their medium-term plans and the National Literacy Project in Figure 5.14.

It is clear that the English subject leader will need to ensure that they oversee this matching and adjusting process carefully in order to meet the requirements of external projects whilst utilising the best of the school's already established practices.

Chapter summary

In this chapter, we have examined the processes involved in planning at the long-, medium- and short-term stage. There have been two models of planning explored and some key issues concerning developing schemes of work for English raised. We have suggested that the English

	Autumn 1 Tudors	Autumn 2 Stories	Spring 1 Through Dragon's Eye	Spring 2 Through Dragon's Eye	Summer 1 Energy	Spring 1 People
Literacy Project Links	Shakespeare Playscripts Developing a play		Imagined worlds -fantasy Stories in series			Comparing stories by the same author Comparing themes in stories from a range of cultures Stories raising issues e.g. bullying
Resources	Animated Shakespeare scripts and video. Novel: Y 3/4 "Meteorite Spoon" - Philip Ridley Look at dialogue Oxford Reading Tree playscripts		"Through the Dragon's Eye" - read chapter by chapter. Novel: Year 3 and 4: "The Secret of Platform 13" by Eva Ibbottson		Focus on authors: Rita Philips Mitchell and Anthony Browne Poems by Michael Rosen Novel: "Dakota of the White Flats" - Philip Ridley (compare with "Krindlekrax"). Issues raised.	
Reading fiction	Sort use of: setting characters Use in stories. Varieties of *narrative order.*		Setting of T.D.E. Making and following a map of the story. Plot map of events. Group reading of chapters.		Discuss issues raised in "Dakota" Settings of stories from a range of cultures	
Writing fiction	Write scripted dialogue. Letter to T.V./Radio/Paper		Fantasy stories *Figurative* language Character descriptions.		Writing on issues, drawing themes from Rosen e.g. jealousy, getting in trouble.	
Reading non fiction	Reading reports - "The Mirror", "The Star"- look at opening sentences. Invite journalist to discuss work.		Select and investigate a theme Scanning a text - locating key words.		Looking at persuasive writing leaflets, adverts. Leaflets info. - Y.E.B. leaflets/ adverts	
Writing non fiction	Reporting historical events. Write opinions and reviews of events. "Review" writing frame		Devising and comparing characters "Persuasive" writing frame		Persuasive writing Note making Information on energy	
Sentence level work	Use of verbs in depicting action Narrative sentences compared with info. texts		Adjectives-use in characterisation words and phrases of time/place/cause		Revise *nouns* Introduce *pronouns* Sentence transformation	

Figure 5.14. Springfield's scheme of work

co-ordinator needs to oversee the whole-school process of planning in order to ensure continuity and progression.

It is clear that we are in a period of immense change and development in the teaching of English. The five-year moratorium on changes to the National Curriculum is fast approaching its end and there has been much talk about how the time allocation for English needs to be extended because of the demands of the literacy hour. Whatever changes are impending, it is clear that there is a major role for the English subject leader in managing this process of change. Schemes of work will always be evolving because of the nature of the educational process. Literacies are constantly developing and changing (Lankshear *et al.*, 1997) and the literacy skills needed in the future may not necessarily be the same as those needed today. The co-ordinator needs to keep up with developments and ensure that the school is delivering an appropriate curriculum. And once the scheme is in place, she must ensure that it is implemented appropriately. In the next chapter, we turn to issues which need to be considered when implementing, monitoring and evaluating curriculum change.

6

Implementing, Monitoring and Evaluating Curriculum Change

In this chapter, we address a number of issues concerning the implementation of curriculum development and the subsequent monitoring and evaluation of this development. Any process of curriculum change needs to be kept under review in order to assess how far the aims of the initiative have been met. This chapter will provide the English subject leader with a range of strategies for facilitating that process in school.

We begin by looking at issues involved in the implementation of curriculum change. We examine the terms 'monitoring' and 'evaluation'. We then move on to look at a range of models of school self-evaluation in order to develop a sense of what the best practices are in the field. These various models of the evaluation process are applied to the English curriculum and we work through a number of examples in order to present a picture of the complexities at work in any evaluation process. The chapter ends by examining how evaluation feeds back into the curriculum development process.

Because of the interrelated nature of many of the chapters in this book, some of the themes and issues which appear in this chapter have been raised in earlier parts of the text. However, it is important to provide an in-depth coverage of this essential part of the change process at this point.

The implementation of curriculum change

If policy development goes hand in hand with curriculum development, then a school needs to ensure that it successfully implements the changes in the curriculum which the policy or action plan proposes. It is much easier, of course, when the proposed changes are owned by the school and not imposed on them by outside agencies. In Chapter 2 we looked at the factors that were necessary for successful implementation of change. It may be necessary to remind ourselves of the key factors:

- Change should be 'owned' by all staff, working in a collaborative and professional school context.
- Change should be carefully managed and planned so that there are not too many demands on colleagues at any one time.
- Change should be supported by relevant professional dialogue including in-service and related staff development.
- Change is most likely to be lasting when there is a clear need to change and a strong element of practicality.
- Change should be sensitive to the internal and external educational context.

When change is imposed by external forces, then the school has to adapt them to meet the needs of their own situation (see Chapter 8). In this chapter, we focus on implementing change that has been owned by the school staff, which can either refer to changes imposed on them or otherwise. The important factor is that the change has been seen as necessary in order to improve educational provision.

So, how is change best implemented? In some cases, it needs to be done slowly, with staff and children alike adapting to the changes made. For example, if a school decides to change the recording format for the assessment of reading, it may be best to start with a particular year group, Reception or Y3. This year group will then move through the school with the changed format whilst other classes would keep the old one. This would mean that teachers would not have to spend hours moving information from one set of recording formats to another. It will also mean consistency of approach for those children who have had many years of records completed in one particular way – much less confusing for feeder schools! This kind of change is gradual and *staged*.

However, in other cases, it may be wiser to implement change at the same time throughout the school. If a school decided to discourage the children from using word books and adapt a developmental approach to spelling, this would obviously be better approached by implementing the change at once. The whole-school staff could then discuss any issues which may arise as a result of the development rather than various class teachers having different methods and therefore different agendas. It would also mean that parents would be clear about what the school policy was with regard to spelling instead of receiving confusing messages. This kind of change is *transformational*.

As we have already seen, you will need a range of strategies for working with colleagues in implementing new classroom practices. The management of change requires a sensitive understanding of inter-personal behaviour in institutional settings. In Chapter 2 we listed a variety of strategies that could be drawn upon by the subject leader.

Here we provide more detail.

Subject leader as model of good practice

One strategy for ensuring the smooth implementation of any curriculum change is for the subject leader to provide a model of good practice. This could involve the subject leader working alongside class teachers and demonstrating particular methods or models. For example, if a school wanted to develop the use of big books for whole-class reading sessions, they might have some staff meetings devoted to the subject. This would allow time for exploration of the topic through discussion, with perhaps some input from advisers or consultants. A further strategy would be for the subject leader to demonstrate the use of big books with a whole class and the class teacher to observe the session. We often learn much from watching other skilled teachers. Such demonstration of teaching could take place in the subject leader's classroom or with the class of the teacher she was working with. This strategy would need a commitment from the headteacher to provide non-contact time for the subject leader in order for her to do this.

Problem-solving

Inevitably, the process of curriculum development will not always run smoothly. Shared relating of experiences can lead to the identification of particular problems with the implementation of certain curriculum changes. One way of dealing with this is to develop 'problem-solving' techniques. A few members of staff, or the whole school if appropriate, could decide to focus on a particular problem and each try different methods of solving it. These different methods could then be evaluated by the whole staff in order to find the most effective ones. For example, if it was found, through detailed evaluation, that the new policy of parents writing in children's reading record books was not working because some children did not receive any comments, staff could each try one of the following techniques:

- children take home letter reminding parents of the procedure
- children allowed to write in the comments book themselves
- children asked to let other members of the family write in the book, e.g. older siblings
- parents asked to hear their child read and write in the book first thing in the morning if they bring their child to school
- other members of staff write in particular children's books instead of parents.

If any of these techniques worked, the staff could then adopt them throughout the school. If none of them worked effectively, then the school needs to review whether or not they are adopting a fair policy.

Resistance to curriculum developments

There may be teachers on the staff who, despite the careful way in which the subject leader has introduced change, are still resistant (see Chapter 2 and Chapter 7). These members of staff need support and encouragement to try out new ideas. People who resist change are often unconfident and fearful of the consequences. That is why thoroughly planned change which is based on careful research is the only model to present to staff. Rushing into the staffroom and saying, 'I've just read somewhere that chanting the alphabet backwards every day works wonders for reading... should we try it?' is most definitely not the model of change upon which this book rests! For unconfident staff, or teachers cynical about the proposed changes, it may be necessary for the subject leader to work alongside them more often. These staff could be given a specific role in the monitoring and evaluation of the change. They would then feel that they are not being silenced but given a chance to have a voice in the process. For example, if the school had introduced a new reading scheme which a member of staff felt resistant to, he or she could be asked to be responsible for garnering the views of children throughout the school on the new scheme. If the children's reactions were favourable, this might help allay the fears of this member of staff. If the response was not favourable, perhaps the scheme should be reassessed by the whole staff! We will, of course, be looking at different methods of monitoring and evaluation later in the chapter.

It is necessary that any implementation of change is communicated to all relevant people – parents, governors, educational psychologists who work with the school, LEA link advisers and so on. One of the ways in which this could be done is to plan and advertise an open morning, or open evening, in which visitors can come to look at the changes made. Displays could be organised around the specific change of focus and leaflets provided which explain the key changes and why they have been implemented. This would enable any worries and concerns to be addressed in an open and honest way.

Once change has been implemented, it needs to be monitored and evaluated in order to ensure that it is meeting the needs of the school. We move on now to look at ways in which this can be done effectively.

What is the difference between monitoring and evaluation?

Monitoring is an essential part of the process of curriculum development. It is a means of assessing how far policies and schemes of work are adhered to by staff. It can be used to identify areas in need of a more in-depth evaluation. For example, one school had decided to extend the range of non-narrative forms of writing that teachers planned for. The monitoring process then consisted of the subject leader checking that termly planning included a wide range. Teachers monitored how often, and what forms of writing, they included in their daily planning. An **evaluation** of the issue, on the other hand, would have included a more in-depth study of how well the non-narrative forms of writing were introduced to the children and supported in the classroom.

Russell (1996) states that:

> In performing an evaluation, information has to be analysed and interpreted to make judgements about the nature, impact and value of the provision being studied.

(Russell, 1996, p. 38)

Evaluation, then, can be seen as a systematic, in-depth analysis of the impact and value of an innovation whereas **monitoring** is a quick check to ensure that something is happening. Evaluation looks at not, 'are we doing this?', but 'how well are we doing this?' For evaluation to be useful and reliable, a range of evidence would need to be collected in order to present a rounded picture of the issues raised through implementation.

In terms of curriculum development, a period of intense activity such as the review and rewriting of policies and schemes of work would be more likely to be followed by a period of monitoring than evaluation. For instance, it would make little sense to begin evaluating how well a new spelling policy was being implemented before teachers had a chance to develop it in their classrooms. For some months, then, staff may be involved in a monitoring process in which they see how things are going before feeding their observations into the evaluation.

Evaluation can be internal or external. That is to say, it is either a process in which schools themselves evaluate how well they are doing, or one in which an outside agency, such as OFSTED, an LEA adviser or a consultant, makes judgements. The focus of this chapter is on internal evaluation. Evaluation by OFSTED forms the basis of Chapter 12 on the inspection process.

How does monitoring and evaluation fit into policy and curriculum development?

In the Introduction we presented a cyclical model of curriculum change. As Figure 1 shows, monitoring and evaluation feed into the cyclical process of curriculum development referred to in earlier chapters of this book. External evaluation may occur at *any stage* in this process and as long as the subject leader can clearly define where the school is in that cycle, she has nothing to worry about. There will never be a 'perfect time' for an inspection or a consultant's visit and it would be foolish to try and rush the school towards an end result. There is no end result! Schools are in a constant state of development and flux and if not, they are likely to be stagnant and in need of immediate change.

Some teachers may ask, 'What is the difference, in this model, between evaluation and review or audit?' They are, of course, closely related concepts. We see a review, or audit, as an in-depth look at the curriculum or a specific area of it in action. (For an extensive exploration of the process of an audit, refer to Chapter 3.) A review or audit is undertaken in order to identify strengths and weaknesses in current provision and to look at what is actually going on in classrooms. Essentially it is a fact-finding exercise. On the other hand, evaluation is a process in which curriculum changes are examined in order to see how worthwhile they are. The results from evaluations can, of course, feed into a review or audit.

When one subject area is the focus of a review or audit, it should take priority in terms of overall school objectives and this should be reflected in the School Development Plan. When a curriculum area has already been reviewed and changes suggested and implemented, the focus would be on monitoring and evaluation – thus leaving room for the review of another subject. A school would then have a rolling programme of subject review and revision. Of course, the time and energy devoted to this method of curriculum development would need to reflect the nature of the subject. The core subjects, for example, would need a more frequent and in-depth focus than the foundation subjects.

Some may feel that this is an exhaustive model of curriculum change. After all, since the introduction of the National Curriculum in 1988, teachers have had to face change and development at an incredible rate. This raises questions about consolidation. We have some sympathy with this point of view and are not advocating change for the sake of it. Once a well-thought-through policy and scheme of work is in place for each subject, a subsequent review or audit should identify only relatively small areas for further work (that is, until the National Curriculum changes again). It is inevitable that the curriculum is constantly evolving as our ideas are developing all the time based on recent and relevant research. Added to this, society's demands on young people are constantly changing and our curriculum must respond to this. Technological advances mean that we have to respond to developments in order adequately to prepare children for their future life. We need to get used to the idea that change is a constant process although it is clear that the rate of the process is crucial if teachers are going to be able to cope with it.

It is clear, then, that evaluation of the English curriculum in terms of policy and practice is an ongoing process that focuses on different areas at any one time. We cannot evaluate everything at once. Subject leaders need to decide what needs to be evaluated. Areas may suggest themselves due to the process of monitoring. For instance, to return to our example of non-narrative writing, if the subject leader noticed that some teachers were not including a wide range of non-narrative forms in their planning over a long period of time, she might feel that it would be worth doing some evaluation in the area. Collection of data might then suggest that the reasons for this were that some staff were not very confident about planning non-narrative writing, and they needed further advice and support.

In order to evaluate, we need to have clear criteria for evaluation. How would we know if a new spelling policy is working? By the children being better spellers? By them being more self-reliant in checking spellings in dictionaries? What methods can we use for collecting this evidence? Are the results of the SATs spelling tests enough? Before evaluating a new development, staff need to decide on the criteria against which the change is being assessed. Once this criteria is agreed, the means of evaluating can take many different forms. Staff could use the range of evaluation tools explored in Chapter 3. These include:

- peer observation
- examination of children's work, sampling
- analysis of children's records
- observation of children
- analysis of test results
- talking to children
- talking to staff
- talking to parents.

In addition to these methods of gathering information, we also advocate the use of a number of other evaluative tools. These are portfolios, journals, mentoring and quality circles. We examine each one in turn.

Portfolios

This technique involves building up a portfolio featuring the specific area of focus. For example, if a school wanted to evaluate how effective their new scheme of work was in developing the teaching of poetry, a portfolio of children's poetry work could be collected over time. At the end of an agreed period, perhaps two terms, the staff could look at this portfolio in order to assess how the scheme of work was working in practice. Was there evidence of continuity and progression in children's poetry work, or was it still rather *ad hoc* and dependent upon individual teachers' interests?

Journals

In this method of evaluation, teachers would be asked to make weekly journal entries which would reflect upon the particular area being evaluated. These entries could consist of anything the staff thought was appropriate – observations, recollections, thoughts, even examples of children's work with comments. These journals could then be brought to a staff meeting set to discuss the particular issue and significant entries analysed and discussed. Here is an example of a typical journal entry. The issue of focus is the use of structured role-play areas to develop speaking and listening skills. The staff had decided to set specific tasks in the area in order to develop the children's talk.'

> May 7th
> The children seemed to be enjoying working in the 'newsagents' this afternoon. I had set up a particular situation, whereby one child had to be a customer who was complaining about a newspaper which had been scribbled on. The newsagent had to make sure it hadn't been done by the customer's children. I didn't have chance to see how it went. I had to stay with yellow group on the maths task. The area was very noisy and busy, but I don't know if the children were using the scenario I had set up.

If other staff had had similar experiences, they could perhaps devise a more effective whole-school system of monitoring and assessing the use of talk in the role-play areas. If it was just this particular teacher having difficulties, the other staff could share their ideas on that particular problem.

Mentoring

Mentoring can be used as a form of support – for example, when supervising students or inducting NQTs into the school – but it can also be used as a means of curriculum evaluation. Members of staff could be assigned a particular mentor for a specific subject area. Their mentor would necessarily be someone who felt more comfortable and confident in that particular subject. In a larger school, for example, members of the English working party could act as mentors to the rest of the staff. In a smaller school, it is likely that all the responsibility will fall upon the English subject leader. The beauty of a mentorship scheme is that all teachers can have the chance to share their expertise. It also allows those with skills and interest in a particular area (not the subject leader) to take part in developing practice in that area. The subject leader's role in this system is to organise the mentoring system and have regular meetings with mentors to discuss any issues arising from this method of evaluation. Meetings with mentors could be used for a number of reasons, not simply for evaluation purposes. Once a relationship has been built up with mentors, staff may use the sessions for discussing a variety of issues and concerns. However, for evaluation purposes, the mentor may wish to provide a little more structure for the meeting.

For example, a school wanted to evaluate how the staff were finding the task of completing the new records for reading, writing, speaking and listening. At the meeting of English mentors in the working party, it was decided to ask the staff at their mentor meeting:

- What are the advantages of the new system?
- What are the disadvantages of the new system?
- Is there any advice you would like on completing the records?
- How would you like the records changed?
- Anything else you would like to discuss concerning the records?

Any issues arising from these meetings could be taken back to a staff meeting in which the new records were evaluated through a process of feedback, discussion and the examination of a sample of written records.

It is important to recognise equal opportunities issues when setting up mentoring partners. Staff need to feel that they can relate to and trust the member of staff they are being mentored by. For black and ethnic minority staff, this may be a particularly important issue as they may have experienced racism from a white member of staff in the school. It would obviously not be productive to team them up with that person. Similarly, a female member of staff may have suffered sexual harassment or discrimination from a male member of staff and so may not feel comfortable with that person. Staff should have a major voice in who their mentor will be. We also intend the term 'staff' to be an inclusive one. It is important that all members of the teaching staff are involved in the curriculum evaluation process and so classroom assistants must also have a voice.

The advantage of using mentoring as a method of evaluation is that it allows all staff to participate in the evaluation process and feel as if they have had chance to put across their point of view. This may not always happen in a large staff meeting. Mentorship also offers possibilities for individual help where it is needed. Not all staff will need the same kind of help. If the English mentors felt that common elements were occurring as problems, then the English subject leader could organise a staff meeting to deal with that issue.

Quality circles

Quality circles have been introduced in a number of educational institutions and other organisations as a means of encouraging staff to reflect on their work and to target areas for improvement. This is done in a collaborative way, with groups working on the same areas together. Sallis (1996) describes quality circles as:

> small groups based upon mutual trust, which voluntarily perform quality control activities within the work place, and which use quality control methods and techniques.
>
> (Sallis, 1996, p. 87)

They are *not* a means of a co-ordinator evaluating the curriculum. However, we have included them because they present a potentially empowering method of teachers monitoring and evaluating their own work. And the more thoroughly teachers monitor and evaluate their own work, the less onerous is the task for the co-ordinator. The key feature of the 'quality circle' is that the use of it should be entirely voluntary. It should not be used as a means of quality control by the senior management team. Sallis suggests that it works best when used by 'natural' work groups which are self-selected. In the context of a primary school, this could be across a year group or, in the case of a small school, a key stage. Quality circles have also been found to work best when provided with resources such as the time and space to meet. Institutions that have initiated the use of such circles have reported excellent results with increased motivation by staff. The English co-ordinator could provide information about this method and model the use of it by starting off a quality circle with interested colleagues.

Planning the monitoring and evaluation process

It is clear that monitoring and evaluation of curriculum development has to be done thoroughly and systematically if it is to be effective. The subject leader needs to draw up a programme of action which will prioritise areas for monitoring and evaluation and decide with staff how and when that evaluation will be carried out. All staff should be clear about the criteria on which the success or failure of the curriculum development will be decided. It is better if they are involved in the development of those criteria. A programme for monitoring and evaluation should arise naturally from the action plan (see Chapter 3). Figure 6.1 is an example of an action plan and the programme for monitoring and evaluation drawn from it.

Outcomes of monitoring and evaluation

Once the results of any curriculum evaluation have been analysed by the subject leader and staff, action should be instigated to address those areas identified as unsuccessful or problematic. If, during the evaluation process, an area is seen to be causing great concern, then a full-scale review or audit of that area could go ahead. We saw in Chapter 3 how this would work in practice. It should always be clear to staff how the results of the curriculum monitoring and evaluation will be compiled, who they will be relayed to and what will be done with the information. This ensures whole-school ownership of the process.

Using the model of curriculum development discussed in this and previous chapters, it can be seen that a school will be continually developing, monitoring, evaluating and reviewing what it is doing. An effective school accepts this as part of its professional duty to deliver the best possible service. It also views the process as a shared one. The

Area for evaluation	Success criteria	How will it be evaluated?	When?	By whom?
Use of new library	• all classes using it regularly • children's library skills developed systematically • children use information-retrieval strategies effectively	• timetable filled in weekly • teachers keep a journal recording their use of the library • children's reading records (information-retrieval skills) • borrowing record of library books	Term 1	All staff SL looks at all pupils' reading records and database of loans
Spelling policy	• all classes adopt new policy • children's spelling skills developed • children able to use range of strategies for checking spelling – dictionaries, word banks, etc. • children's writing demonstrates ability to take risks	• monitoring of use of policy – peer observation • analysis of children's writing • analysis of children's writing records • analysis of tests, SATs, etc. • talking to staff and children	Terms 2 and 3	Class teachers – analysis of work, records, peer observation SL – talking to staff and children, analysis of test results
Use of group reading packs	• all classes set up group reading systems using the packs developed • teachers make effective use of group reading to develop reading skills • children able to conduct group reading independently of staff, where appropriate • children's reading skills developed, e.g. key skills, ability to discuss texts	• monitoring of use of packs in teachers' planning • observation of teachers leading a group reading session and feedback • observation of independent groups analysis of reading records	Terms 1, 2 and 3	Class teachers – observation of groups, analysis of children's records SL – monitoring planning Peer observation of teacher-led group reading

Figure 6.1. Monitoring and evaluating the curriculum

English subject leader will take the ultimate responsibility for monitoring and evaluation of the English curriculum – but this can only be done if the staff work as a whole in an atmosphere of open trust and shared concerns. The evaluation process should not be viewed as something imposed on the staff, an indirect form of individual appraisal, but as a means to examine collectively the quality of provision the whole school is making. Nixon (1992) advocates a 'collegial' approach to whole-school evaluation:

> For what a collegiate approach to evaluation means in practice is that teachers should relate to one another first and foremost as colleagues, not as fixed points

within a hierarchical structure; that they should work towards a definition of their own interests, rather than accept uncritically interests that are externally imposed upon schools; and that their prime concern should be the quality of learning of the young people they teach, rather than the bureaucratic vagaries of cost analysis and systems management.

(Nixon, 1992, p. 23)

It takes skilled senior managers to ensure that the staff of a school do take this approach to monitoring and evaluation, managers who can improve the quality of teaching and learning which goes on in their school at the same time as developing the confidence and expertise of staff. Subject leaders have a role to play here too. If you are aware that some staff are having difficulties in certain areas of the English curriculum, you need to work out strategies to support them rather than making them feel like failures.

We have discussed certain techniques for supporting colleagues at various points in this book (e.g. working alongside colleagues in order to provide a model of good practice; finding something that members of staff are good at and building upon those strengths; reassuring members of staff that other people have difficulties in a particular area too). However, perhaps the most important thing the subject leader should do is to be human, admit her own failings and weak areas and be honest about these to others. After all, we all have areas for possible improvement! People will not open up about the difficulties they are having to someone who appears to be very successful, or perhaps even tells everyone how successful they are! Instead, if the subject leader comes across as a teacher who is very knowledgeable in the area but is active in self-analysis, honest about her own failings and willing to act upon them, staff may be more willing to join in with the reflective approach. We realise that this approach is becoming more difficult in a climate of increasing competitiveness and the tendency to blame teachers for 'falling standards', but unless we attempt to break this cycle of defensiveness, attack and counter-attack, any monitoring and evaluation process will be hampered by superficiality.

It is clear that there will be a very small number of teachers who cannot be helped by the subject leader if, after all the support given, she is still not managing an aspect of the English curriculum. This matter has then to move out of the subject leader's hands and becomes the responsibility of the senior management team. Of course, in some schools, a member of senior management may be the English subject leader and needs to deal with both roles.

Monitoring and evaluation can be an exciting process which develops the research, reflective and analytical skills of all staff. Schools do not have to do it alone. If they want to work with people outside the school in order to develop an effective monitoring programme, there are a range of options. LEA advisers will be willing to spend some time working with schools they are in partnership with if they are allocated such time on their busy schedules. External consultants can be used to look at specific areas. HE institutions may be willing to work in partnership with a school on an evaluation project if it is mutually beneficial. In practice, this could mean that the school works alongside HE colleagues, devising effective monitoring systems and analysing the results, perhaps even jointly publishing them in order to disseminate the work more widely. The options open to a school depend on their particular needs and concerns and the resources they have to hand.

Chapter summary

Throughout this chapter, we have emphasised that the monitoring and evaluation process should take place in a supportive and collegiate environment. The changes in recent years have given rise to a particular climate of blame and recrimination in schools which has led to demoralisation. Effective curriculum changes cannot take place in such a climate. We need to support colleagues and build confidence and self-esteem in order to raise the standards of teaching and learning in our schools. In this chapter, we have considered a number of tools which can be used for monitoring and evaluation purposes. If used sensitively, they can provide the subject leader with a clear picture of the nature and delivery of the English curriculum. This knowledge can then be used to make sound plans for future progress.

As we have suggested previously, an essential aspect of the implementation of curriculum change is staff development. In the next chapter, we discuss ways in which the English subject leader can plan and deliver staff meetings and organise other forms of staff development.

7

Staff Meetings, School-focused Training and INSET

This chapter examines the principles and practicalities of developing whole-school initiatives in the English curriculum through working parties, staff meetings and school-focused INSET. These activities are important contexts for developing the kinds of professional dialogue that are an essential part of curriculum change. Our main aim is to provide guidance for in-house work, although the final section also looks at the role of external agencies. We begin by establishing general guiding principles before moving on to considerations concerning the organisation and management of staff meetings. Examples of how co-ordinators have planned such events are used as illustration.

No discussion of this topic would be complete without an exploration of the difficulties that may arise in professional development settings. The third section looks at some of these difficulties and suggests strategies for working with them. We then look at the kinds of support which are available from agencies external to the school and how these can be utilised in staff meetings. The chapter concludes with a more general look at INSET provision.

Principles

As we have stated throughout this book, school policy and practice in English, as in other curriculum areas, will develop most effectively if staff have a sense of ownership of change and a clear direction or goal. The importance of staff involvement in discussing, adapting and agreeing policy is a central theme in the curriculum development literature (for example, Fullan, 1983; Day, Whitaker and Johnston, 1990). In Chapter 2 we highlighted the importance of creating a variety of contexts for professional dialogue. We argued that this kind of dialogue is central to the change process. So, although the responsibility for establishing policy and leading development rests with the head and the English co-ordinator, consultation is an essential part of the process.

Ideally, consultation will take place in a variety of ways, both informally and formally, and will involve individual discussions, the more structured deliberations of a small working group (Campbell, 1985; Corson, 1990) as well as wider consultation with all colleagues. In small schools it will be necessary to involve part-time staff. Establishing a working group may not be appropriate. However, the involvement of all colleagues, in the context of a staff meeting or training day, is vital for policy development whatever the size of the school.

Striking the balance between direction and ownership is key to the success of a staff meeting. Direction, in this context, means being clear and realistic about what you wish to achieve and the timescale for achieving it. These considerations will have already been addressed in your action planning (see Chapter 3). It also means making sure that you have the full support of the management team and your head.

Primary school teachers, already over-burdened with government directives, large classes and a crowded curriculum, are all too prone to 'innovation fatigue'. They may themselves be carrying the responsibility of another curriculum area and may perceive work on English as 'competition' for the time and resources of the school and its staff. It is therefore important that colleagues understand how work on English fits into the school's overall priorities as reflected in the School Development Plan. Where a large external initiative is involved, staff also need to be familiar with the wider context (for example, the National Literacy Strategy, 1997).

So, improving policy and practice needs to take place within the context of the School Development Plan and the co-ordinator should maintain a clear focus and formulate agreed points of action. For this process to run smoothly a positive staff climate is important. Day *et al.* (1993) suggest that this sort of positivity is characterised by 'a climate of trust and openness' in which teachers:

> plan and work together to improve teaching; reflect on practice and experiment with new ways of teaching (without feeling that mistakes will be frowned upon);

and that:

> those affected by decisions should be involved in making them.
>
> (Day *et al.*, 1993, p. 60)

As we saw in Chapter 4, it is unlikely that all the staff in a large school will be involved in writing a policy for English. Indeed, for many this would be a daunting task. The head, the co-ordinator and her working group are more likely to provide the direction. This means that in a staff meeting, they will be the ones responsible for generating the agenda for discussion or the policy for agreement. In other words they will provide the goals for the session and it is the appropriateness of these goals which will be instrumental in determining the success of the staff meeting.

Although one of the purposes of the staff meeting is to give colleagues a sense of ownership of policy and practice as it develops, this ownership will only be established if meetings are skilfully handled. Specific guidance is given later on in the chapter, but at this point it is important to look at some general issues that relate to the functioning of groups in professional and educational settings.

An effective group

Whether a co-ordinator's immediate focus is on the management of a small working party or a whole-school staff meeting, it is worth looking at factors that facilitate the effectiveness of a professional group. The literature dealing with the organisation and management of working groups is extensive, and it would be an impossible task to provide an overview here. However, we do recognise that it is an important topic for the co-ordinator and wish to draw attention to some fundamental considerations.

Participation

In order to reach agreement on policy and practice and to feel part of the decision-making process, staff need to have plenty of opportunities to draw on their experiences and to develop their point of view. This does not necessarily involve contributing to whole-group discussion, but usually means being active in some way (e.g. through paired discussion or as a scribe). Some members of staff may have an important role to play in preparing or providing materials for a staff meeting.

Discussion

The most valuable work in professional groups takes place through discussion. It is important that we recognise from the start that a number of factors influence the individual's willingness to engage in group discussion. Some people will tend to dominate and others may either lack the confidence to join in or be content to take a back seat. The skilled co-ordinator will have thought through various strategies for involving particular individuals in discussion and will have planned activities to facilitate group discussion (see below).

Time and task

An important aspect of effective group work is defining and maintaining a focus. The co-ordinator needs to establish clear aims for the meeting and, if appropriate, to share her thoughts about specific outcomes. It is helpful to regularly remind participants of aims and proposed outcomes. Groups work most effectively when time boundaries are agreed and adhered to.

Conflict and consensus

Our better social instincts often tempt us to the view that group meetings should be harmonious and marked by plenty of agreement. Of course, if this were the case then there would be little point in discussion in the first place! Part of the process of the staff meeting is to clarify thinking, to articulate differences in opinion and to work out a way forward in the light of this. Conflict is almost inevitable and whilst it may be uncomfortable it is usually productive. Individuals may agree to differ but a workable consensus is the desired end product.

Working parties

Convening a working party to support aspects of the co-ordinator's job can be a useful strategy. Of course, if you work in a small school this way of working is difficult. However, you might consider how permanent staff could work on proposals for a larger meeting that included part-time or support teachers, parents, governors and non-teaching staff. From the co-ordinator's point of view a small group of colleagues that can be depended upon to provide back-up in whole-school staff meetings, as well as to help in the preparation and evaluation of work, is invaluable. From the whole-school point of view, working parties can be a great time-saver. For instance, the drafting of a policy is far easier in a small group, progress is quicker and new thinking can be explored prior to a full staff meeting. In some settings, however, a working party can seem divisive and may not help staffroom dynamics.

The considerations set out in the previous section are equally applicable to running a working party or a staff meeting. However, our experience suggests that there are further practical matters to be taken into account when setting up a working party. These are listed below.

- Try to ensure that the composition of the working party represents a variety of interests (for instance, a cross-section of year groups should be represented, or if working in a multilingual school, a bilingual teacher or EAL specialist should be invited to join the group). It will probably be impossible to represent all interests and it is only reasonable to expect volunteers to take part in a working party.

- The working party needs a clear brief and a regular meeting time (e.g. every other Tuesday lunchtime), so that people keep it clear and the head and other colleagues know not to make demands at that time.

- Encourage a colleague to keep minutes of each meeting – working groups can often jump from one subject to another and it is important to keep a track of discussions. It can be very useful to make the minutes available to other colleagues and the head to keep them informed of progress.

- Invite members of the working group to share responsibilities such as looking at resources or keeping minutes, and be prepared to delegate, but remember that the co-ordinator is ultimately responsible for writing up and disseminating the working group's plans or proposals.

Structuring staff meetings

Few co-ordinators receive any proper training or guidance on how to run staff meetings. Nevertheless, it is increasingly common to meet English specialists who have been asked to report to staff on the progress of their working party, to chair a staff meeting on policy or to present a summary of what they have gained from an out-of-school INSET event. In some primary schools, the co-ordinator is given the full responsibility of organising a school-focused training day. For many, such work may seem like a daunting task. Our aim here is to help to simplify this task by taking a step-by-step approach.

Step one: timescale

Initially you need a long-term view. This will include considering how much time is available for your subject area. This may already be laid out in your School Development Plan. Questions to ask yourself include:

- How many staff meetings are available to me during the year?
- What do I need to achieve as a matter of priority?
- What will the focus of different sessions be?
- Do I need to devote more than one meeting to a particular topic in order to follow through ideas?

Step two: aims

To begin with, you need a clear idea of what you hope to achieve during the staff meeting. For instance, you might just need a small amount of time to communicate some basic information (e.g. the location of new resources). Alternatively, there may be issues related to policy-making, such as the recommendations of your working party, that require discussion. Or, following on from INSET or your own monitoring work, you may need to address matters of classroom practice, challenging your colleagues to rethink their teaching approaches. It is important to recognise that different kinds of INSET activity serve different purposes.

Step three: negotiation

With your head or management team it is important to work out the timing of the proposed staff meeting. You need to make sure that you will have long enough to prepare thoroughly and that there will be sufficient time available for you to achieve your aims. If you are working within the confines of a regular weekly staff meeting, try to ensure that you will not be 'crowded out' or even postponed by the emergence of other 'more important' matters. Remember that the evening before the school play may not be the best spot for a challenging discussion on your colleagues' approaches to the teaching of spelling! Similarly, a time in the day when staff are not too tired or pressured by other matters is preferable.

Step four: planning and preparation

At this stage, you need to revisit your aims and give them a sharper focus. It is helpful to think about specific outcomes and how you hope to achieve them. Preparation may include involving your colleagues in some way, such as acting as 'teacher researchers', bringing their findings to the meeting. For example, when planning a session on assessment and recording pupil progress in reading, you might ask colleagues to bring all the reading records that they keep. Staff could also be asked to report on their own approach to assessment (how they plan for assessment, what time is given to it and what they are looking for). This sort of preparatory work can then form the basis for the kind of discussion that focuses on 'live' classroom issues. During the planning stage you should consider the kinds of activity or task that will help you to achieve your objectives. Figure 7.1 shows an English co-ordinator's plan for a staff meeting on choosing and using information books.

Step five: resources

As in planning for classroom activity, you need to think beforehand about the resources you will need, whether they are children's work, published resources, handouts or audio-visual aids. The right choice of resources will help to make the meeting run smoothly.

Step six: setting

The comfort and atmosphere of the physical location are important considerations. For whole-day meetings, it is sometimes worth thinking about an alternative venue. Some schools have started to take advantage of special deals at local hotels or conference centres; others book rooms at the nearest teachers' centre. However, it is likely that most meetings will take place in the school. Although staffrooms are usually quite comfortable, they may not be the ideal place. In some schools a staffroom

9/10/98   **Staff Meeting: Information Books**
4.00 – 5.15pm

Aims: raising awareness about the quality of non-fiction resources in school

looking at the kind of reading skills used in an information search

starting to explore teaching approaches

Resources: a range of non-fiction books for both key stages for activities; large piece of paper, blu-tak and felt pen; handout on information search; Honeybee (All Aboard Ginn big book)

Plan:

1. Introduce the topic (needs as identified through audit) and the aims of the meeting. Stress the need for discussion and how activities are intended to trigger discussion. (3 minutes)

2. Choosing information books
For 3 minutes talk with partner about what you are looking for when choosing non-fiction. (Keep to time!)
Use large sheet of paper to make a composite list of criteria (remember to keep this). (5 minutes)
With partner apply criteria to a selection of books (5 minutes – remind colleagues when there is 1 min. left)
Report back around the room and then discuss action to be taken to improve the stock. (10 minutes)

3. Looking at reading skills
Use handout from INSET course to talk about the stages that may be involved in an information search. Give handout at end. Involve colleagues by asking them what sort of reading skill applies at each stage. (Refer to books: David Wray; Bobbie Neate and the ideas in the Scholastic Curriculum Bank – Reading). (15 minutes)

4. Exploring teaching approaches
Introduce the idea of teaching children about the presentational features of non-fiction that can help an information search. In groups of 3 complete a chart which shows which of the books you have brought have: a contents page; an index; a glossary; sub-headings; diagrams; bibliography. (10 minutes)
Discuss adaptation of this activity to different age ranges. Use big book (Honeybee: Ginn) to illustrate how young children can discuss non-fiction.(10 minutes).

5. Conclusion
Recap on aims and any decisions/conclusions reached.
Alert staff to forthcoming one-day course – Using Non-Fiction run by the English Advisory Service. Arrange for feedback from this. End. (5 minutes)

Figure 7.1. **Plan for a staff meeting on choosing and using information books**

can take on the characteristics of a rest room – a kind of safe haven in which the curriculum or wider educational debate is frowned upon. This sort of ambience may have an important function in the day-to-day life of the school, but is certainly not conducive to staff development work. Staffrooms can also provide the physical setting for familiar patterns of behaviour and interaction (for instance, where the young or enthusiastic sit or the dissenters' corner). You may find that an alternative location, such as the school library or your own classroom, will allow colleagues to interact in different ways.

Step seven: running the meeting

Important groundwork can be done in the opening minutes of a meeting. It is a good idea to have worked out a clear introduction which states your intentions and gives an idea of the intended outcomes of the session. You should also give an overview of the process involved and what you expect from colleagues (for instance, open discussion, practical suggestions or a willingness to share experiences). We find it helpful to provide an early opportunity for colleagues to be active either in discussion, or through a short task done in pairs or small groups. This can help to warm up the group as a whole and to set the climate of participation through discussion. During the course of the meeting you need to listen carefully to contributions from colleagues and ask for clarification if necessary. At the same time it is necessary to keep to time and to move more or less systematically through your plan. You may find it useful to summarise at key points during the meeting. This will help you to draw ideas together and enable you to move on through your schedule. For certain kinds of meetings – particularly those where decisions are to be made – it will be important to keep a record. It is a good idea to ask someone else to take on this task so that you can concentrate on facilitating discussion. If these notes can be copied and circulated to colleagues soon after the meeting, the ideas are likely to stay fresh in people's minds.

At the end of the meeting, you will need to summarise the main points of the discussion and agree any future action. Again, it is essential to note this as the papers can be produced if someone subsequently says that they don't remember agreeing to a particular action!

Training packs

Curriculum developers now have the capacity to publish sophisticated training packs which often contain sound advice for those leading sessions. Photocopiable handouts, transparencies and audio and video support materials may be included. Despite the high quality of some of these packs, we advise co-ordinators to think carefully before using them. The main problem with using training packs that someone else has designed is one of match. Published materials can never take into account the specific needs of your school, the existing level of expertise amongst your colleagues or their various learning styles. However, they can provide useful in-service ideas for the co-ordinator who is faced with the prospect of planning a training day.

We suggest you use packs selectively and take plenty of time to familiarise yourself with any material you choose. Ideas for starting discussion are often quite useful to borrow but we would advise you to consider the use of video very carefully. Videos of another teacher's classroom practice are easy targets for ridicule. The school context of the video may be very different from yours (prompting the 'it wouldn't work here' response), the classrooms may look unnaturally tidy or so well-resourced that they provoke envy, and the number of children shown may suggest that the video depicts an 'artificial' situation of small group teaching with no distractions.

If you do choose to use video material, think carefully about how your colleagues can be active rather than passive viewers. 'Whilst you're watching the video jot notes on ...' or 'Look out for how the teacher uses...' or 'How are the children responding to ...?' are good ways in. And finally remember that showing a video in an after-school meeting or immediately after lunch on a training day is an invitation for colleagues to doze!

Anticipating difficulties and how to deal with them

Staff meetings don't always run smoothly, and sometimes we know only too well the kind of reaction we are going to get. Sometimes it is possible to think through strategies for dealing with predictable comments or behaviour in advance. However, it is also worth recognising that not everyone may be equally enthusiastic about developing the English curriculum.

Staff who fit the description of 'the cynic' ('It won't work with my children.' 'Seen it all before (yawn).' may be particularly difficult to deal with. We have noticed how they can often underestimate what the children can do. When pressed they may make comments such as: 'It won't work because my children wouldn't be able to concentrate/follow instructions/work independently, etc.'. If the co-ordinator or a more confident member of staff can work alongside this teacher, she may be able to see what children are capable of.

'The block' ('What's the point?' 'I've always done it this way.' 'It's another bandwagon.') may well lack confidence and feel threatened by change. It may help to find out their particular strength and capitalise on it. This may help to win them over. For instance, if M works well on teaching information skills you might try: 'Well, M, you are really good at getting your children to use the cataloguing system in the library, would you like to talk about your approach at our next meeting?'

Evaluation

As we have already emphasised, evaluation must be seen as an integral part of the process of school development. Day *et al.* (1993) suggest that:

> Checks on implementation and success mean continually asking the question 'How well are we doing?' Curriculum review and development is rather like painting the Forth Bridge – never completed. Having discussed and agreed change and attempted to put that change into practice, evaluation of that practice will more often than not reveal other aspects of practice that require attention.
>
> (Day *et al.*, 1993, p. 126)

It follows, then, that evaluation of the staff meeting or school-focused training should be more concerned with how the event has contributed to teachers' thinking and practice than with the abilities of the co-ordinator. However, because of the high level of personal investment in running a meeting, it is quite common to see evaluation as feedback on our performance. Although there is, undoubtedly, a role for this sort of professional feedback, regularly returning to the question: 'How well are we doing?' and planning for future needs are of central importance.

External agencies

So far in this section we have concentrated on ways in which the subject leader can organise and run her own staff meeting. There are, however, occasions when curriculum development in English will benefit from the contribution of specialists from external agencies. LEA advisory staff, lecturers from HE institutions and other INSET providers are often a useful catalyst in the process of change. They cannot be expected to do all the work for you, but an experienced 'outsider' can give colleagues food for thought, generate enthusiasm and give practical hints. A well-chosen outside speaker can show staff that the English co-ordinator is not alone in her philosophy and approach and is, as a result, harder to ignore.

It is worth giving careful thought to the sort of follow-up that may be needed after a session with an external provider. There may be issues to pick up on or resource matters to address. The outside speaker may be able to provide a momentum to change which the co-ordinator can capitalise on.

School-focused training

Once you have found a suitable trainer, you can organise a school-focused training day or session. In some ways, this is much more effective than individual staff attending outside INSET sessions because input can be tailored to meet the needs of the school. For example, if the staff as a whole need some staff development in planning and assessing speaking and listening, then an outside trainer could be asked to plan a day's INSET session around this, taking into account the particular needs and circumstances of the school. As we have said earlier, it is often useful to have these sessions outside the usual environment of the staffroom.

INSET

There will also be the need for individual teachers to attend courses which meet their own individual development needs. If the co-ordinator is effective in auditing the strengths and weaknesses of the staff (see Chapter 3 and Chapter 10), then she will be aware of which courses will suit particular people. The co-ordinator therefore needs to ensure that relevant INSET sessions are pointed out to staff. There will, of course, be a limited budget for INSET and not everyone will be able to attend the sessions they need. There may be courses which individuals would be willing to fund themselves, such as NATE regional conferences which often take place at the weekend. Whenever a member of staff attends an external INSET session, they need to be prepared to feed back information to the co-ordinator and the rest of the staff. If this does not happen, useful information is lost to the school community as a whole. In analysing staff development needs it is easy to overlook your own. As we have noted on a number of occasions, it is important that you keep up to date with developments in the English area. This will involve attending conferences and short courses. You may need to strengthen aspects of your own subject knowledge or you may just want to find out about new approaches to teaching English. Part of this could involve finding out what your local HE institutions provide in terms of award-bearing courses. You may be able to study useful units of work that count towards a Masters degree. This sort of qualification will be useful as your career develops and will develop your knowledge base as a subject leader.

Chapter summary

In this chapter we have taken a close look at how to facilitate the development of colleagues' thinking and practice by establishing professional dialogue in staff meetings and in-service events. Subject leaders need to develop both training and leadership skills. We have argued that these skills will be based on an understanding of interpersonal relationships in an institutional setting. Because of this we have included advice on the factors which lead to the development of an effective working group. We have also given practical guidance on how to plan for professional development work in school. Finally, we considered external in-service provision. Some of the issues concerning the relationship between external influence and internal school needs will be raised again in the following chapter as we turn our attention to the co-ordinator's role with respect to external projects.

8

The External Context

In examining the process of change (Chapter 2), we considered both the internal and external forces at work. This chapter looks at responding to external initiatives. So far, we have argued quite strongly for the primacy of a school-based model of curriculum and professional development. However, schools are not autonomous institutions. They are part of an education system with broader ranging values, concerns and goals influenced by a variety of interest groups in society. Although schools enjoy a certain amount of autonomy, they are always subject to the direct force of legislation as well as the more indirect pressures of public opinion and political interest. In addition to this, of course, there is the advice, recommendation and encouragement that comes from the educational community of curriculum developers, theorists and researchers.

At times it seems as if everyone is an expert in the field of education. And matters can seem worse when we focus on the English curriculum: that aspect of school which concerns the teaching and learning of the national language. Needless to say many have strong feelings about English and its varieties, as well as its relationship to the other languages spoken in the British Isles. Perhaps the teaching and learning of language will always be contentious. The subject co-ordinator will need to recognise this and to develop a clear view of the subject and its relationship with the rest of the curriculum.

This chapter looks at the impact of external influences on the primary English curriculum. We begin with an attempt to categorise the sorts of initiatives that are around at the moment. We then turn our attention to the difficult task of evaluating an external project in terms of your school's needs. This is followed by a brief exploration of the issues involved in negotiating and managing collaboration with an external agency. We conclude by looking at the tension between the pressure and support from project work using a case study that looks at an English co-ordinator's own experience of implementing the National Literacy Project.

Types of external influence

For a number of years our school system has enjoyed a creative relationship with a wide range of funding bodies and interest groups. More recently, economic circumstances have pushed schools and LEAs into looking at new ways of funding innovation and curriculum development by establishing partnerships with other agencies, local businesses and industry, and organisations with charitable status. One of the unfortunate side-effects of this can be to create a culture in which the availability of funding and resources becomes the driving force for curriculum change.

As a subject leader you may need to make some hard choices, steering a course between the school's immediate needs and the kinds of support that are available from external sources. External initiatives vary considerably in their level of demand and the degree to which they can support what you do. For example, some funding bodies expect quite detailed evaluative feedback from curriculum development work as a prerequisite for continuation. Others may simply expect a lot of hard work but have the advantage of providing high quality advice and support. Before we go into more detail, however, it will be useful to look at different sorts of external initiative.

Central government

Through Education Acts and statutory instruments (including curriculum Orders) central government provides the legal framework for education and the curriculum. These are, of course, *requirements* which every teacher should be aware of in providing for children's educational entitlement. As well as these requirements, central government also gives advice and direction in DFEE circulars and through special initiatives. The establishment of Reading Recovery centres and more recently the piloting of the 'literacy hour' under the guidance of the National Literacy Project (NLP) represents this second kind of government-led external initiative. Under slightly different conditions, curriculum development was centrally guided through the work of the Language in the National Curriculum Project (LINC, 1989–92); the National Oracy Project (NOP, 1989–92), and the National Writing Project (NWP, 1985–89). Central initiatives such as these constitute high status external pressure to change.

It is now quite likely that new central initiatives will be sponsored by other government agencies given the growing influence of the Teacher Training Agency (TTA) and the establishment of the Qualifications and Curriculum Authority (QCA).

Local government

Although the role of the LEA in curriculum development has diminished in recent years, it still continues to play an important part in the change process. In some cases the LEA acts as a gatekeeper for national developments – for instance, in deciding whether or not to bid for curriculum initiatives (for example, the NLP) or GEST-funded INSET provision. Alternatively, LEA advisory services may take the lead by establishing smaller projects that are responsive to local need. Funding may be made available by the local authority for such projects. Professional networking through cluster-groups of schools, sometimes with support from external funding, provides a different model for change.

Institutions of further and higher education

Partnerships with other educational institutions have considerable potential. Both further and higher education students are often interested in a period of school placement, either for work experience or as an integral part of a course leading to a professional qualification. Although some of these course may have quite specific expectations of school placement (for example, BA or PGCE courses leading to Qualified Teacher Status), there is often the scope for working with the institutions and the students on particular initiatives. The advantages of extra adult help (the students) is an important source of support, as long as their own learning is not compromised. So, for example, such a project may provide small groups of children with the opportunity to work closely with students on planning, assembling and drafting extended pieces of writing, giving pupils the sort of close attention that is often difficult to organise when teachers are working on their own.

Higher education institutions may also wish to establish partnership projects with primary schools for the purposes of research. When an institution can attract funding, support can usually be made available to participating schools either to release teachers, or to provide equipment. For example, our work with the Laptop Literacy Project (Merchant and Monteith, 1997) provided schools with portable computers in order to develop the use of IT in home–school literacy work. The role of individual researchers may also be useful in developing English work in the school. For an example of this, see the impact that work on structured role play based on popular culture had on the literacy activities of a class (Marsh, Payne and Atkinson, 1997).

The successes of some family literacy programmes have come about as a result of the involvement of further education (FE). Not only have FE colleges provided training and guidance for adult tutors, but also they have been able to give on-going support to parents who wish to develop their own skills and educational qualifications.

Professional groups

A number of interest groups and associations can provide advice and support for primary English. Although they may not be able to provide financial support, many of these groups have a strong professional interest in curriculum development projects. Their input or interest may help your networking with other schools and may lend some external legitimacy to practices that you are trying to develop in school. A list of such groups and associations is given in the annotated bibliography at the end of this book

In Chapter 12 we will be considering the management and development of resources. Part of this work will involve establishing a working relationship with educational publishers. Our concern here, however, remains at the level of external initiatives and it is from this perspective that we wish to explore the contribution of publishers. There are two ways in which this sort of work can happen. First, and more commonly, your involvement with a publisher may lead to your being asked to trial some materials to test their appropriateness and effectiveness. Again, this external impetus may be just what you need to boost colleagues' sense of motivation. So, for example, being involved in trialling collections of non-fiction for a group reading set will involve colleagues in professional dialogue about reading and may have important spin-offs as you develop a reading policy and schemes of work. A less common but vital kind of contact with publishers arises out of work that you and your colleagues are developing that you think would be applicable to teachers working in other schools. Often publishers are more interested in this kind of work than teachers realise. You don't need several degrees and a doctorate to publish curriculum materials!

Evaluating external projects

If we were completely dependent upon external initiatives we would be continually changing direction in the wake of the latest wave of publicity inviting us to bid for new projects. Although, as we saw in Chapter 2, part of the change process involves external pressure and support, there is a dynamic tension between external and internal forces. In other words, the sort of priorities in English that the staff agree upon are every bit as important as the new trends set by external initiatives. So we are left with some important strategic decisions as an English co-ordinator. Although the head and sometimes the LEA may have strong ideas about the direction the school should take, the co-ordinator, with her overview of the English curriculum, has an important voice.

Making sense of an external project may not always be easy. Where should we start? In order to answer this question we have drawn up a checklist (see Figure 8.1) to help co-ordinators to work out how a particular initiative may or may not benefit the school.

Inevitably there is a degree of compromise in deciding to become involved in an external initiative. It is unlikely that what is on offer will fit in neatly with the school's own priorities. However, part of the skill of

1. How does the project fit with our existing policy and practice?

2. How does the project fit with our action plan and development priorities?

3. What investment of time and resources does it require?

4. What are the likely benefits for staff/pupils/parents?

5. Who will be involved?

6. What kinds of training and support are offered by the project?

7. What scale of change is suggested?

8. What is the timescale for implementation?

Figure 8.1. Checklist for assessing an external project

managing change is to be flexible enough to modify development plans without completely losing direction. Using the checklist will help you to weigh up the advantages and disadvantages of working with an external agency and to gather sufficient information to make an informed decision.

Negotiating and managing projects

Assuming that you have been through the process suggested above, and have come to the conclusion that involvement in an external initiative would be fruitful, a number of possibilities are open to you. An important first step will be to consult with the head, the management team and the staff.

In liaising with external agencies, the active support of the head is essential. So, before taking any action you need to discuss the proposal and its implications for the school. You need to keep the head informed as regularly as possible. Some projects may involve individual teachers on a rolling programme, or teams of staff (such as year groups), or may work progressively with the whole teaching staff. Even if only one teacher is involved, it is important that all colleagues are informed. A larger-scale initiative should be discussed first with the staff, since their co-operation will be essential if new practices are to be adopted.

If you are to be involved in negotiating the school's involvement with an external agency, it is worth thinking through this process first. We will look at two different scenarios. The first is a situation in which the initiative needs participants. The second scenario involves competitive bidding. In other words, the project has a specified number of schools or teachers to work with and is in a position to select participants.

An example of the first situation is a project offered by a local HE institution. They have a small grant to develop materials for teaching grammar at Key Stage 2. The project team are looking for schools to trial and adapt these materials. Since grammar, language study and standard English already feature on your action plan, the project seems to match your needs. Your exploratory discussions give you the impression that the suggested teaching approach and draft materials may make considerable demands on colleagues' time and may not, as a result, be popular. However, at the same time it appears that the project team desperately need volunteers. Clearly you are in a strong position. You can point out your reservations whilst still expressing interest. As a result of further discussions you are able to persuade the project team to make an input on a forthcoming training day and also to arrange student placement so that teachers have additional support during the trialling of materials.

An example of the second situation is a literacy project offered by an LEA, funded through the Single Regeneration Budget (SRB). Their funding is limited and their targets are quite specific. You will be bidding, competitively, against other schools in the authority. You are required to submit a proposal to the English Inspector. The first step here is to try to find out the criteria for selection and the kind of format and detail required of a 'good' bid. This may involve talking directly with the inspector or her advisory team as well as other schools and co-ordinators – particularly those who you know have been successful. After this period of information-gathering, you can then make decisions about your involvement. There is an 'opportunity cost': it will take time and energy to put your proposal together and you may not necessarily be successful. You will also need to consider how well the project's specific literacy targets match your school's needs and whether the level of support will be sufficient for you to capitalise on the potential for change.

By comparing these two contrasting scenarios we have been able to explore the varying demands and opportunities offered by external initiatives. However, it would be misleading to conclude that projects can be divided into two simple categories. We have used the examples as an illustration of the bidding and negotiating processes.

If you are successful in becoming involved in a project, you will also need to think about what it means in terms of in-school management. Given the quite specific requirements of some projects, it is difficult to talk in general terms about aspects of management, so we conclude this section with some broad issues for consideration.

Responsibility

As we suggested above, it is normal for the headteacher to have direct responsibility when an external agency is involved. The head will normally delegate some of this responsibility to you, but it is essential to ensure that management is fully aware of any financial implications of project work.

Contact person

You may decide that, although you are the co-ordinator, it would be more helpful to directly involve a colleague as the named contact person. This can have advantages. It gives greater staff involvement in the English curriculum, it may free you up to do other work and it will certainly have benefits in terms of staff development for your colleague. It may also be more appropriate to involve another member of staff. For some initiatives, a year group co-ordinator may be more suitable. Finally, since communication is a two-way process, you need to try to make sure that you have got a reliable point of contact with the external agency you are involved with.

Staff involvement

Even with a small-scale initiative which perhaps only focuses on one or two classes, you will want to try to involve more staff. This may take the form of a programme of classroom visits in which colleagues can see new work 'in progress' or of a report back by teachers who have been involved. This sort of dissemination helps to capitalise on project work so that it begins to influence practice throughout the school.

Keeping colleagues on target

External projects often work to quite tight deadlines. Their deadlines may not be flexible enough to take into account busy times in your school calendar. So, first of all it is important to be clear about the expectations and targets of the project as well as the particular timescales that they are working to. This sort of information needs to be communicated to colleagues who are involved – probably on more than one occasion. You, or whoever is responsible for managing this aspect of the project, will need a clear time-line. This should have reminders and progress checks built into it and should allow some slippage time to help you to meet the deadlines. Colleagues will also need encouragement, support and praise to maintain their morale.

Ownership

One of the indicators of a successful project is the degree to which schools 'take ownership' of new ideas. At this point you begin to feel that what you have contributed as a staff has been worthwhile and that you have developed something that is to some extent tailored to the needs of your school and fashioned by the values and skills of your colleagues. If projects publish materials to disseminate their work to a wider audience, try to make sure that the contribution that you and your colleagues have made is acknowledged. It may only be a small claim to fame but it can generate considerable pride in the achievements of your staff.

Evaluation and reporting

Most projects involve some level of evaluation. This may involve teachers in report-writing, monitoring visits by the project team or an independent evaluation study. Make sure what will be required of you in advance so that you know what to expect.

Implementing the National Literacy Project – a case study

We now turn our attention to the key role played by the subject co-ordinator in implementing and adopting changes that are initiated by external agencies. Based on a case study of a primary school's involvement with the National Literacy Project, we trace the sequence of events concluding with a step-by-step guide to the implementation process.

Keeping colleagues informed

As the teacher responsible for the English curriculum, it is part of your function to keep colleagues informed about new developments. Whether these developments take the form of media debate, government pronouncements, national projects or local initiatives, or are concerned with new teaching approaches or resources, staff will look to you for guidance. So it is important that you keep up to date on primary English. Through your formal and informal networks, your membership of subject associations and your journal subscriptions you will be well-informed and sometimes it will be important to share information with the whole staff. Only you can decide how much information colleagues need and what is appropriate. Schools' needs are different and the extent to which teaching staff are aware of new developments varies quite considerably.

Although teachers will look to you as the expert, there are bound to be times when you just don't know. Be honest about this – admit that you don't know and then try to find out. When we interviewed an English co-ordinator about introducing the National Literacy Project, we were surprised by the ways in which information travels:

> Funnily enough I first found out about it from my next door neighbour – she works in a local comp. and must have been looking at the educational press...I phoned the English adviser when I got back to school – she didn't know how things were going to shape up but did say that they were holding interviews for literacy consultants. She didn't say much more but said she'd keep me posted.

As it became clear that this was going to be a major national initiative, the co-ordinator decided that all colleagues should know about it. At this stage there seemed to be little idea about what it might entail and there was no indication that the school might wish to become involved. It was just a case of keeping colleagues informed.

> I looked up the *TES* report and got hold of some more bits and pieces. I copied these for everyone to read and asked the head if I could have five minutes at the next staff meeting....people should at least know what's going on.

Coming to a decision

In most innovations there comes a point at which the school must make a decision as to whether to get involved or not. When the external pressure is strong, as is the case in the National Literacy Project pilot LEAs, the decision may not actually be *if* to get involved but *when* to get involved. In our case study, it seemed that there was already a willingness – at least amongst some members of the staff – to be involved in an initiative which addressed the teaching of reading:

> I think we'd been worried about the reading for some time – well at least I had ...and the head. After OFSTED and all the stuff in the press...it gets to you in the end. Even if we were doing OK we were beginning to have doubts!

The actual decision-making process and the way this is handled is very important. Teachers do not like to feel bullied into accepting more work, and although the co-ordinator in our case study was involved in discussion with the headteacher, the final decision to join the project was taken in a staff meeting.

> Anyway the head got all the information through the post and talked things over with our adviser. I was asked what I thought and talked for quite a bit with the head about whether this was the right thing for us. It's no good just jumping on bandwagons, and we didn't want to unsettle people who were just beginning to build up a bit of confidence after the INSET day on curriculum planning. We decided to take it to the staff – it's the best way really – let them decide. It was a long one – an after-school meeting. To be quite honest, there were one or two in the juniors who were a bit cheesed off – more work, more interference, that sort of thing – but there was a feeling from others that we should give it a go. We'd had Reading Recovery and this sounded similar-ish...except with the whole class. In the end we decided. It was getting on, there were still some concerns and she (the head) just sort of said 'So we're all agreed then we'll give it a try and see what we think.' – not bossy – just sorting things out. It was good. Fortunately for us, we were accepted as part of the first cohort of schools. Then we had to work out which teachers were going to be trained. We had to have two – one from each year group, that's the way it was.

Getting involved

The level of participation that typifies this sort of decision-making process does, of course, raise the expectation that information on further developments will be shared in a similar fashion. The advantage of this way of working is that all teachers are included – the staff as a whole own the innovation, and as we shall see, this became important later on. Only two teachers were to be trained for the project in the first place and it was important that this wasn't just seen as 'their thing'.

> As soon as we knew that we were in the first group of schools to have the Literacy Project it seemed important to let everyone know.....so I asked for some time at the next staff meeting – by then everyone knew anyway – but it sort of made it official. I'd made my own action plan, but I didn't show it because quite a few things weren't settled. I just took a bit of time to talk about what was certain....going on the course, the year groups, the assessments, that sort of thing, and then my thoughts about how things might develop.

Training and networking

As we saw in Chapter 2, successful curriculum change is always accompanied by some sort of professional development. We defined professional development in terms of 'a dialogue about our working practices' and gave examples that included both the formal and informal contexts in which this took place. In our case study, the language co-ordinator's informal professional network included an ex-colleague who provided peer support at various stages during the implementation. This support proved to be invaluable.

> Well I'd known D. for a long time – since we worked together – we're both co-ordinators now you see. A while back we used to have this thing where co-ordinators in the cluster met twice a half term – it was great, really useful – but people have moved on, everyone's too busy. Anyway I'm still in touch with D. – on the phone and we meet up – so it was quite natural that we started talking together about the Literacy Project.

Training provided by the National Literacy Project was given a high status and the direction and challenge that this provided clearly set things going for the two teachers involved. This demonstrates how a professionally run course that provides plenty of food for thought can provide powerful momentum for change.

> D. was on the course as well, so it was only natural that we kept up the link. The week was exhausting, my head was spinning, it was good but very intensive. There were some difficult moments. It was clear quite early on that you would need to be good at class management if it was going to work. We've got some quite difficult children. You know, you'd be worried about group reading if some of the class were a bit disruptive. And some of the videos – you know what they're like – a small group of attentive children sitting round and you're

wondering 'Where's the rest of the class?'

However, it was clear that at this stage, there were still issues to be resolved. The ideas, although well-received, would need to be put into practice. Regular professional dialogue, planning and support would be necessary.

Planning and implementing

At the next stage, new ways of working are actually tried out. This can be a very difficult time. Not only does it mean that the teachers are treading on unfamiliar ground, it also involves children in new routines and this can be unsettling. In the Literacy Project, teachers had to familiarise themselves with new ways of planning and, at first, it was this that seemed to be their main focus of concern.

> It was a bit daunting at first – all the extra planning we had to do and there were problems about matching it up with our existing schemes of work. It would have been really useful from my point of view if they'd put references to the National Curriculum in the framework. We were worried about resources – well we still are. You can't make something as important as this work on a shoestring.

It was apparent from quite an early stage that involvement in the project would eventually lead to whole-school adoption of a literacy hour, and this was clearly at the forefront of the co-ordinator's mind at the time. As well as making a positive start, he was concerned about familiarising colleagues with the style of classroom work and the constituent parts of a literacy hour.

> At first we were only focusing on those two year groups, so I talked with the head about how we were going to introduce the others to it. We wanted to keep the others on board – keep the momentum going and prepare those who were going to be next into the project.

Although these ways of working could easily be explained to the staff and would eventually be the subject of a school-based INSET session, the co-ordinator decided that first-hand experience through observation and participation would be a better introduction.

> In the end the head talked to everyone at a lunchtime meeting. We agreed to have a settling-in time followed by a timetable of visits so that others could see a literacy hour for themselves – they'd be better prepared then when it was their turn – they'd know what to expect. That worked out well when we got our INSET day with the consultant...people were asking her good questions – like they already knew.

At this point, more of the staff were keen to join in with the project. It had begun to generate its own momentum. The co-ordinator gradually introduced more year groups, allowing staff to implement the literacy hour at half-termly intervals. By working in this way he was able to capitalise on enthusiasm as well as controlling the pace of change.

Curriculum innovation rarely runs smoothly; this is because of the complexities of the change process. So we were not surprised to find that some staff were not so keen to adopt the literacy hour.

One teacher was not at all happy, being concerned about what she described as the loss of 'quality time' – the child's individual reading with an adult. In the end the situation was resolved through negotiation. The teacher was allocated additional CCA support in order to continue with individual reading and it was agreed that this would be a good complement to the literacy hour. This solution acknowledged a valid criticism as well as offering practical support.

Sharing

Just as the co-ordinator had benefited from talking things over with his friends and colleagues in the early stages, so it was important for staff to keep up the dialogue in school.

> I organised regular meetings where those of us involved could talk about what was going on – how we were finding it. This was nothing to do with the planning – that happened in the year group – it was more informal than that, but we found it useful.

As more year groups became involved, it was still important to include all staff in discussion. The co-ordinator was keen for it to be seen as whole-school involvement by including those teachers who were not yet running a literacy hour.

Later on, the idea of talking with teachers from another school was suggested. Fortunately, the links had already been established.

> Then we had a get-together with the teachers in D.'s school. That was really good...some of the problems were the same and we also got some good ideas about resources from them. Both schools were concerned that individual children were spending less time reading to the teacher. There were worries too about how parents might feel about this. Of course, there was also a lot of enthusiasm around too...It was like we were all in the same boat helping each other out.

Again we see the importance of professional dialogue. In this instance it was informal, in the sense that it was not organised by the National Literacy Project. It was simply a case of interested teachers from two schools talking about their experience of adopting a literacy hour.

Monitoring

As we saw in Chapter 6, monitoring is central to the work of an effective subject co-ordinator. We described it as the mechanism by which the co-ordinator finds out what is actually being taught and how it is being taught. In our case study, the co-ordinator as a designated 'project teacher' was able to work out a system that involved monitoring, support and feedback.

> It was like I was genuinely interested in what other people were up to and after a bit we were all committed to making a success of it, so I got the head to do my session once a week – that was good – and I joined in with the other classes in rotation. It was like I was helping out but we agreed to have break together afterwards so we could go through things. A lot of the concerns at that stage were about getting our heads round the framework and speeding up the planning process.

After a while, he was also beginning to build up a picture of the strengths and weaknesses of the school's literacy programme. By asking the questions: 'where's it going well?' and 'where's it not going so well?', monitoring was beginning to throw up some interesting issues. These were seen as problems *of* the literacy hour rather than particular teachers problems *with* the literacy hour.

> One of the things I noticed was how some of the kids were getting really drawn into things – but we were also worried about some of the quieter ones particularly in the whole-class work...those who were just cruising along. But the big thing seemed to be about management and control, getting the work right, what to do about groups finishing early. I think we're better at our group work now and we're looking at how we pitch our questions in the whole-class parts. We used a problem-solving approach, watching each other – seeing what solutions we could find. It was as if no one had the right answer, we were just finding out. That's a good position to be in.

Support

Support for curriculum development may come either from within the school or from external sources. As we have already seen, external support in the form of material resources was meagre in the early stages of this project and the school had little of its own money to support the initiative. Similarly, staffing resources were stretched. Two CCAs were involved in the literacy hour and a graduate who worked as a volunteer. The school was, however, keen to draw on any source of support.

> It's great because it's a big thing – a new thing and everyone wants to know about it, so you can say: 'Well, it's complicated to explain but you could always come along and see a session' – and if they like that idea then you just slip in: 'but you'll have to help out...look after a group.' We've got some parents and students involved in that way. With parents, we've found it difficult to

encourage them to make a regular commitment – after all, they've got things to do, lives to lead!

The school also made good use of the LEA's literacy consultants, usually being the ones to make contact in the first place.

> We've had the consultants in quite a lot – well they're the experts and they're getting paid for it. We tend to go out to them...ask them to come and see new things were doing – like the work on magazines or ask them to show us things or give advice on resources – it's better than them coming along all serious and pointing out what we've not got right.

Review and evaluation

In a large national project the question 'is it worthwhile?' has to be rigorously addressed for the purposes of accountability. A large-scale evaluation of this kind is likely to draw on a whole range of information, including indicators of pupil performance, effectiveness of in-service training and support as well as the qualitative accounts of pupils, their parents and their teachers. Of necessity, this sort of evaluation will provide an overall national picture and will be produced, primarily, for the stake-holders of the project.

Important as this sort of study is, there is also a key role for the school's own evaluation. The question is the same: is it worthwhile; has it been worth all the effort? Although the co-ordinator may not have access to the advice of academics, statisticians and professional evaluators, the question is, of course, still worth asking.

> I do want to get a clear idea of what we're getting out of the literacy hour. I know it's supposed to be great and we've enjoyed it – we've put a lot of hard work into it, don't get me wrong – but is it helping our kids? And if it is – how's it helping them, who's succeeding, who's still struggling? And how could it be changed to help our kids more...some of this'll go into the report for the Project. It won't all be sugary sweet – that wouldn't be right. But in school we need to know how to make the best of it, how to adapt it and how to improve it. And, on a personal level I'd like to know something about the active ingredient – you know, is it the shared reading or is it the group reading or is it simply the fact that we're doing the hour a day with a sense of purpose!

We can see here that there are both questions about how to improve provision and questions of genuine professional interest. One of the hallmarks of a reflective teacher is the ability to ask questions about what works, what doesn't and why.

Celebrating achievement

The old adage, 'giving credit where credit is due', was an important part of the co-ordinator's approach to the school's work with the National

Literacy Project. It was, after all, a whole-school initiative and those teachers who put in the hard work were given plenty of recognition.

> I think it's important that the people who do the hard work get the credit for it. You know what it's sometimes like – it's the adviser's baby and your school's the jewel in the crown – the adviser's crown and you're just the poor lackeys who did the hard work...then it's something new and you're forgotten. Well, I've been there before so this time I've been quite hard about it. It's the teachers who've done the work – done it for the kids and the school – so we'll take the credit first off and that's the way it's happened.

As a result of their introduction of the literacy hour the teachers were mentioned in reports to governors and parents and even in an article in the local press. Alongside this, the effort and commitment has been praised by the headteacher, advisers and the project's consultants. This has been important, happening at a time when primary school teachers' morale is generally quite low.

Development

As we have already suggested, it is unlikely that teaching and curriculum development will ever reach a steady state. There is always room for improvement and always the need to respond to changing circumstances. In this case study, we have seen that at each stage of the implementation process problems have been generated and it is clearly the co-ordinator's view that further developments are anticipated.

> There are still the resource issues too – the head, the LEA, the project – someone's got to find some more money and no one seems to have any. But we'll also be concerned about how to get it just right for our kids. They've got their own ways, their own interests and they come from different cultural backgrounds. It's a community – a different sort of community from down the road and something like a literacy hour has got to be part of their world...otherwise it'll never last.

There will be a need for more staff training, focused on more specific elements in the literacy framework where there are particular demands in terms of subject knowledge and its application. Some staff will continue to need extra support on aspects of classroom management and organisation. Sharing new ideas and building up resources for literacy work will be a priority for all teaching and support staff.

Chapter summary

From this case study of one school's implementation of a literacy hour, we are able to identify some key themes for the language co-ordinator. These are incorporated in the step-by-step guide for responding to the external context. The successful adoption of a new approach that we have described has been typified by the co-ordinator's concern to keep all staff informed of developments, to ensure full ownership of the project work and to take a problem-solving approach to any difficulties encountered.

Step-by-step guide	
1. Keeping colleagues informed	What is important for colleagues to know about?
2. Coming to a decision	When is it appropriate to decide to get involved?
3. Getting involved	How will you keep colleagues informed as you start?
4. Training and networking	What training and networking can you access?
5. Planning and implementing	How will you start things off in your school?
6. Sharing	What opportunities will there be for sharing practice?
7. Monitoring	How will you know what is happening in classrooms?
8. Support	What internal and external support is available?
9. Review and evaluation	How will you know whether it was worthwhile?
10. Development	How will you continue and improve your work?

9

Managing the Assessment, Recording, Reporting and Accountability Process

The English subject leader has a number of roles in these processes. The areas of assessment, recording, reporting and accountability need to be looked at separately as each has its own particular set of tasks and responsibilities. In this chapter, therefore, we take a focused look at each area in turn. We begin by considering the assessment of English. How can the subject leader co-ordinate the whole-school assessment process? What are the key issues in the assessment of speaking and listening, reading and writing? Assessments need to be recorded in a practical and useful way and so we move on to the issue of developing appropriate recording formats. Reporting and accountability are dealt with together as they overlap in many ways. This final section contains a consideration of issues relating to the reporting of achievement to parents. We begin, however, by considering the tasks involved in the whole-school management of assessment in English.

Assessment

The English subject leader has a number of roles and responsibilities with regard to assessment of English in the school. One of the principal ones is supporting staff in the monitoring and assessment of pupils. The assessment of English is a complex process and the co-ordinator cannot assume that all staff feel confident about assessing every aspect of English. There are a number of questions to be asked about the assessment of oracy and literacy such as:

- What are we assessing and why?

- What is the best way to assess each aspect of children's skills, knowledge and understanding in English?

- When and how should we use the various types of assessment, e.g. informal, formative, summative, diagnostic?

- How can we ensure that the assessment process informs future planning?
- In what other ways can we make use of assessments?

If you are an English subject leader, are you confident that all the staff in school are clear about the answers to these questions in relation to English? If not, you will need to organise time when you can discuss these issues as a group and agree on common policies and practices. If the staff have already had these discussions and the school has established common assessment practices, the co-ordinator's task is to ensure that all staff are using them appropriately. If, for example, your school has agreed to conduct reading conferences with each child once a term, you need to ensure that this is, in fact, actually happening. It should not be done in a manner which suggests to staff that you are watching them in order to detect faults. It should be done in a supportive way. A simple discussion, in which you ask the staff whether they are managing the reading assessment process, will suffice. We do not think it is appropriate to 'check up' on staff by asking to look at the records of individual children in the class in order to ensure that they are up to date. This will simply indicate to teachers that you do not trust them to carry out their professional duties and may prove to be counter-productive when trying to raise standards of assessment practices.

However, it may be the case that an individual member of staff is giving you cause for concern. You may be aware that they are not keeping on top of the assessment procedures. In this case, a close monitoring of the situation is needed, but again it has to be done in a supportive manner if it is to be useful to the individual concerned.

We suggest that you set up a monitoring system which is based upon trust and sends messages to all concerned that it is part of a collective effort to maintain standards. Asking colleagues regularly if they are managing the process is one method. If you are trusted, staff will let you know if they are having problems and you can then organise appropriate support for them. This may mean working with the colleague, or providing them with details about an appropriate in-service course. You can also suggest they consult relevant materials such as teacher handbooks. If a large number of staff are having problems with the same aspect of assessment, then this indicates that there is an issue that needs dealing with at the whole-school level. Have staff had sufficient training in that particular aspect of assessment in English? Could it be that the task is, after having considered every other aspect, simply unmanageable and so needs reviewing?

If assessment in English is a staff development priority for the year, another method of monitoring new initiatives is to look at a sample of teachers' records in order to identify patterns and areas that need further attention. You can decide as a staff what a representative sample could be; for instance, records for six children in each class, across the ability range, could be sufficient to build up a picture. You can then analyse these records to find out if there is a consistency in the way assessment in English is addressed throughout the school, or if staff have particular professional development needs. There are two ways in which you can discuss your findings from this with the staff. First, you can provide individual feedback, in a supportive and positive manner. This can be written or verbal, for example:

Shelley, your English assessment is very good. You are obviously thorough in your approach and appear to leave no stone unturned! However, I think you need to question if, in fact, you are too thorough? Is your assessment of English taking far more time than is feasible? You must be careful of wearing yourself out! For example, you provide much more detail in your speaking and listening records than other staff do. I have given you an (anonymous) sample from other classes so that you can see what the 'norm' is. It may be that you want to provide this much detail for your own purposes, if so, that is your decision!

Or, second, you could provide more general feedback to the staff as a whole, being careful not to name individual colleagues in the feedback given to everyone. Again, the feedback can be given orally or in writing. Ensure that it mentions the positives, as well as indicating where practice could be improved. For example:

Thanks for letting me loose on the English records! Here is a summary of what it revealed. If you do want more specific feedback on your individual records, do ask me. Otherwise, here goes:

– The standard of assessment across the school is very good. I think the process we have been through this year has had a huge effect.

– We need to think about the assessment of speaking and listening. This is the weakest area across the school. Some of us are not linking assessment to the programmes of study, but are assessing random skills. Perhaps we need to revise the recording format further. I'll organise a staff meeting on it early next term, if we can fit it in. I know maths has the priority now, I won't poach that time! If we can't fit it in, I'll provide some written guidance.

– Reading records are detailed. Most people are providing very specific comments about skills and attitudes on the reading conferences. Some people are forgetting to attach the appropriate running record to the conference! Try not to forget, as they complement each other.

– Writing assessment is excellent! The journal system is working well. Do remember to put the date on each piece of work in the journal. Written feedback to children in the journals varies – we need to look at this as a staff again. I'll dig out the advice the English adviser gave us.

Thanks to everyone for co-operating I know you have enough on already. I hope you agree it has been a useful exercise. I think we ought to discuss the possibility of doing this once a year – could you bear it?!

Cheers, Brian

If staff do need further development on particular areas of assessment, you could provide training following the procedures outlined in Chapter 7. In the next section, we provide specific advice about the assessment of each of the three attainment targets in order to outline the key issues in each. For a more detailed look at assessment in English, please consult the relevant section of our annotated bibliography at the end of the book.

Assessment of speaking and listening

Shorrocks (1993) reminds us that the National Curriculum Working Group (1989) suggested five essential criteria for assessing speaking and listening:

- The nature of the skills requires that they be assessed in a *continuous* way and as *informally* as possible.
- The assessments should be in the context of activities and experiences *familiar* to the child.
- The speaking and listening dimensions are closely *related* to each other and this should be reflected in any assessment.
- The assessments should both reflect and promote *a wide range of classroom activities*.
- The assessments should be as free as possible from the influence of *social and cultural bias*.

Teachers need to focus on what children can do rather than what they cannot do. They also need to ensure that their own prejudices and assumptions are not clouding their judgements. For instance, the fact that a child has a strong local accent does not necessarily mean that they are not able to speak standard English.

The assessment of bilingual children needs careful consideration. Teachers cannot assess a child's competence in his or her first language if they are not users of that language, but they can obtain information about the child's attainment in that language from the class teachers, parents or relatives. This will help them to form a fuller picture. Teacher assessment of the child's skills in English should focus on their achievements and identify what English they do know and can use. Remember that bilingual children in the early stages of acquiring English can often understand much more than they can say (Barrs, Ellis and Thomas, 1990).

What are we assessing when we are focusing on oracy? The Programme of Study has three sections: Range, Key Skills and Standard English and Language Study. In Figure 9.1, we outline what skills, knowledge and concepts children need to develop in each area and pose key questions.

Range	Key Skills	Standard English and Language Study
How far can children:	How far can children:	How far can children:
– use talk for a range of purposes, e.g. narrating, explaining, hypothesising, clarifying ideas? – communicate to individuals, in small and large groups and to a class? – communicate to known and unknown audiences? – use language appropriate to the audience? – listen to others and respond appropriately? – use language appropriate to a role or situation in drama? – reflect on how other speakers adapt vocabulary, tone, pace and style to the needs of different audiences?	– speak with confidence and clarity? – incorporate relevant detail, appropriate to the needs of their audience? – take turns in conversation and not dominate? – take the views of others into account? – ask relevant questions of others? – use talk to develop their thinking and extend their ideas? – structure their talk appropriately? – evaluate their own talk? – summarise others' talk?	– adapt what they say to the needs of the audience and the purpose of the talk? – recognise differences in language, e.g. dialect and standard English? – understand how language varies according to context and purpose? – know when it is appropriate to use informal and formal talk and begin to use SE in formal situations? – recognise similarities and differences between written and spoken forms of standard English? – use an increasingly varied vocabulary?

Figure. 9.1.   Assessment of speaking and listening

The evidence of attainment in speaking and listening is very often ephemeral. Teachers therefore need to develop a range of strategies for the assessment of talk. The types of evidence which can be collected are:

- notes of observations, sometimes including direct quotes
- tape recordings of children
- video recordings
- children's written work related to speaking and listening activities, e.g., talk diaries, language maps.

This evidence can be collected in a variety of ways:

- Observing children in a particular activity, e.g. talking in pairs, groups or presenting information to the whole class. This can be an activity focusing solely on oracy or talk as an integral part of a curriculum activity, e.g. science experiment.
- Talking with a child informally, e.g. chatting when they come into the class in the morning.
- Conducting a planned discussion or conference with a child or group of children.
- Asking children to record a discussion, retelling of a story, themselves giving instructions, interviewing others, etc.
- Video recording a performance or presentation.
- Asking children to note down their observations of their own and others' talk.

Assessment of listening skills is much more difficult than the assessment of speaking skills. We can assess how well a child is listening by:

- Observing their body language – are they attentive?
- Analysing the questions they ask and the comments they make – are they appropriate? Do they reflect the comments of previous speakers?
- Asking them to act on the information they have been given, e.g. carry out that instruction, tell Ayesha what I have just said, now go and do that yourself, etc.
- Asking them to summarise what has just been said.

Children should be encouraged to assess their own oracy development through the use of talk diaries, or other strategies which allow them to reflect on, and make comments about, their speaking and listening skills.

Assessment of reading

Learning to read is a complex process and so our assessment of reading should reflect this. We need a variety of methods and modes which will provide a full and rounded picture of a child's reading development. We need to assess a child's attitude to, and interest in, reading as a crucial aspect of the process. Schools need to help children develop as active readers and not simply as children who can decode and read mechanically.

The assessment of reading can take many forms. The main modes of assessment that can be used are:

- observation of children browsing, reading silently, reading in pairs or groups, whole-class interactive sessions

Range	Key Skills	Standard English and Language Study
Do children:	How far can children:	How far can children:
– listen to literature being read aloud, and read themselves, from a wide range of genres? – read information in printed texts and on screen? – use a range of sources of information, including information texts, dictionaries, newspapers, CD ROMs? – read, or have read to them, texts written by key children's authors (past and present), stories from a range of cultures, classic poetry, myths and legends?	– read with fluency, accuracy, enjoyment and understanding? – use a range of knowledge, understanding and skills when reading, e.g. *phonic knowledge* (includes phonological awareness, knowledge of names of letters of alphabet and the sounds they can make, identifying initial and final sounds), *graphic knowledge* (letter patterns), *word recognition* (sight vocabulary), *grammatical knowledge*, (syntactic cues – use word order and structure of sentence to check meaning) *contextual understanding* (semantic cues – meaning derived from the text as a whole)? – talk about characters, plot, language used in the text? – predict? – retell stories? – use inference and deduction? – evaluate what they have read? – use the text to support their opinions? – use reference materials and their organisational devices? – skim and scan texts to find relevant information? – use research skills?	– discuss the characteristics and features of different kinds of texts? – use relevant vocabulary in order to aid discussion, e.g. author, setting, etc.? – use knowledge gained from reading to develop their under-standing of the structure, vocabulary and grammar of Standard English?

Figure 9.2.   Assessment of reading

- listening to individual children read either alone or in group reading sessions

- reading conferences – talking with a child about their reading

- running record/miscue analysis – in-depth analysis of cues used in reading

- standardised reading tests

- analysis of children's written and oral responses to materials they have read.

We need to assess a range of skills, knowledge and attitudes if we are to get a rounded picture of a child's reading abilities. Again, if we look at the Programmes of Study, it is useful to ask key questions under each of the three headings – Range, Key Skills, Standard English and Language Study (see Figure 9.2).

Running records

Another useful diagnostic tool is the use of a running record or miscue analysis. This is a process whereby a teacher notes down what strategies a child is using in tackling familiar and unfamiliar words. The teacher then analyses these strategies in order to plan focused reading work with the child. There are a variety of methods of carrying one out. The most familiar method involves marking a photocopy of a passage from the text the child is reading. The adult listens to the child read, and as he reads the adult notes down on the copy a series of abbreviations which record the types of miscues being made. Symbols for miscues can vary and it will be necessary for your staff to develop a set which are agreed upon. The symbols used in the reading SATs can be used as a starting point. Here, we indicate some of the most common ones:

- If a child omits a word, put the letter 'o' above the word:

    o
    she sat on the chair

- If you tell the child what a word is, put the letter 't' above the word:

    t
    she laughed loudly

- If the child substitutes one word for another, cross out the original word and write the word which was substituted above:

    wide
    The ~~wild~~ sea

- If the child self-corrects, insert the letters 'sc' over the word which was corrected and add the miscue:

Sc (this)
He put it in the box

- If a child inserts an extra word, write it above the line:

own
Come to my ^ house

- If a child takes a long pause before reading a word, insert a stroke before it:

she went to the /fridge

The running record can then be analysed later by the teacher in order to make a careful assessment of what strategies the child is using when reading and where his or her strengths and weaknesses lie. For example, in this short extract from a running record, it is clear that this child is reading for meaning as her substitutions, insertions and omissions do not alter the sense of the text:

quickly   O   T   that
She went ~~quietly~~ out of the small room, expecting to hear ^ Sam shout her back.

The observations made using a running record can then be used to inform future planning for children. Strategies which were over- or under-used could be noted, as well as how well the child orchestrates his use of the key skills. Appropriate teaching strategies could then be devised.

Reading conference

A reading conference provides an opportunity for an adult to have a detailed discussion with a child about his reading habits, likes and dislikes and his own self-assessment of reading. The session could include the child reading aloud to the adult and the adult conducting a running record and making notes about the child's reading skills and the discussion of the text. You need to develop a whole-school policy on how often you conduct a reading conference with children. Figure 9.3 contains an extract from a reading conference conducted with a Year 3 child.

Reading conferences can provide a wealth of information that is not easy to collect in the daily running of a busy classroom. However, they can be very time consuming and need careful organisation if they are to be manageable. They are also not appropriate for young bilingual children in the very early stages of learning English. Of course, they could always be conducted in the child's first language if the school has the appropriate staff. For younger children in general, the questions asked need careful consideration if they are to be appropriate for their level of understanding. Reading conferences are often used in conjunction with a running record (Barrs, Ellis and Thomas, 1990).

Attitude to reading	Barry said that he doesn't like reading books at home unless they are about sharks. He likes reading computer comics. He likes reading 'Goosebumps' books at school.
Text	*Gerbil Crazy* by Tony Bradman. Barry had previously read to Chapter 3. He had forgotten the details of the story – was able to retell key events.
Key skills (reading observation)	Barry read quite competently but did not read with any enthusiasm or expression. Had difficulty with silent ks, e.g. knelt, knife. Used phonic cues when necessary, checked meaning.

Figure 9.3.   Reading conference extract

Reading and comprehension tests

Children's reading skills are often tested in schools through the use of standardised reading tests. Although this is a fairly widespread practice, we would want to suggest that schools think seriously about it before deciding if and when it is appropriate to use tests, and which ones to use (see SCAA, 1996b, for a useful overview). They can provide the teacher with a picture of the pattern of attainment in a class, but there are also questions to consider such as:

- Does the test assess reading skills or is it a vocabulary test?

- What reading skills does the test assess? Could these be assessed in a different way?

- Is the test culturally biased? For example, does it ask children to respond to pictures and scenarios they may never have encountered?

Most schools use tests as a means of acquiring a broad picture of reading attainment across a year group. We look in a later section at how the English subject leader can use the results of tests to set whole-school targets.

Comprehension tests are another form of reading assessment. There are many examples of poorly constructed and unbearably dull comprehension tests. These tests do not always depend upon a child having understood and responded to texts and indeed promote a rather functional view of reading. If a teacher wants to check how well children are able to understand what they have read, or how well developed their inferential reading skills are, a discussion after a running record is probably more accurate. Some teachers use cloze procedures in order to encourage children to read for meaning. This involves presenting the child with a text in which words are erased at regular intervals. The child then has to predict the missing words and, assuming that they are well constructed, they do this by having to read and understand the surrounding text.

Assessment of writing

When assessing children's writing, we have to look at a variety of features – the child's attitudes to writing, the structure and content of the writing, the spelling, grammar, punctuation and handwriting. Of course, teachers will need to focus on one or two of these aspects at a time rather than trying to assess everything at once.

We can assess writing using the following strategies:

- observation of child writing alone and collaboratively

- discussion with child whilst he is engaged in writing task, or on completion

- analysis of child's drafts, redrafts and finished pieces of work

- discussion with child about his writing progress

What are we assessing when looking at children's writing? Again, we need to examine the Programme of Study for writing (see Figure 9.4).

Writing conferences

Writing conferences perform the same function as reading conferences in that they allow the child to discuss their work in depth with an adult. This helps to develop their self-assessment skills as well as providing the teacher with information about the child's perception of their development. It can also allow the teacher to assess the child's metalinguistic skills – are they able to talk about writing in a meaningful way, using appropriate terminology? Figure 9.5 contains an extract from a conference with a Reception child.

When teachers have completed the writing conference, they should attach some examples of the child's writing to the conference. These pieces of writing should be annotated with the dates and comments about the context of the writing, e.g. '6/5/98. First draft of a poem. Elijah has been given some words, e.g. 'was', 'some' and has attempted others himself.' Some schools have developed the use of journals or writing portfolios to provide an on-going record of children's writing develop-ment. The children write in the journals, or contribute a piece of writing to a portfolio, at regular intervals. This writing is always completed without teacher assistance. The entries are dated and immediately provide a clear record of a child's development over time.

Range	Key Skills:	Standard English and Language Study
How far can children:	How far can children:	How far can children:
−understand the value of writing? −write in response to a variety of stimuli? −write for a range of purposes and audiences? −write using a wide range of forms, incorporating relevant characteristics?	−differentiate between print and pictures? −understand the connections between speech and writing? −write their own name? −write each letter of the alphabet? −experiment using known letters and words? −spell commonly occurring words? −recognise and use simple spelling patterns? −use knowledge of spelling patterns, rules and word families to spell unknown words? −check the accuracy of their spelling using word banks and dictionaries? −write with confidence, fluency and accuracy? −plan, draft and revise their writing on screen and paper? −organise and structure their writing according to form and purpose? −read their work aloud and evaluate it? −make choices about particular tone, style, format, choice of vocabulary? −use punctuation marks correctly in their writing (full stops, question and exclamation marks, commas, apostrophes)? −use legible handwriting in both printed and joined up styles? −use different forms of handwriting for different purposes?	−reflect on their use of language? −analyse how written Standard English varies in degrees of formality? −use their grammatical knowledge to inform their writing? −discuss their vocabulary and stylistic choices?

Figure 9.4. Assessment of writing

Part 1: Discussion with child about writing	Elijah stated that he likes writing but he finds it difficult. ('It makes my hand hurt.') He likes writing about Power Rangers.
Part 2: Assessment using portfolio of child's work and observations	
Compositional aspects	Elijah seldom chooses to enter the writing area although he is happy to take part in writing activities if directed. Elijah's writing skills are still at the emergent stage. He uses strings of random letters to convey words. He is able to assign meaning to the letters, assigning simple sentences which are modelled on speech. He is able to understand the structure of some non-narrative forms of writing, e.g. lists, posters. He can plan writing through discussion.
Transcriptional aspects	Elijah is not yet able to spell phonetically. He recognises some letters of the alphabet but is not using them in his writing to denote associated sounds. He does leave spaces between his 'words'. Elijah has control over the size and shape of some letters but still has difficulty with those letters he is not familiar with. He uses upper and lower case letters inappropriately. He is not yet using punctuation in his writing.

Figure 9.5. Extract from writing conference

Spelling tests

Many schools use spelling tests as a means of checking which children are able to spell correctly. Most teachers are now aware of the pitfalls of setting one test for all the children in the class. It would be very unusual if all 30 children in a class needed to learn the same words. Group spelling tests, in which groups are given differentiated lists to learn, are much more suitable. Some schools incorporate the words to be tested into a dictated passage in order to contextualise the words. This helps children to develop a sense of the meanings of words as well as how they are spelt. Other schools have developed systems whereby children are assigned a spelling partner with whom they work on learning new words and testing each other throughout the week.

Sharing assessment criteria with children

As we saw in Chapter 5, it is important when planning to link the criteria for assessment to the learning objectives for your lesson or activity. Learning objectives for each English session should be clear and unambiguous as well as achievable. Too many learning objectives leads to confused teaching! It is also not good practice to move whole-heartedly towards focusing upon *teaching* objectives to the exclusion of *learning* objectives. Good teachers link both together in a cohesive manner. It is obvious, but perhaps cannot be said often enough, that what we teach should be based upon what children need to learn. It is also appropriate to share criteria for assessment with children, so that they are aware of what the teacher will be looking for in any particular session. So, for example, a class of children might be told,

> Today you are going to rewrite the story we have been working on this week, *The Iron Man*, from the point of view of the Iron Man himself. I want to see if you can imagine what it would be like to be that character. Think about what happens to him at each stage of the story. How does he feel? What might he be thinking? I want to assess how well you can get inside the head of a character and put yourself in their shoes. This is a first draft. I will not be looking at the spelling, handwriting or grammar first of all, that will come later. Today I am going to be looking at your work and assessing how well you can empathise with a character, how well you can express what that character might think or feel.

If children are clear about what you are going to assess, they will be able to direct an appropriate amount of their energies and effort towards achieving that objective.

It is not feasible to examine the issues relating to the assessment of English any further in this chapter. We recommend in the bibliography a variety of books which pursue the subject in depth. In a later section of this chapter, we return to the aspects of assessment that we have not discussed so far: using assessment to inform future planning and Standard Attainment Tasks. We now move on to discuss the various tasks the English subject leader has in relation to recording of attainment in English.

Recording

Once staff are clear about the key principles in the assessment of English, they need to be able to record their assessments using a system which is manageable and provides useful information to a range of people. Records can be used to inform other teachers, support staff, feeder schools, parents, educational psychologists, outside agencies. LEAs and inspectors.

Developing recording formats

If you are working in a large school, this is best done through the use of a working party. Refer to Chapter 7 for a discussion of the key principles involved in setting up and running working parties. If you work in a small school, you may find that you have to devise suitable formats yourself. There are many recording formats around and indeed your LEA may suggest a set of particular ones which they recommend. However, we feel that formats which are developed by staff, to suit particular schools' needs, are ultimately more useful and acceptable to staff. When developing recording formats, the following questions need to be considered:

- What assessments do we want to record?

- What sort of information do we need?

- How much information is needed to provide appropriate evidence?

- How best is this information collected? Through the use of checklists/ticklists? By using written comments? By collecting examples of children's work?

- If we use a combination of methods, can the different information be held on one sheet or do we need different sheets for different aspects?

- How can we quickly access information in order to plan for progress?

- What distinctions, if any, are to be made between a teacher's own pupil records and those that are passed on at the end of the year?

It is useful to trial drafts of formats before adopting them as the school's records. There will always be something you haven't considered, or information needed which is not contained on the form. The use of the formats should also be carefully monitored. You need to ask yourselves whether they are manageable and whether they provide useful information. This can be done through discussions with staff, but also through the use of surveys of completed forms. If you take a sample of records and find that, in general, teachers are making generalised and brief comments you may need to consider whether the assessment and recording load is overburdening. It may be that staff need further training in using the formats, or it may simply be that they have so many records to fill in that none of them get done thoroughly enough. If this is the case, it obviously is an area that needs attention.

Below, we present a variety of recording formats for English. They are presented merely as examples to inform staff discussion. We would envisage that most schools would want to develop their own, using a range of ideas from different sources. We look at each of the three programmes of study in turn.

Speaking and listening

Many schools use simple checklists which contain statements which the teachers tick once the child has attained that particular skill. However, we also feel that teachers need to collect more qualitative evidence of a child's oracy skills. This could consist of an observation sheet which a teacher completes occasionally. The frequency of observations can be decided as a staff. Figure 9.6 is an example of a completed observation sheet.

Some schools also encourage the children to assess their own developing skills in oracy. They can do this through the use of a 'Talk diary' in which they record comments about the oracy activities they have been involved in and how well they did in them. Examples of children's work in oracy can also be used to inform the recording process, such as copies of tapes or videos that children have made.

Reading

It is useful to keep a record of each time a child reads, either as an individual to a teacher or in a group reading situation. This can then be used to build up a picture of the child's skills and inform daily planning. If the child is able to write independently, they can add their own

Date	Social context, e.g. pair/ small group/ with adult	Audience (if different)	Learning context, e.g. role play/ science investigation	Purpose of talk, e.g. hypothesising, reporting, narrating, predicting	Observations, e.g. notes on confidence, ability to listen, take turns, ability to incorporate details, awareness of audience, etc
2.4. 98	In pairs	–	Paired reading	Discuss characters and justify opinions	Shona was able to use talk to clarify her thoughts and she changed her mind about the mother during the discussion. She asked M. relevant questions about her opinions. She was able to justify her opinions well, e.g. she said 'I think that Lou is selfish because he didn't ask Frank about the holiday.'
10.4. 98	Group (of 4)	Class	Presentation of findings from an investigation into the use of land in the local area	Reporting findings, explaining findings, answering questions	Shona spoke confidently and clearly. She was able to wait for her turn in the presentation and explained clearly what her task had been. She missed a few details from her report but was able to remember them when I questioned her. She used the key vocabulary, e.g. survey, leisure, appropriate.

Figure 9.6. Shona's speaking and listening record

comments. Children sometimes keep a 'reading diary' in which they note down comments about the texts they read. Figure 9.7 is an example of a typical on-going reading assessment format, with each heading explained. Figure 9.8 is an example of a reading observation of a Year 2 child, using the format outlined.

One school has adapted the headings and placed them in a small, bound, booklet. Each child has their name on the front of the booklet, along with a photograph of them in the book corner, reading. This promotes an image of each child as an active reader and is much loved by children, staff and parents alike.

Reading conference formats vary enormously and need to be adapted to meet individual schools' needs. An example is given in Figure 9.9.

Date	Text	Genre	Context	Comments	Where next?	Child's comments
	Note down the title and author	What type of text is it, e.g. poetry, information, fiction, comic?	Individual or group reading?	Here, write specific observations about the child's reading rather than using superficial comments such as 'read well'!	Make one or two brief suggestions for future development of the child's reading.	The child can add his comments about the text, or his self-assessment of reading.

Figure 9.7.   The reading assessment format explained

Date	Text	Genre	Context	Comments	Where next?	Child's comments
3.2. 98	'Funny-bones' by Allan and Janet Ahlberg	Humorous story	Group reading	Sajad read the first four pages of the text and a couple of pages towards the end. He recognised most words and used phonic and semantic cues when meeting unknown words. He is not yet using intonation/ expression. He was able to discuss the plot and identify favourite parts of the story. He responded well to the humour of the text.	Sajad needs to develop intonation. I will draw his attention to how the punctuation can give us clues.	It was a good story. I liked it when the dog was mixed up. I was good at reading.

Figure 9.8.   Sajad's reading record.

Reading Conference – Prompt Sheet

Use these prompt questions to inform your discussion with the child. These questions are only *guidelines*. We expect you to adapt them to suit the age/ability of the child or focus of the conference. They are not intended to be asked in order – it is a conference, not an inquisition! A few questions answered in depth are more valuable than a list of short answers. *DO NOT* use as a checklist!

	Possible questions
Attitude to reading	What do you like or not like about reading? What is your favourite book? Do you have a favourite author? How good a reader do you think you are? Where and when do you like to read? Do you like being read to? Do you like reading aloud?
Range of reading	What sort of books do you read? Do you read comics, magazines, newspapers? Do you like information books, poetry, horror stories? Do you read anything on computers? What? Where? How do you choose a book? Do you read different sorts of things at home than you do in school?
Text	Note the title, author and genre of the text chosen. Note whether the text is known or unknown to the child.
Key skills (observation of reading)	Observe the child reading and make notes on his/her reading behaviour and use of cues. For example, can/does the child: Handle books correctly, appropriate to directionality of print? Turn pages at the appropriate time? Know the difference between text and pictures? Join in with known words and phrases? Point to the words, with accurate word/sound correspondence? Use picture clues where appropriate? Have some knowledge of the basic sight words? Use phonic cues where appropriate? Use syntactic cues (i.e. use the structure of the sentence to guess the word)? User semantic cues (i.e. use the meaning of the sentence to guess the word? Self-correct? *(YOU NEED ONLY COMMENT ON A FEW KEY SKILLS. DO NOT USE THIS SECTION AS A CHECKLIST!)*
Discussion before and after the reading	Before reading: If it is a known book, ask the child to summarise what they know about it so far. If it is an unknown book, ask the child to predict what they think it is about, using the cover as a clue. Talk about the author/illustrator. After reading: Ask the child key questions about the text in order to assess how involved they have been with it. If it is fiction, can they talk about the plot, characters, etc. in a thoughtful way? Are they developing inferential reading skills? If the text is non-fiction, can they discuss it appropriately?
Overall impression	Make notes on your overall impression of the child as a reader, e.g. did they read with enjoyment and enthusiasm? Did they read confidently and fluently? Did they read with appropriate intonation and expression?
Where next?	Make a few suggestions for what the child needs next in order to develop their reading skills further. For example, do they need to widen their choice of texts? Are there any key skills which need working on? Do they need to develop the ability to talk about the texts they have read?

Figure 9.9. Reading conference (part 1)

Reading Conference

Name of child.. Class................   Year..........
(Use the prompt sheet of questions to complete the conference.)

	Comments
Attitude to reading	
Range of reading	
Text	
Key skills (observation of reading)	
Discussion before and after the reading	
Overall impression	
Where next?	

Figure 9.9.   Reading conference (part 2)

Most schools also use a quick checklist of key reading skills which provides an overview of a child's attainment. Teachers can also use examples of children's written work that they have done in response to reading if they want to provide further evidence of attainment. This could be placed in a reading portfolio.

Further advice on recording formats can be found in Barrs, Ellis and Thomas (1990) and Karavais and Davies (1995).

Writing

Many schools use a checklist which provides a developmental model of a child's skills. However, checklists need to be supplemented by some qualitative evidence and so schools can either incorporate a format which includes space for written comments, or conduct regular writing conferences, an example of which is provided in Figure 9.10. The analysis of a child's written work does not have to be completed at the same time as the discussion conducted with the child.

Obviously, with regard to writing, examples of children's work should inform the recording process and we have already mentioned the use of journals and portfolios.

Whole school portfolios

Schools need to develop portfolios of work in English which should inform the teacher assessment process. Examples of children's work need to be analysed and discussed with all staff in order to establish shared levels of assessment. Some schools have also cross-moderated with other schools in the cluster. SCAA/QCA have provided a range of exemplification materials so that the task of assigning levels should be easier. One co-ordinator has said:

> We spent ages getting together a portfolio for spelling and handwriting. It was very useful to do it, though. We spent a long time arguing over particular pieces! But the discussion we had was worth it and I think we are all a bit sharper now in our assessment of these skills.

We feel that the development of portfolios needs to be carefully organised so that a range of specific areas can be targeted for such work. For example, rather than having just one portfolio on writing in general, there could be portfolios developed in a number of areas such as drafting and revising, handwriting, narrative writing, non-narrative writing, spelling, punctuation and grammar. Work can then be carefully chosen to demonstrate achievement in that particular area.

Setting targets

Assessments of children are used to inform the teaching and learning

Writing Conference – Prompt Sheet

Part 1 – use the questions to inform your discussion with the child. Adapt the questions to suit the child. These are merely guidelines. DO NOT use as a checklist!
Part 2 – choose a range of written work from the child's portfolio. Assess the work and make comments in each section. There are some prompt questions to help you.

	Comments
Part 1: Discussion with child about writing	The discussion is a chance to talk with the child about writing in general and his/her own perceptions about how much progress he or she has made. Useful questions: What do you like/not like about writing? What kinds of writing do you find easy? Why? What kinds of writing do you find difficult? Why? What to you do when you don't know how to spell a word? Do you plan your writing? What do you do if you change your ideas when writing? What could you do better? What would help you to do it better? What do you think you have got better at doing? Do you like writing with other children? Can you write in a language other than English? Where do you learn it?
Part 2: Assessment using portfolio of child's work and observations	
Attitude to writing	From your observations, comment about how you think the child approaches writing. Does he/she find it a chore? Does he/she enjoy it? Does he/she like writing collaboratively? What experience does the child have using a word processor?
Forms/ purposes/ audiences	Does the child approach a range of forms and purposes for writing confidently? Which forms does he/she have difficulties with? Is the child able to assess and meet the needs of the audience when writing?
Process	Is the child able to plan, draft and revise writing, on screen as well as in print? Can the child discuss each stage of their writing appropriately?
Structure	Is the child able to incorporate the characteristics of different forms of writing appropriately (e.g. structure letters, stories, instructions, reports using appropriate conventions)? Is the organisation of writing appropriate to form and purpose?
Style	Comment about the child's vocabulary choices – varied? Deliberately chosen to suit purpose? What about syntactical features? Is writing generally confined to simple sentences or does child make use of more complex forms (clauses joined by connectives, sentences using main and subordinate clauses, etc.)? Are adjectives and adverbs used to refine meaning? Are a variety of verb forms used (past, present, passive, etc.)?
Spelling	Does child use random letters to represent words? Is child able to spell simple monosyllable words phonetically? Does the child have a range of words they can spell from memory? Is child beginning to use knowledge of spelling patterns and rules? Does the child use the look-cover-write-check method? Does child check spellings in dictionaries, thesauri, etc.?
Hand-writing	Has the child some control over shape and size of letters? Can child space letters and words appropriately? How legible and fluent is the script, print or cursive, the child produces? Can child use different styles of handwriting for different purposes?
Punctuation and graphics	What understanding of punctuation does the child demonstrate in their writing? Which punctuation marks can the child use with confidence and general accuracy? Can child use paragraphing accurately in their work? Can the child plan and layout a page appropriately?

Figure 9.10   Writing conference (part 1)

Writing Conference

Name of child.. Class.............. Year...........
(Use the prompt sheet of questions to complete the conference)

	Comments
Part 1: Discussion with child about writing	
Part 2: Assessment using portfolio of child's work and observations	
Attitude to writing	
Compositional aspects (Comment on features of: structure and organisation, style, use of variety of forms, ability to write appropriately for different purposes and audiences, use of processes of writing etc.)	
Transcriptional aspects (Comment on: spelling, handwriting, punctuation)	
Where next?	

Figure 9.10. Writing conference (part 2)

cycle. The framework produced by the National Literacy Project has stated that teachers need to set literacy targets for individual children. Teachers may not need any advice on setting literacy targets as most teachers have been involved in devising Individual Educational Plans for children who have Special Educational Needs and all teachers have had experience of planning work for individual children. However, NQTs may need some support in setting literacy targets for individual children and so the co-ordinator needs to ensure that if this is the case, the NQT is provided with appropriate advice. The subject leader may also feel that it would be useful to have a staff meeting on the subject so that there is some consistency across the school in the number of targets set and their nature.

The individual targets set for children should be shared with the children and their parents. Obviously, the sharing of targets with children needs sensitivity and care. The aim is to engage the child in the process of reflecting upon and evaluating his own performance, not to overwhelm him with a long list of skills he needs to learn. Work on targets should also celebrate achievements; for example, by outlining to a child what they are doing well and then how to improve on that:

> The way in which you now can redraft work and think about how to improve it is excellent. You can see where you need to check spelling and can think of ways in which to improve the words you choose. You now need to think about how you structure the writing. You need to work on putting the writing into paragraphs. Should we have that as this half term's target?

Children could also be involved in the process of setting their own targets. If they own them, they are more likely to be motivated to achieve them. Sharing targets with parents also needs careful handling. Again, the emphasis should be on celebrating achievements and providing information about achievable targets. Parents can be involved in helping their child to meet those targets but will need guidance in this. Care needs to be taken to ensure that parents do not undermine the work of school by pressurising their child to reach targets in such a way that he becomes demotivated or stressed.

Reporting and accountability

The English subject leader will need to consider the range of audiences for the reports on children's progress:

- teachers who will be teaching the child next
- support staff
- parents
- feeder schools
- relevant outside agencies, e.g. educational psychologists
- governors
- LEA.

Reporting to governors

Governors need to be informed of whole-school formal assessments but also need more qualitative data about how the school is doing. Data will need to be provided which details how the school's results compare with national results, but test scores should always be given with 'value added' information, such as the number of children having free school meals or the number of children who speak English as an additional language. Many LEAs also provide information about a school's performance in relation to that of other schools of a similar nature. However, this needs care and consideration as such data is sometimes misleading or unreliable. It is useful if the English subject leader can present information relating to school performance in English to the governing body herself. She could then present the governing body with more detailed information and be ready to answer further questions. It is useful to present other information to governors from time to time in order to keep them in touch with developments. For example, if the school has had a particularly successful book or poetry week, the English co-ordinator could prepare a display of photographs and children's work which can be presented at a meeting of the governing body.

Reporting to parents

Schools have a statutory duty to report children's progress to parents. The two modes of reporting achievement to parents, orally and through written texts, need to be monitored by the English subject leader in order to ensure that there is consistency in the practice across the school.

In the case of written reports, it is useful to circulate a range of written comments which will illustrate the types of things which should be said and provide models of language use which can be adopted by all. This is not to suggest that there should be a list of stock phrases, although some schools have certainly found this approach useful. Rather, there should be an agreement about how specific comments need to be and how to ensure that reports remain positive and encouraging in tone whilst being clear about children's future targets in English. NQTs may need additional support from the co-ordinator in writing these reports for English. A collection of examples of good practice, covering a range of abilities and age ranges, would be useful for any new staff in the school. When writing for parents, it is important that acronyms, jargon and technical terms relating to literacy skills are avoided. For parents who speak English as an additional language, it may be possible to have the reports translated although there is not usually sufficient time between them being written and when they go out for this to happen. It is our belief that results of standardised tests, such as SATs scores, always need to be contextualised for parents. This may reassure them. For example, when the parents of a bilingual child at Stage 1 of learning English (using Hilary Hester's model, 1990) find that their child has achieved

Level 1 in reading when the national norm is Level 2, they may panic and worry if this information is presented without any discussion. But when the parents are informed that their child does not, in fact, speak English to a sufficient extent to achieve Level 2 in reading, but that he is doing very well in acquiring English and has achieved to the best of his ability, they may feel less worried. This would be especially the case if, at the same time, the school outlined how the child's needs were being met.

Most teachers have had extensive experience of orally reporting progress to parents and so the language co-ordinator may not need to play a pivotal role in this area. However, it would be good practice to ensure that all staff were agreed on the key principles of reporting achievement in English to parents and so the subject could inform a brief staff meeting. The key principles of orally reporting achievement to parents need to decided upon by individual schools but should include:

- being positive; focusing upon what a child can do rather than cannot do

- listening to what parents have to say – they have a much broader experience with the child and can provide important information about literacy practices and interests at home

- answering parents' questions openly and honestly, with tact

- being specific about future targets and providing ideas about ways in which the parents can help

- avoiding technical jargon and a patronising tone

- developing a partnership approach to a child's literacy development – teachers need to establish a relationship of trust and honesty with parents

- backing up the discussion by reference to the child's work – have examples/portfolios present.

NQTs will need particular help and guidance and we suggest that the open evenings are timed to enable the NQT to sit and observe the English subject leader reporting to the parents of children in her class. Student teachers working in the school would also find it useful to sit in on such sessions and even contribute to them under the guidance of the teacher.

Some schools use open evenings as an opportunity to communicate with parents about a particular feature of school. Interviews with parents take place within classrooms whilst a central area is used to set up displays or talks which feature on a particular aspect of the curriculum. The English subject leader could use such opportunities to set up displays based on a specific area of English. One co-ordinator outlines how she organised an evening based on children's literature:

On one open evening, I used the central hall area to set up a display of children's books – mainly picture books and poems. I then put up a range of children's work relating to books such as writing, models and puppets. I got a few computers and set up the talking books we have. They turned out to be the most popular bit of the display! I had borrowed some old books from the school museum service and set up a display on old and new books. There were quite a few there that the parents remembered! The children's librarian from the local library came with a range of books they have and talked to parents about joining if they hadn't already. We got a local bookshop to run a stall for the evening and they sold quite a few books. I set up a video which ran a few times which was aimed at parents and provided ideas about reading with children. The head said that it was a brilliant event – I was in my classroom talking to parents all night – and most of the parents who came said that they had never realised how many good children's books there were.

Reporting to other agencies

Outside agencies will need detailed reports about individual children and these will need to be compiled by the teachers working with the child. Records kept on individual children will be passed on to new teachers or feeder schools using systems already set up by the school. It is important to have good links with feeder schools in order to evaluate the usefulness of records passed on to them. They may have some valuable feedback about the effectiveness of particular forms of record-keeping. This may be the role of the senior management team, however, or a teacher with responsibility for transition. They can oversee the whole process rather than subject by subject.

Chapter summary

In this chapter, we have discussed the role of the English subject leader in relation to assessment, recording, reporting and accountability. It is a major role and one which needs reviewing constantly in order to ensure that the school is a model of good practice. The co-ordinator also needs to keep abreast of new developments and respond to local and national initiatives relating to the area in an appropriate way. She also needs to ensure that her own standards in assessment, recording and reporting are high enough to provide a role model for those staff that may need further support. For those co-ordinators who are beginning to think that this role is unmanageable, we have some sympathy. However, we want to reassure you that with careful organisation and a realistic overview of what can be done in the time allocated to the post, it can be done. In the conclusion to the book, we provide some advice about how to manage this diverse and challenging role.

10

Subject Knowledge

There is a lack of hard evidence about the level of knowledge that we need in order to teach the various subjects that make up the primary curriculum. Questions about which areas of knowledge are most useful and the depth to which they should be studied have been discussed by teacher trainers, HMI and INSET providers over a number of years. So, in this chapter we will be exploring the concept of subject knowledge and the ways in which it relates to the role of the English co-ordinator. We begin by taking a look at the distinction between generalist and specialist teachers and the complex issues that this raises. This leads us on to questions about the kind of English subject knowledge that all teachers should have. We then turn our attention to the topic of specialist subject knowledge – in other words, the knowledge and understanding that you as a curriculum co-ordinator will be building up. Auditing your own subject knowledge as well as that of your colleagues is an important aspect of your role. We conclude by giving guidance on how to approach this task as well as how to plan for the professional development needs that this process will identify.

Generalist and specialist knowledge

The idea that you should be familiar with a subject before you begin to teach it is hard to dispute; the question of *how* familiar you should be with that subject is more problematic. How helpful is a knowledge of approaches to literary criticism, grammatical description or reading theory to our primary colleagues? Teachers, teacher trainers and the various bodies that give professional advice and guidance have expressed quite diverse opinions on this matter.

Despite this, a succession of HMI reports (HMI, 1987; 1988; 1991) and summaries of inspection findings have suggested that students in training, newly qualified and experienced teachers need more depth of subject knowledge to increase their effectiveness. The work of Shulman and his colleagues helps us to be rather more specific about what we mean by subject knowledge. Shulman (1987) identifies seven areas of teacher knowledge. Of these, two are important to our discussion here. They are described as 'content knowledge' and 'pedagogical-content knowledge'. Content knowledge is about the subject itself, and the ways in which its basic concepts and principles are framed. Pedagogical-content knowledge relates to the understandings necessary to present and explain the subject to pupils.

In Initial Teacher Education this debate has resulted in some models of training that aim to produce 'generalists' – all-rounders who are confident in teaching at least six curriculum subjects – and other models that aim to introduce student-teachers to the whole curriculum whilst, at the same time, placing an emphasis on the study of a main or 'specialist' subject. This specialist subject is usually studied to degree level in graduate courses; in postgraduate courses (PGCEs) the student's first degree is usually seen as the specialist subject.

We tend to find that generalist teachers are well-equipped to teach most subjects in the primary curriculum. They may well have an enthusiasm for some subjects and admit to a lack of confidence in others.

Specialists, on the other hand, are more likely to have enthusiasm, confidence and a good working knowledge of their subject but may, in a similar way, need support in other areas of the curriculum. A small-scale study of trainee teachers (Bennett and Carre, 1993) points to the important role that subject knowledge plays in students' teaching performance. A group of students with high levels of appropriate subject knowledge consistently out-performed those peers who had less familiarity with their subject.

But what exactly is specialist knowledge? It is not altogether convincing to argue that a degree in a subject or degree-level study (in the case of a BA or BEd) necessarily equips a teacher with the right kind of subject knowledge to be a specialist. What aspects of literature studied at degree-level will be most useful in informing primary practice? What role should language and linguistics play – and what approaches to these topics are most helpful? What sort of under-standings of drama are appropriate? These are not easy questions to answer and to some extent they depend on the kind of curriculum that teachers are required to deliver. However, most experts are agreed that subject specialists need a broad view of their subject, an appreciation of that subject as studied at their own level and an understanding of how that subject develops beyond the primary years.

Specifying the kind of English knowledge that *all* teachers should have is also a complex undertaking. Again, curriculum design is likely to influence our view. Partly as a result of the rich debate over the content of the English curriculum, subject knowledge has had a high profile in recent years. As we saw in Chapter 2, the reports of the Kingman and Cox committees were not well received by the Conservative government (Cox, 1991). Similarly, the ideas underpinning the Knowledge about Language training materials designed by the LINC project were unpopular and never published in a complete form. The *kind* of subject knowledge that LINC was promoting was not what the government of the day had in mind.

Despite all this controversy, teachers' subject knowledge about English language is still seen as important. The recent emphasis on children's understanding of grammar and the attention given to Standard English and language study in the Programmes of Study mean that all teachers need to be confident about the terminology used and have the necessary skills to teach these topics. Further changes are embodied in the *National Literacy Project Framework for Teaching* (NLP, 1997). This will require additional subject knowledge. For instance, to teach about verb tenses (in Year 4), the use of the apostrophe (Year 5) or the term 'phoneme' (Year 1) demands a particular kind of subject knowledge.

In June 1997, the Teacher Training Agency (TTA, 1997a) published the National Curriculum for Initial Teacher Training, a document that lays down the subject knowledge requirements of all those who are to attain Qualified Teacher Status from September 1998. This means that all newly qualified teachers will have demonstrated that they can achieve specific levels of subject knowledge. It is hoped that these standards will be sufficient for a clear understanding of the primary English curriculum in its current and developing form. However, this will only reach new members of the profession (13,000 were recruited to primary training courses in 1996) – there are, of course, training implications for those teachers who qualified prior to that date (some 190,000 serving teachers), and this is an issue that we will be addressing later in this chapter under the heading Auditing Subject Knowledge.

At this point, then, we can only go so far as to suggest that *all* teachers (generalists) should have sufficient subject knowledge to teach English effectively and that *co-ordinators* (specialists) will need a broader and deeper view of their subject, a view that is at least sufficient to guide school policy development and to offer practical guidance and direction to teaching colleagues. Clearly continuing professional development has a key function here. It is central in updating the subject knowledge of generalists, both to clarify 'difficult' subject matter and to prepare for curriculum change (see, for example, *The Implementation of the National Literacy Strategy*, ss 25–40, Literacy Task Force, 1997). It is also central in strengthening the work of curriculum leaders, in establishing a secure knowledge base for those who develop an English specialism as part of their career development and in 'topping up' the subject knowledge of trained specialists.

English subject knowledge for all teachers

So far we have suggested that the knowledge that teachers need in order to teach English effectively will, to a large extent, be dependent upon curricular requirements. As well as this, however, we assume that all primary colleagues will understand basic aspects of children's language development. For instance, they will recognise the crucial role that they take as teachers in providing a context for children to learn to *use* language effectively, to learn *through* language and to learn *about* language. They will also know how to develop the skills of oracy and literacy in different subject areas. They will recognise the significance of spoken and written language in thinking and learning, whether the subject matter is mathematics, geography, science or indeed any other part of the curriculum.

In addition to this we might expect all primary teachers to have a clear view of the developmental patterns of oral language and an under-standing of the processes and skills involved in learning to read and write. All teachers should be able to demonstrate an enjoyment and enthusiasm in children's literature and poetry and we would also expect that they would understand the importance of drama and role play and be able to incorporate this in their planning and teaching. As we begin to explore these different areas of knowledge we become aware of the scale of the task – and this is before we even begin to consider the specific needs of the children we teach and how to plan, teach and assess their learning.

We cannot, however, be certain that even these basic understandings are shared by all our colleagues. In fact, there is evidence to suggest that they are not. Annual summaries of inspection reports attempt to identify important issues for the profession. For example, for a number of years these reports have raised concerns about teachers' knowledge about the teaching of reading at Key Stage 2 (OFSTED, 1994). More recent reports have highlighted the lack of progression in phonics and spelling (OFSTED, 1997). Other sources of information also point to specific subject-based professional development. SCAA's publication *Boys and English* on the influence of gender on children's performance in primary English suggests that teachers could be more sensitive to the ways in which gender-related attitudes to literacy are constructed in the classroom (SCAA, 1996a).

It will be useful for English co-ordinators to become familiar with the new *Standards for the Award of Qualified Teacher Status* (TTA, 1997a) because these will now constitute a basic minimum for all teachers entering the profession. We begin with the structure of the document. The English section of the standards document is subdivided into three parts. These are concerned with the knowledge and understanding required to secure pupil progress; effective teaching and assessment methods and knowledge and understanding of English. The final part of the third section is concerned with subject knowledge and understanding. This is shown in its entirety in Figure 10.1.

English subject knowledge for co-ordinators

From our discussion so far, it follows that curriculum co-ordinators will need a thorough understanding of the subject knowledge required to teach English at Key Stage 1, Key Stage 2 and probably the early stages

As part of all courses, trainees must demonstrate that they know and understand:	To underpin the teaching of Key Stage 1 and Key Stage 2 programmes of study, including:
i. **phonology** – the sound system of language ii. **graphology** – the writing system, i.e. the English alphabetic system iii. **how the writing system** represents the sound system	*for example:* • *to teach pupils to read and spell using phonological strategies.*
iv. **morphology** – word structure and derivations	• *to enable pupils to break down words into their constituents, e.g. compound words – head/ache, prefixes and suffixes;* • *to make links between words in order to derive meaning and spelling.*
v. **word meanings** and how words relate to each other	• *meanings, use and interpretation of words in contexts;* • *vocabulary characteristics of Standard English;* • *choosing vocabulary for different contexts, purposes and audiences.*

Grammatical

As part of all courses, trainees must demonstrate that they know and understand:	To underpin the teaching of Key Stage 1 and Key Stage 2 programmes of study, including:
vi. the **grammar** of spoken and written English, including: • the grammatical function of words/ phrases in clauses and sentences, e.g. subject, conjunctions, verbs, nouns, adverbs, predicates, etc; • word order and cohesion within sentences; • types of sentences – statements, questions, commands, exclamations; • simple, compound and complex sentences in writing	*for example:* • *to show pupils different ways in which ideas can be ordered and organised into sentences;* • *to help pupils read and re-read texts to establish, confirm or checking meaning;* • *to improve pupils' understanding of the grammatical structures appropriate for different purposes, and their ability to write in a variety of forms and styles;* • *to contribute to pupils' acquisition of Standard English in speech and writing;* • *to stimulate pupils' interest in the ways in which language works;* • *to analyse pupils' writing in order to determine what has been achieved and what needs to be taught for pupils to progress.*
vii. **punctuation** – its main functions and conventions	• *to help pupils understand the role and importance of punctuation and in marking grammatical boundaries, and the relationship between grammar and punctuation in establishing and clarifying meaning, e.g. where different punctuation can change the meaning or alter the emphasis of a sentence even if the word order remains unchanged.*

Textual

As part of all courses, trainees must demonstrate that they know and understand:	To underpin the teaching of Key Stage 1 and Key Stage 2 programmes of study, including:
viii. **cohesion** – the way that individual words, sentences and paragraphs work together to convey meaning including the logic and sequences of ideas;	*for example:* • *to enable pupils to understand the importance of vocabulary and grammar in creating coherent and cohesive texts, such as by helping them to understand that words and phrases such as 'first', 'second', 'third' suggest sequence, 'thus', or 'therefore' suggest logic, and 'as a result' suggests causation, and to help pupils understand the purpose and effect of the use of pronouns or topic sentences.*
As part of all courses, trainees must demonstrate that they know and understand:	To underpin the teaching of Key Stage 1 and Key Stage 2 programmes of study, including:
ix. **layout** including paragraphs and conventions associated with particular forms of writing	• *to help pupils understand how meaning can be conveyed by the layout of text;* • *conventions, e.g. the layout of a formal letter.*
x. **organisation** including the structure of written text, the order of para- graphs, and the chronology of plot;	• *to help pupils to understand the choices available to them in the way they organise their writing, e.g. in the order of the key points for and against in an argument; the way ideas can be grouped for emphasis or effect.*

Figure 10.1. Initial Teacher Training National Curriculum: English subject knowledge

of Key Stage 3. Not only will they need to be secure in this knowledge, they will also need to be able to monitor the subject knowledge of colleagues and provide appropriate advice or explanation. But co-ordinators will also need a wider understanding of their subject and its place in the school curriculum.

Co-ordinators who have studied English to degree level or who have followed it as a subject specialism during their training may already have some of the appropriate subject knowledge. However, the situation is complicated by the fact that many teachers may, as their career progresses, take on the leadership of a subject other than their original specialism. So, both generalist-trained teachers and those who originally specialised in another subject (for instance, history or technology) may end up as English co-ordinators or may even carry the responsibility for several subjects.

It will be important, then, for you to reflect on your own level of subject knowledge. The co-ordinator whose work is often focused on the needs of colleagues can sometimes forget about her own professional development. Figure 10.2 lists areas that we feel are important for you. You can use this in order to assess your own needs.

Given the diverse background of many primary co-ordinators it is quite likely that you will be able to identify your own strengths and weaknesses against this list. You will then want to work out ways in which you can strengthen your own subject knowledge. For example, this may be through self-study or attending a course (see the final section of this chapter for more detail).

Recent moves to strengthen the professional role of the co-ordinator (TTA, 1997b) have, as we have seen, emphasised the importance of specialist subject knowledge and one hopes that more opportunities for development will become available to English co-ordinators. Of course, any specialist training for subject co-ordinators will need to take into account the diversity of subject knowledge and the varied needs of participants.

Auditing subject knowledge

As a co-ordinator you will also need to have a clear view of the subject knowledge of your colleagues and an informed view of whether or not this is sufficient to teach the English curriculum and to meet the requirements for the assessment, recording and reporting of children's attainment and progress. The professional development needs that you identify as part of an audit will be an essential part of turning your school policy into practice.

We suggest that the subject knowledge framework set out in Figure 10.1 constitutes a good starting point for auditing purposes. Co-ordinators might wish to add to this in ways that reflect the specific needs of the school or the particular policies that it agrees. For example, a school's commitment to raising the achievement of specific groups of

- A broad understanding of the subject, its place in the curriculum and the influences that have shaped it.

- An in-depth knowledge of the processes and skills involved in the development of children's literacy.

- A thorough understanding of the development of children's oral language and the teacher's role in this process.

- An understanding of the place of drama and role play in the curriculum both as a tool for learning and as a subject in its own right.

- An extensive knowledge of children's literature and poetry and significant authors for the age range.

- An appreciation of the range of resources for reading for information including a good working knowledge of non-fiction and ICT resources.

- A clear understanding of language variation including the learning needs of bilingual children, the concepts of accent, dialect and standard.

- A detailed knowledge of the language system, particularly with respect to text organisation and cohesion, sentence grammar, morphology and phonology.

- Familiarity with a wide range of teaching approaches for Key Stage 1, 2 and at transfer to Key Stage 3 and new developments in classroom practice in English and literacy.

- An in-depth understanding of a variety of approaches to pupil assessment and the subject-specific issues of recording and reporting.

- A knowledge of appropriate ways of representing subject knowledge to pupils of different ages and an understanding of particular difficulties that they may experience.

- A knowledge of key research in English teaching and its related areas.

Figure 10.2.   Subject knowledge for English co-ordinators

pupils such as bilingual children will make different demands on subject knowledge.

The auditing process can be approached in a variety of ways. Incorporating the principles referred to in Chapter 3, we would advocate informal professional discussion about subject knowledge. This might be done on an individual, year-group or whole-school basis. The extract from the Initial Teacher Training National Curriculum on subject knowledge (Figure 10.1) could be used to give structure to your discussion. As a co-ordinator you would need to keep a record of areas in which colleagues' knowledge was weak and be aware of the steps they are taking to improve their knowledge.

A more formal approach to this information-gathering is a self-audit, in which colleagues are required to assess their own level of subject knowledge. This is a model which is currently being explored in initial teacher education. A detailed audit and self-study has been produced by Wray and Medwell (1997).

There are two difficulties with the self-audit approach. First, it can seem rather unfriendly. It is by nature impersonal, and sometimes the questions may be difficult to interpret. After all, it is rather like a test, the last thing that colleagues may want to do after a hard day's work! The second difficulty with this kind of audit is the reliability of colleagues' self-reports. In the end a self-audit is only of any use if you are able to provide the guidance that colleagues need to update their knowledge.

Planning for professional development

Auditing your own and your colleagues' subject knowledge is, of course, only half the story. Having completed this you will need to look at how you can use the various strengths that you have identified, and to what extent you can build on subject knowledge in your school. The principles and practices will be the same as those we have referred to earlier in our discussions of professional development (Chapter 2 and Chapter 7), although it may be worth noting that some aspects of subject knowledge are commonly perceived as being 'heavy-going'. An example of this is the topic of sentence grammar – an area that many primary school teachers lack confidence in. An awareness of your colleagues' feelings about particular topic areas will help you to choose materials or course provision that is clear, carefully structured and has relevance to the classroom.

In some cases you will be able to take the lead in professional development by providing in-school training and support. You may also find that some of your colleagues can help. A subject knowledge audit not only identifies need, but may also highlight areas of expertise. As in other developments, you may be able to support colleagues in the application of their subject knowledge through coaching and by example. And alongside this you will be in a position to co-ordinate external training provision, whether this is through the LEA, higher education or subject associations.

As with other facets of the co-ordinator's work, monitoring and developing subject knowledge is an on-going process. You will need to consider the subject knowledge needs of trainees, newly qualified teachers as well as newly appointed staff. In addition to this, as we have already observed, changes in the English National Curriculum or specific school-based initiatives may require new subject knowledge for all.

Chapter summary

In this chapter we have focused our attention on the issue of teachers' subject knowledge in English. We have underlined the problems in defining subject knowledge requirements for primary teachers and commented on a variety of new initiatives. By considering the distinction between the needs of all teachers, whom we referred to as generalists, and the needs of subject specialists we have identified another dimension to the role of the co-ordinator. This involves both the identification of needs through the auditing process and the management of appropriate professional development.

English subject knowledge is an important area and there are clear indications that it will remain so. However, it is worth reflecting on the role of such knowledge in school development. The processes of policy-making, planning, monitoring and evaluation that we have referred to in earlier chapters will, quite naturally, raise issues about teachers' own knowledge base and it may well be the case that key aspects of subject knowledge will be addressed in this context. So, although monitoring subject knowledge is an important aspect of the co-ordinator's role it may not necessarily be tackled in isolation.

11

Partnership with Parents and Families

In this chapter we look at parental involvement in the literacy development of children. This is an important aspect of the work of the English subject leader, yet one which has had relatively little coverage in books of this kind. We begin by exploring the concept of 'parent' and broadening the definition of the term. The nature of the relationship between home and school is then examined and the needs of different groups of parents explored. We then move on to exploring the role of the subject leader in developing home–school partnerships by focusing on communication with parents about the literacy curriculum and the co-ordination of the school's liaison with parents. Family literacy projects are an increasingly important feature of the contact between schools and families and we take a brief look at some of the major considerations to be made in the development of such projects.

Family partnerships

First of all, we would like to qualify the term 'parent'. British schools serve an ever-changing society. Less than half of all British families consist of two married parents and children living together. Those children who are living with two parents may not necessarily be with their birth mother and father. For instance, children may live with a birth parent and step-parent or they may be living with adoptive or foster parents. They may be living with gay men or lesbians who are co-parenting. Children may live in an extended family grouping where their grandparents or aunts and uncles are their main carers. Once we have disabused ourselves of the notion that there is such thing as a 'normal' family and that anything outside those parameters is in some way 'abnormal', then we will be a long way towards being able to work with all of the families we serve in our schools.

Whenever we refer to 'parents' in this chapter, we would like the term to include all of these possibilities. In fact, we would like to see the term 'partnerships with parents' replaced by the broader term, 'partnerships with families'. This helps us to recognise the significance of members of an extended family in a child's literacy development. Uncles, aunts, grandparents, older brothers and sisters, family friends: all of these groups of people may be involved in reading or writing with a child, or providing a role model for literacy. However, for the sake of brevity and clarity, we will use the term 'parent' throughout this chapter to refer to family involvement.

Working with parents is a mutually beneficial activity. The parents receive information about the school, its practices and their child's place within it, but teachers also gain much from a close relationship with families. For instance, we get to know more about the children, what their likes and dislikes are and what they do at home. The English subject leader has an important role to play in the development of these relationships. She will be responsible for a range of activities which will enable effective communication between schools and families concerning the English. This could include:

- producing booklets which provide information on helping children to read and write

- organising parent workshops, or family literacy projects

- organising displays which are aimed at communicating aspects of the English curriculum to parents

- co-ordinating parent volunteers in the library, book shop or book club

- developing a group of parents who are willing to work on a particular project, e.g. making 'storybags'

- identifying parents who have particular skills and expertise they can contribute, e.g. storytelling in first language, computer skills, drama skills.

Reading and writing are of key importance to most parents. It can be the one area which busy parents are prepared to work at with their children and as key projects have shown (Belfield Reading Project, Hannon and Jackson, 1987), parental help can have beneficial effects on children's performances. Browne (1996) states that, amongst other things, the aims of involving parents in literacy development should include:

> informing teachers about the child as a learner outside school...fostering mutual respect, understanding and openness between parents and teachers...enabling children to apply learning in the world outside school...extending the curriculum to include contributions from parents and members of the community....

> (Browne, 1996, p. 209)

It is clear, then, that gains are to be made on both sides of the equation and this needs to be acknowledged by schools if parental involvement is to be any more than a token gesture. Parental involvement should be thoroughly planned and thought through if it is to work effectively. In developing a whole-school literacy strategy, the co-ordinator will need to pay careful attention to parental and community involvement. For as the Literacy Task Force document (1997) emphasises:

> Parents have a vital role in supporting and encouraging children's learning, perhaps most of all in helping that child to read. Attitudes to literacy in the community as a whole are crucial.
>
> (Literacy Task Force, 1997, p. 32)

The literacy co-ordinator should identify the literacy patterns of the school communities in order to develop her understanding of the role of literacy in the children's lives. As one co-ordinator has said:

> I was amazed to find out that Asia in my class not only goes to the mosque for lessons after school but also is taught Urdu at home by someone who is paid for by the family. They do not have much money, her dad is unemployed, so they obviously have that as a priority. It made me wonder about the rest of the class – what reading and writing activities do they do at home that I have no idea about?

It may be that you work in an area with parents who are enthusiastic readers and have established reading circles; on the other hand, a high proportion of your parents may have literacy difficulties themselves. As Brice-Heath (1983), Merchant (1992) and Barton (1994) make clear, there is a wide variety of literacy practices in the diverse communities that make up contemporary society. If the language co-ordinator is clear about the types of literacy events which occur in the community, she will be able to ensure that the English curriculum acknowledges and values these practices and builds upon them.

We want now to look at the many ways in which parents can be involved in the literacy curriculum and outline what steps a subject leader must take in order to ensure that this involvement is meaningful and extensive. We want to examine first the role that parents could play in the development of language policy and planning and the work a school has to do in order to provide parents with sufficient information about these documents.

Language policies and curriculum planning

As we saw in Chapters 4 and 5, designing language policies and schemes of work should be a developmental process in which the whole of a school's staff is involved. Corson (1990) thinks that parents should also be involved in this process, having a voice in the formation of them. However, involving parents in writing policies is not that easy. How could it be realistically achieved? A starting point might be to ask parent representatives to join the relevant working party. However, there are sometimes many different communities involved in the life of one school and there are bound to be some voices left unheard. Many parents lack the confidence to participate in this sort of group. One school's way around this was to hold an open evening once the policy documents had been fully drafted and invite the parents to make comments and contributions. Of course, if parents had wanted to include something that the school objected to, the school would have had the final say. There is always this tension in work with parents. Teachers would like to be as co-operative as possible but, as professionals, we sometimes feel that we should have the last word about pedagogical issues. However, this can at times lead to underestimating parents' knowledge and expertise and we need to ensure that this process is undertaken with care and sensitivity.

If the involvement of parents in the writing of policies and schemes of work is problematic, then the co-ordinator has to be sure that these schemes and policies are communicated to the parents in effective ways. This is the way in which one school approached the task:

> We had spent a long time revising our English curriculum and had ended up with what we thought was a comprehensive and exciting programme of work. We decided to let the parents know about our curriculum and policy through an open evening. We set it up carefully. We set out reading and writing activities in each of the school's classrooms. Next to each activity, we placed a card which detailed why we did that particular task, what we were hoping to achieve. The parents were encouraged to go in each classroom, from Reception to Year 2. The progression and continuity was clear to see. We then handed out copies of the policy and talked it through with parents. Once they had seen things for themselves, the policy made much more sense to them.

Many of the school's parents were bilingual and so the head ensured that she had translators attending the open evening. The parents were informed well in advance that translators would be present. This is important, otherwise some bilingual parents will assume that there is little point in attending such events.

Of course, this process can lead to difficulties. Parents can object to an aspect of a school's English curriculum. What are the options when parents really object to an aspect of a school's policy? There are a number of ways around this. First of all, it may be that parents have not seen the necessity for a particular piece of work and so have objected without understanding all of the issues at stake. Therefore the first step should be to ensure that these issues are fully outlined in as clear manner as possible. Parents who still object, even after further clarification, can be asked to visit the classrooms to see the particular aspect of the policy which is in question at work. Once parents are convinced that the policy will be effective in practice, they may be reassured. Parents can also be asked to join a group which will be set up to evaluate the particular aspect of the policy under question. Parents will then feel that their objections are being taken on board and not ignored. However, it does mean that if the policy is effective, they will be part of a group which will identify that and then be able to endorse it. If the aspect of the policy is not effective, perhaps the parents were right to object in the first place!

Keeping parents informed

Many schools now have leaflets which explain their policies and practice in developing children's reading and writing. Often, the leaflets contain advice and ideas for those parents who want to help their child with their literacy development. These leaflets need much careful thought and discussion before drafting. It is important to remember the following points:

- Language used should not be too technical (e.g. avoid 'syntactic cues', 'phonemes', 'miscues'!).

- The style should be friendly and personal (e.g. use personal pronouns: 'I', 'we', 'you').

- The tone should not be patronising. (School does not always know best!)

- Insert children's drawings and statements at various points in the book. (This enlivens the booklet and breaks up the text.)

- Do not assume that each home will have the same opportunities for reading. (Don't make generalised statements such as, 'Read to your child before they go to sleep'. Some parents may work at night, others may be too exhausted to read before bedtime, they may be single parents who have other children to see to. You should avoid adding to parents' guilt!)

- Many children have opportunities for interacting with texts written in a variety of scripts at home, in community schools and places of worship. It is important to acknowledge this in the booklet.

- Ensure that the booklet is concise and appealing. (You want to inform and interest parents, not make them want to put the booklet straight in the bin!)

We would suggest that you trial the booklet before you decide on the final version. Some schools have their booklets translated into the languages that parents speak. A school may not be sure how many of the parents read the scripts of those languages, just as they may not be sure how many monolingual and bilingual parents read English confidently, but nonetheless it is important to provide the booklets in a range of languages.

Booklets which deal with reading and writing are well established in many schools. Booklets which refer to speaking and listening are not so common. Some recent initiatives attempt to address this need. Nutbrown and Hannon's (1997) collaboration with Sheffield Education Authority on the REAL project developed a number of ways of working with parents to develop children's literacy skills. As part of this project, Springfield Primary School has produced audio tapes which contain a variety of songs and rhymes in different languages. They have also produced an accompanying booklet of words. This could be extended to producing written material which explains how important talk is in a child's development and give parents many more ideas about how to develop their child's oracy skills.

There are also some good commercially produced booklets aimed at developing parental partnerships (e.g. those produced by NATE or the Reading and Language Information Centre). However, we feel that it is more productive for individual schools to produce their own, tailored to the needs of the particular communities they serve. 'Home-made' books will, of course, reflect the values, ethos and curriculum of the school. In order to produce booklets which meet their needs, schools should ask themselves a number of key questions:

- What are our aims in producing the booklet? To:
  - inform parents of our reading/writing/speaking and listening policy?
  - provide some guidelines for interacting with their child?
  - provide parents with information about how children learn to read/ write/talk?

- Will we involve the parents in writing it, or help them to produce their own booklet?

- Do we want children's voices to be heard in the booklet?

- What kind of, and how many, illustrations or photographs do we want in the booklet?

- Do we want to provide parents with information about facilities in the area, e.g. libraries?

- What languages do we need it translating into?

- How will we disseminate it? Through open evenings?

- How often should we update it?

Displays and newsletters

Central displays are an excellent way of communicating information about the curriculum to parents. The English subject leader can use such displays to:

- exhibit children's work, making appropriate comments, e.g. 'This is an example of planning and drafting. This child planned their story using pictures before producing a first draft...'

- illustrate ways in which parents can interact with their child, e.g. next to photographs of environmental print in the area: 'Next time you walk around the local area with your child, talk about some of the signs you see...'

- focus on a particular author, or a particular theme, e.g. information books

- provide information about the local library (libraries are normally more than happy to lend materials for display)

- relate to whole-school projects, e.g. book weeks, poetry weeks.

Newsletters and noticeboards are another way of communicating with parents regarding the English curriculum. Information could be sent out regarding events and also ideas for games and activities to play at home. Again, all such material needs to be translated for those parents who speak English as an additional language.

Workshops for parents

Most parents want to help their child develop literacy skills but many are not confident that they are giving their child appropriate help. Booklets may help to a certain extent, but often parents would benefit from more direct contact with teachers regarding this. Many schools now offer workshop sessions in which the intention is to educate parents about how children learn to read and write and provide them with ideas for working with their children. The sessions can be held in the evening or during the daytime if staff can be released. The REAL project in Sheffield has worked with a large number of schools to develop the structure and organisation of such workshops. They have now produced an excellent manual which will help schools support such training (Nutbrown and Hannon, 1997). Workshops can be held over a number of weeks in order to deliver a coherent and developmental programme.

The overall aims of such workshops would be to:

- provide parents with an overview of the key stages in development of children's literacy and oracy skills

- enable parents to discuss their own child's progress within this framework

- provide an opportunity to exchange ideas for supporting and developing children's literacy and oracy skills

- allow parents to try out some of these activities in a supportive environment

- provide opportunities for parents to make further resources, e.g. games, book bags

- introduce parents to resources available in the area, e.g. libraries, book shops.

Such training sessions will need to be adapted to meet the needs of the parents you work with. Bilingual parents will need to work with staff who share their first language. If there are no staff in the school who can speak a particular language, then the school should try to get a translator. Resources are scarce and this may not be feasible, but there are sometimes grants and trust funds prepared to support this kind of initiative.

The following key principles should underpin such workshops:

- The staff/parent ratio should be as small as possible. This will enhance small-group and individual work.

- There should be a balance between information-giving, practical 'hands-on' activities and opportunities for discussion and reflection.

- Parents should be encouraged to try out new resources and materials. They should be provided with opportunities to make some resources for their own use.

- Workshop sessions should not be over-long as this can create child-minding difficulties.

- If you run a series of workshops, e.g. some on reading, some on writing and some on oracy, ensure that the programme is not too long. It is difficult for some parents to commit themselves for weeks at a time.

- If you are intending to invite outside speakers, e.g. librarians, advisers etc., ensure that they are provided with relevant information about the intended audience. If, for example, you will be using a translator, the outside speaker will need to be prepared as it necessitates adapting talks.

All workshops need to be evaluated by parents in order to adapt and improve them. Evaluation can take the form of personal interviews or written evaluations. Oral evaluations will be more appropriate for those parents who are not confident with written English. Parents who have taken part in such workshops may be willing to attend future ones in order to pass on their new expertise. One school utilised their skills in this way:

We had a number of parents who had gained in confidence through the workshops. They had particularly enjoyed making environmental print games from food packaging and sweet wrappers. We therefore set up an 'environmental print' workshop in the hall with lots of tables, resources, equipment, and all parents were invited to take part. The parents who had been through the workshops took a major role in guiding other parents. It was very successful all round.

Some schools have included ICT work in the workshops. Parents have been introduced to computers and word processing, some for the first time. Parents have made books for their children using photographs from home and text printed from the computer. This has been beneficial for many parents as it has extended their own skills. In fact, this principle of running workshops which extend parents' own literacy skills is the one underpinning much of the family literacy work which is going on around the country at the present time.

Classroom-based workshops

Workshops which take place with the children in their classrooms need much thought and structure if they are to be successful. The subject leader needs to ensure that there is a cohesive policy and approach throughout the school in order for such workshops to make sense to parents as their children move through the school. There are a range of models for these workshops. Most of them involve a whole class at a time being involved in the sessions. We outline a few models in Figure 11.1, with some key questions to consider on each.

Parent helpers in the classroom

Some parents are willing to work in classrooms on a regular basis and perform such tasks as hearing children read and playing games with them. The English subject leader has an important role to play here. Rather than relying on individual teachers to provide intensive support for parent helpers, the subject leader could put on special workshops aimed at providing helpers with information which could be useful to them. Such information could include:

- strategies to use when hearing children read

- relevant questions to ask children about their reading

- how to fill in reading records

- how to join in with school approaches to reading, e.g. literacy hour, group reading

- introduction to the range of language games in school and some practice in using them

- strategies for reading stories to children

- dealing with difficult behaviour

	Activities	Key questions
Reading workshops	Parents sharing books with their children Playing reading games Writing book reviews Reading on the computer Listening to story tapes	Will parents be expected to read only with their own child? What texts will they use? A reading scheme? Books around the classroom? Specially selected books? How will they record what they have done? Will the teacher choose an appropriate game beforehand? What arrangements will there be for children whose parents do not attend?
Writing workshops	Parents writing with their child Writing books for their child Parent and child working on the computer	What stimulus will be provided for the writing? Will parents be given sufficient input into how to help their child develop writing skills? Will bilingual parents be encouraged to write using the script of their first language? What will happen to the books completed in the workshop – will they all go home? Will computers be used? Will parents need training? What provision will be made for those children whose parents do not attend?
Oracy workshops	Parents playing language games with their children Parents and children learning and taping nursery rhymes, etc.	Will bilingual parents feel encouraged to use their first language? Will the school need to develop a resource bank of a range of tapes of songs, nursery rhymes, etc.? Will the workshops need to take place in a separate room? If so, who will supervise?

Figure 11.1   Classroom-based workshops

- school policies on a range of issues, e.g. Equal Opportunities, Health and Safety.

Parent helpers could work with the subject leader in developing an information booklet for new parent helpers on some of these issues.

Some schools ask parent helpers to run the library or book shops. Again, this needs careful input by the subject leader in order to ensure that parents are given all the information they need and are not left to flounder, unsure about what is required of them.

Some parents may not have the time to help regularly in school, but may be willing to offer their services in a more limited way. For example, bilingual parents could be asked to make story tapes of familiar books for the listening corner. Other parents may be willing to come into school to be interviewed by children on particular topics, e.g. 'My childhood'.

Some schools are wary of involving parents in any major way in classroom life because of the issue of confidentiality. They worry that parents may compare the progress of their child with that of children of their friends or neighbours, or discuss confidential issues outside school. Our view is that this issue should be discussed with parents before they start to help in school and their agreement about confidentiality sought. Parents who are determined to compare their child's progress with others could be persuaded to help out in a different classroom where this type of surveillance will not be possible.

It is clear that parents have much to offer schools in terms of their time, energy and commitment. However, we need to heed the note of caution about the development in using parent volunteers that Hannon (1995) sounds:

> Will this development mask a shortage of properly trained and paid teachers? Is it a consequence of it? There is undoubtedly a case to be made for greater community involvement in schools and it would be wrong to suggest that everyone contributing to the work of schools has to be paid for it. Nonetheless, this problem...should make schools uneasy about too readily promoting the use of volunteers.
>
> (Hannon, 1995, p. 77)

There is little credibility for the proposal made in recent years of promoting a 'mum's army' of unpaid helpers in schools. It is no substitute for trained, professional teachers. Nevertheless, some parents do want to be involved and large numbers have gone on, after many years of gaining confidence and expertise through volunteering in this way, to return to Access courses and universities in order to train as teachers themselves. This sort of empowerment of mature, often working class women is to be welcomed.

Finally, careful consideration should be given to making provision for parents with younger children. It is sometimes difficult for schools to arrange the sort of crèche facilities that are needed if these parents are to help regularly in the school. Nevertheless, if external funding can be found, crèche provision could be offered for occasional events and workshops.

Family literacy

Family literacy programmes aim to go further than those educational workshops which focus solely upon children's developing literacy skills. They provide a means of developing the literacy skills of parents as well by including sessions which have that specific aim. They target parents whose own literacy skills are limited and who lack confidence to take part in the usual classroom workshops. Family literacy projects have three strands: work with the children on their own, work with the parents and children together and separate work with the parents which is co-ordinated by an adult worker. Many family literacy programmes provide accreditation for parents so that they can continue their education once the schemes have finished. The National Literacy Strategy (1997) has indicated that funding family literacy projects will be a priority for the next few years. LEAs will be putting in bids for these initiatives and so your school needs to be prepared for the eventuality of being asked to take part in such a project. Many LEAs put in bids on behalf of schools and then inform them if the bid is successful.

The director of the one of the largest family literacy projects in the country, the *Read On – Write Away!* initiative in Derbyshire, has outlined the implications for schools. Carol Taylor is keen to develop the principle that there are many ways in which such projects can be run. They need to be adapted to meet the needs of the community and the children. She says:

> These projects can be as wide as you want them to be. Some schools have decided to target ten children in Year 3 and do something structured on the reading scheme. Others do less structured things such as environmental print, puppet making, drama, story sacks and book making. They should focus on literacy in the widest sense. Lots of activities – photography, art, IT – can be linked to literacy. Whatever the parents do with the children, the adult worker will then tie it into the work with adults. So if the parents and children had gone on an environmental print walk, the adult literacy worker would say, 'Let's look at environmental print, what is it about?' It's not just about work with mums, it's family literacy in the broad sense. One school concentrated on getting dads in because it is an ex-mining area with high unemployment. Another targeted grandmothers because they are the ones at home who play with the kids. Sometimes the building dictates the kind of work that goes on. One school has open-plan bases, so they couldn't set up an adult group in a separate room, with a crèche in another room. So they did a literacy day every month where they invited all the parents in at once. They got 80 in at a time. The teachers alerted the adult literacy worker to the parents who had limited literacy skills and they targeted them, working alongside them. Gradually, they tried to get them to set up a separate group, once their confidence was built up. So the projects have to be tailored to meet the needs of schools and parents.

It is important to get funding for resources as well as workers. Schools have sometimes found themselves having to buy flipcharts and folders for parents' work. Petty cash needs to be found to fund coffee for parents, as having to pay for refreshments would be difficult for some parents. It also makes the atmosphere less welcoming. If your school does get money to run such a project, it may not be the English subject leader who would co-ordinate it. Even if it is, Carol suggests that it should be a whole-school issue:

> It needs to be a whole-school project. The school must have clear aims. Who are

you going to target and why those parents? You have to target parents with limited levels of literacy and that can be tricky. Some schools are very up front about it because they have that kind of relationship with the parents. Others might ask particular parents but not emphasise the adult literacy side of it. Once they have had some weeks doing art and IT and things like that, they feel more confident to move on to literacy activities. Some schools use the money to get a supply teacher in to run the project. I think that is a shame. The good work and ideas that go on in the project need to permeate the school so that it can carry on in some form after the money has gone. So it's best if a teacher in the school does it.

The teacher co-ordinating the project needs to ensure that there is adequate time for planning, training and liaising with the adult worker. They could visit other projects to see what goes on there and gain ideas. They will need to set up an evaluation of the project which can feed into future action plans. As Carol notes:

> Evaluation should be wider than reading test results. You need to look at literacy in a wider sense. What effect has the project had on literacy habits at home, on the self-esteem of parents and children? And if only three parents turned up when you targeted ten, don't be despondent, that is brilliant. If you get three parents who have been too scared to come to school before, that is wonderful.

Family literacy projects have much to offer the children, parents and schools who take part in them. They usually raise levels of literacy amongst children and parents and most parents go on to take part in other projects and courses. *Read On – Write Away!* have devised a set of guidelines for setting up family literacy projects (see Figure 11.2). They are not overly prescriptive because it is recognised that if such projects are to be successful, there should be scope for creating ones that meet the specific needs of the school and community. Nevertheless, there are certain elements which are essential if such projects are to work effectively.

Parental involvement in the home

Most schools encourage children to take reading books home regularly. This needs to follow a consistent procedure throughout the school in order to avoid confusion. There are various ways in which schools organise this. Some let children choose from a particular range of books rather than the whole classroom collection, while other children take home only reading scheme books. If children are choosing from a range of books, the school needs to adopt a system of sending information home about how to read that particular book with a child. Some books will require more adult assistance than others. Therefore some schools have developed cards which the teacher puts inside the book, detailing how the adult should approach that text with the child.

a strategy to improve literacy in Derbyshire
and Derby City

<u>Draft consultation document</u>

The Read On – Write Away
Model of Family Literacy Provision

The following elements make up the basic structure of a model of Family Literacy provision.
It is accepted that there may be other requirements dependent on funding, target groups etc but we put this forward as the framework.

1. Staff

   – All adult workers adult trained. Minimum requirements: recognised teaching certificate + 9282 + 2 terms' experience in Key Skills groups (when possible, Family Literacy trained).

   – All school staff to be adult friendly, open to new ideas (when possible, Family Literacy trained).

2. On-going training and specific staff development to be available, e.g. the teaching of reading, sharing good Family Literacy practice.

3. An Agreement drawn up between the partners. This will include what is expected of both school and the Adult Service and will include lines of responsibility.

4. Progression routes for adult students – guidance should always be offered.

5. Someone other than the teacher and tutor must have a coordinating role and there must be a support mechanism. This could be a Community Education worker, Read On – Write Away! , an SRB Co-ordinator etc.

6. Time written in for joint planning – minimum whole day before programme begins.

7. On-going liaison (tutor/teacher) time written in to the agreement of minimum one hour a week.

8. Suitable separate work with adults – minimum 2 hours a week – in appropriate accommodation with refreshments easily available. This includes appropriate furniture!

9. Suitable separate work with children.

10. Regular joint work – with the adults and children together, led by both the tutor and the teacher.

11. Baselines for adults and children with targets set with a realistic assessment of progress.

12. Adults will have the opportunity for accreditation.

13. Parental/community involvement in a wider forum should be encouraged.

Carol Taylor

Figure 11.2. Family literacy workshop guidelines

Many schools now send home reading record books in which parents make comments about how their children read. This needs some care, however. If parents are not very confident in their literacy skills, or if English is not their first language, they may find this a rather daunting task. This may result in inequality between the children in any one class and lead some children to feel left out.

If resources permit, children could be encouraged to take home a range of resources, not simply reading books. Park Hill Primary School in Sheffield secured a grant from the local TEC and used the money to buy not only books and story packs but also writing materials. They put a range of materials, including pens, paper, envelopes, forms and ideas for writing, in plastic wallets. These have proved to be as popular as the story packs with the children and their families. In the next section, we take a brief look at what story packs could contain.

Story packs

Some schools send home story packs. These are packs of materials based around one particular story. So, for example, a pack which contains the book *Farmer Duck* by Martin Waddell may also contain some of the following:

- an audio tape of the story
- a toy duck
- toy animals, e.g. cows, sheep, hens
- finger puppets of some of the animals and the farmer
- a board game based on the story
- a crossword containing key words in the book
- a quiz about the book
- an information book about farms and farming
- a farm jigsaw
- poems/nursery rhymes about farm animals
- snap/lotto games based on the book.

Parents are then encouraged to keep the packs for a few days and play with some of the resources with their children. English subject leaders could be responsible for co-ordinating the development of these packs around the school. Parents may be willing to help to devise some of them. Packs could include materials based on an information text. For example, here are some of the contents collected by a school to use in conjunction with an information book on the Tudors:

- a cloze procedure based on a selected passage
- a quiz about the Tudors
- a card game based on Tudor kings and queens
- instructions on how to make a model of a Tudor house
- a board game relating to the Tudors.

Other work which could take place in the home could include joint writing projects or topic work.

Chapter summary

This chapter has been concerned with the variety of ways in which parents can be involved in the literacy development of their child and in the life of the school generally. The English subject leader has a key role to play in this. She needs to ensure that the school has cohesive, unified policies and practices on all the various forms of involvement, policies that are clearly communicated to parents. She also needs to ensure that all new parents to the school are aware of the approaches to the organisation and delivery of the English curriculum taken by the school. Any open evenings which focus upon literacy must be organised/co-ordinated by the English subject leader to ensure that maximum use is made of them. Training/workshops on literacy given to parents and parent helpers should be co-ordinated by the subject leader although they will possibly be delivered by a range of staff. Displays/newsletters concerning literacy could be developed by the subject leader. How much time spent on this aspect of the post will depend on the demands made on the subject leader's time elsewhere. Nevertheless, it is essential that the link with parents is one that is forged carefully and nurtured tenderly. Literacy is a key issue for parents; parents should be a key issue for the English subject leader.

12

Resourcing the English Curriculum

Managing resources for any curriculum area is time consuming, but for English it can be even more demanding and needs careful organisation. In the first part of the chapter, we discuss the tasks a subject leader needs to undertake when resourcing the English curriculum. We then move on to review the ways in which the use of resources can be monitored in order to inform future purchases. The English co-ordinator often has responsibility for the library, so there is a separate section on this area which outlines key tasks. Organising book weeks, poetry weeks and book fairs is a major concern for English co-ordinators, and so the final part of the chapter discusses ways in which this organisation can be made more manageable.

Resourcing the English curriculum

Most schools have suffered severe financial constraints in recent years and the majority do not have sufficient resources for many curriculum areas. The financial climate has serious implications for the English curriculum and many schools are seriously under-resourced in terms of book provision and related resources. Therefore our discussion of the management of resources is underpinned by the understanding that the co-ordinator will be greatly constrained by the school budget and will have to prioritise needs. Some very difficult decisions may need to be made. This chapter will offer a number of suggestions about priority setting. However, we begin by looking at how the budget for English resources can be decided and managed.

It is no longer the case that schools have a set amount for resources, with that amount divided up equally amongst the curriculum areas. The overall resources budget is too small for that and it would not be an effective way to manage finances. Instead, the allocation for each subject will depend upon the place of that subject within the School Development Plan. If the subject is a priority for a particular academic year, then it should be given extra funding from the budget. This means that the amount allocated to English may change from year to year. The

English subject leader should always be aware of what the overall amount is and should have a major say in how it is spent. You may be working with a head who does not like to delegate budget decisions. If this is the case, then getting together with other curriculum co-ordinators and presenting a united front to the head in your request for more financial responsibility would be the wisest option. It may be that you have responsibility for a number of curriculum areas and so have a few budgets to manage. You will need an effective filing system to ensure that each area is accounted for separately and should guard against leaking money from one budget to cover overspend in another! However, given the relatively small amounts of money you will be dealing with, you will not need extensively complicated accounting systems.

Once English has been allocated a budget, you will need to decide how it is going to be spent. This should, of course, not be your decision alone. The whole staff needs to be involved in deciding what is required in any subject area; your role will be to consider what may be competing and conflicting requests and make the ultimate decision. The decision about what to buy with a very limited sum of money, an amount that in no way corresponds with what you need to spend, will not be easy. It is a decision which should be based on a careful assessment of what is needed in order to enhance the teaching and learning in school. If, for example, you have decided that you want to develop the time spent on shared reading, a decision which many schools have taken since the introduction of the literacy hour, then you will need to allocate funds to purchasing big books and multiple copies of the same text. However, if you decide that your main focus needs to be on developing children's information skills, then you will need to purchase a range of suitable texts. Any purchases which are made with respect to curriculum development should be related to the subject action plan.

At times, it is necessary to replenish stock which has aged, been broken or disappeared. For example, schools regularly need to update reading schemes and replace torn or worn reading books. Rather than leaving damaged stock to go unreplaced for many years, thus leading to the need for a large amount of a budget in one year allocated for this purpose, co-ordinators should set aside a small amount of each year's budget for replacing stock. Again, this will need to be prioritised. It should also be linked to a resource audit.

A resource audit

Because of the scarcity of resources, the subject leader needs to ensure that she is clear about how resources are being used throughout the school. This will provide the co-ordinator with a picture of what is being used and how, whether some resources are under-used or over-used and if there are particular patterns emerging in particular year groups. The audit needs to be carried out regularly if it is to be useful – at least once a year, and more often if it can be fitted into the schedule. An audit can take a number of forms. Some co-ordinators give staff a questionnaire which asks them to detail how resources are being used. This questionnaire is different every year, as a section of it may focus on one particular resource the co-ordinator wants to know about, or a new resource that has been recently introduced.

Once the audit has been completed, the subject leader can analyse the responses and make decisions about resources accordingly. For example, if it is clear that the early years teachers use one reading scheme more often than any other, and that this is a different one from the predominant choice of other year groups, then when it is time to replace that scheme in the early years classroom, it may not need replacing elsewhere. Similarly, if a particular resource is used heavily by an older year group but less frequently in the early years, then the resource which has been placed in the early years classroom can be moved to supplement those of the other classes. If a resource is being under-used across the school, then the co-ordinator needs to find out why. Is it too cumbersome to use? Does organising its use involve too much teacher time? Does it not fulfil its purpose? Do staff need further training in its use? The co-ordinator can then act upon these findings. Doing such an audit gave one co-ordinator a surprise:

> I found out that staff never used the school's video camera. Only I used it, to film drama activities, to develop media studies work and so on. When I asked why, it turned out that everyone was too nervous to use it as they had never been shown how to. The camera had been in the stock cupboard when I came to the school and I just assumed they knew how to use it. After the audit, I arranged to train everyone individually – actually, it's so easy to use, just press a few buttons. I also did a staff meeting on ways in which the camera could support work on speaking and listening skills. I won't pretend everyone is enthused, but certainly a couple of upper school staff are now using it more.

Apart from the self-audit, it can also be useful for the co-ordinator to monitor the use of resources through classroom observation. If you are to monitor the use of resources, the principles outlined in Chapter 3 would apply in terms of informing staff about what is happening. You need to devise a monitoring checklist related to the resource you are focusing upon. It is, of course, very difficult to monitor the *amount of use* a particular resource gets because the teacher may not be using this resource when you come in, but may use it at another time. However, you can monitor *how* a particular resource gets used. For example, do the staff set certain tasks to do at the listening centre? Are these related to what is happening in the rest of the classroom? Or is the centre just used randomly, the children choosing any particular tape they want to listen to? How is the computer used for English work? Are the children given specific tasks to do or are they left to move randomly from program to program? Is there a gender imbalance in the use of ICT in English work? You need to approach this sort of audit in a collaborative way. You should not be perceived as a spy, but as a trusted colleague who needs to identify areas for future staff development. As we have said before, this approach needs a whole-school policy and agreement if it is to work effectively.

From the audit, whether it is a questionnaire, visits to classrooms or a mixture of both, the co-ordinator will need to draw up a list of priorities for ordering and purchasing. This should be combined with an understanding of what is needed for particular areas of curriculum development and so it is inextricably linked to the action plan for English.

Fundraising is obviously one way in which a co-ordinator may increase resources for a subject area, but this needs much careful thought. If your school is in a poor socio-economic area, you need to question how fair it is to ask parents to contribute to the school's funds. They will probably have little money, if any, to spare and may feel guilty if they cannot contribute. Targeting local businesses may be one way in which to raise money. Often, local businesses prefer to respond to a request for contributions towards a particular item rather than being asked to give money to a general fund. There are sometimes particular grants you can apply for, but these are fiercely competitive and schools are often disappointed. If you do apply for a particular grant or fund, do ensure that your request meets the criteria for funding. In addition, your case is helped if you detail exactly how you will evaluate a particular project and how you will disseminate these findings.

In the next sections, we consider the issues relating to the purchase of major items in any English resources budget: reading schemes and ICT hardware and software.

Reading schemes

Occasionally, schools decide that they are going to invest in a new reading scheme. It is usually the language co-ordinator's responsibility to carry out research into the latest schemes available and perhaps even be ultimately responsible for deciding upon which one. If this is the case for you, then we would suggest that you begin by asking the LEA English adviser if he or she has a range of schemes for you to look at. If possible, you should borrow a few titles and try them out with children in the class.

Publishers are more than willing to bring a range of schemes into the school for a lunchtime or after-school staff meeting. Some publishers are happy to leave a sample on approval for a few days. You would be well advised to ask other schools that you have contacts with. It would be useful to find out whether or not they had bought the scheme you were thinking of purchasing and if they had, how well it had been received by children. Having said that, it is worth remembering that each school is different and no reading scheme will be suited to all. A scheme that inner-city multilingual children enjoy may be very different from one liked by children living in a small village.

There are a number of issues to consider when choosing a new scheme. Does the scheme:

- contain books with interesting stories?
- contain a range of genres, e.g. poetry, information texts?
- offer flexibility, e.g. big books, group reading sets?
- reflect children's lives and current interests?
- use appropriate language?
- have interesting, good quality illustrations which support the text?
- have well-developed characters?
- have an awareness of equal opportunities issues?
- develop a range of key skills rather than focusing on one, e.g. phonics?
- have supplementary materials which extend response to texts and are more interesting than the usual set of photocopiable worksheets?

Bromley (1997) has a range of other questions which she suggests are important when choosing new schemes and her article includes a review of some of the more popular schemes. Of course, the co-ordinator and school staff need not assess the range of schemes on offer using the criteria suggested above. They may wish to devise criteria which suits the school's particular needs and indeed we would encourage this. Schemes should be supplemented with a range of high quality children's books. In the annotated bibliography, we suggest a range of sources of information regarding these which will help in the selection of a good range of texts.

ICT resources

ICT resourcing for English would include tape recorders, video cameras, photographic cameras and computers, amongst other things. There is not the space within this book to deal adequately with issues relating to these. Instead, we have included a section in the annotated bibliography which details key texts for advice on ICT. In terms of resourcing ICT in the English curriculum, we would recommend the NCET (1997) booklet, developed in conjunction with NATE, *IT in English: Resources for Learning* (see also Abbot, 1994). This deals with a range of issues in relation to word processing, information handling, desktop publishing, e-mails and multimedia authoring. It discusses the criteria which should be used when buying CD ROM books and provides guidance to schools on accessing the Internet.

When providing staff development in ICT and English, you will need to ensure that you focus on manageable topics, one at a time, rather than overfacing staff. It is better to use a small selection of hardware or software programs well than have a wide range of hardware and software that is used inconsistently. If you are not very confident with

ICT yourself, it will be important to develop your skills through attending relevant courses. Much is changing in the world of English and the new media literacies are something which every English co-ordinator should be at least familiar with, if not expert!

Organisation of resources

This task is not as simple as it may appear. As a co-ordinator, you may need to make some difficult, even at times unpopular, decisions. Because of the restricted budget, there will be a limited number of resources for the school. Some resources may need to be held centrally, and teachers borrow them when they need to use them. This system can cause problems, particularly when some teachers hang on to the resources longer than they should, or borrow parts of larger sets. For example, if the school has invested in group reading texts, it would be very frustrating if a teacher went to use a particular set only to find half of them were dispersed around school. You will need to keep an eye on such matters and provide gentle reminders when things need returning. You need to ensure that you have an effective monitoring system; for example, a book in which teachers sign and date their loans. Over time, if you notice that a particular teacher uses a resource much more frequently than anyone else, you could order that resource just for that class. At least you will be sure it will be used regularly. Resources held centrally pose storage problems. If items are too inaccessible, people may forget about them and they will be little used. You need to organise a general inventory of the English stock. Of course, it is not feasible, nor desirable, to list every single item. However, you need to know what the school has and where it is. You can be more specific about larger items, e.g. tape recorders, magnet boards. This system means that, if one class needs extra resources for a particular activity, you know where to get them from. This list should be given to every teacher so that they too are aware of what the school has.

In addition to classroom resources which can be held centrally, it is also a good idea to develop a collection of professional development material which can be loaned to staff. This could include teachers' manuals from schemes, but also textbooks which provide information on the teaching and learning of English, as well as the more practical manuals which provide banks of ideas for the classroom. In addition to this, it is also useful for the English co-ordinator to develop and circulate a regular newsletter for staff on the English curriculum that presents relevant information such as summaries of recent research and OFSTED findings relating to the English curriculum. It can also contain a diary of school events as well as news about English training in the area.

Resources distributed around the school need to be shared fairly if teachers are to feel that the system is working. Of course, this does not mean that every class has exactly the same resources. What is needed in a Reception classroom is very different from what is needed in a Year 6 classroom. However, each class needs to be stocked, as far as the budget will allow, with resources which meet its needs and a fair programme of renewal/replenishment established. It is not good for public relations, nor the educational welfare of the school, for the English co-ordinator's classroom to be well stocked with the latest books whilst everyone else makes do with tattered copies of old titles!

Maintaining the school library

This can be a very time-consuming task for the English subject leader. The library will need regular stock checks, ordering of new stock, processing of new titles, records of loans and returns kept up to date, tidying and the organisation of displays, amongst many other tasks. The first step is to consider which of these tasks can be delegated to others. Tidying the library could be a task allocated to classes of children, for example. Once children are familiar with the coding system, they will be able to return books to the correct place on the shelves. Your role could then be to do a regular 'spot check' to see if everything is in order.

Putting in place an effective record system could save you hours of work. You need to develop a system which can be run by classes themselves when they are using the library. The teacher in charge of the class could then be responsible for ensuring that the records for their class are kept up to date. There are many different systems which can be used. Some schools give each child tickets which are kept in the library and the books are stamped for two weeks. Other schools keep filing cards for each child on which the books they borrow are noted. In some small schools, class teachers are responsible for keeping records on books their children have borrowed. And of course, some schools are so short of resources that their library is kept for reference books only. If a central borrowing record system is kept, it will be useful for the English co-ordinator to monitor it to see which texts are borrowed most frequently. Further copies of those texts may be needed.

Co-ordinators need to consider the cataloguing system they use, for both fiction and non-fiction. It is useful if this correlates with the system used by the local library so that children can find their way around the shelves with little confusion. Some public libraries do not use the Dewey system in the children's section but instead have picture/colour categories. Teachers may have their own personal views about what is the most effective system, but our advice would be to use the public library cataloguing system and point out your objections to the librarians if you don't agree with it. Doing this will prevent the children from becoming confused by having to use two different systems. The School Library service in your LEA may provide help with cataloguing. They will certainly be happy to talk over any issues in relation to school libraries with you.

The stock kept in the library needs careful monitoring in terms of equal opportunities. If books do contain offensive or stereotyped

---

'Race'

Does the book contain stereotypical images of black people?

Are the drawings of black people realistic, or are they simply white characters with the skin coloured brown (or lines drawn across to darken the skin colour)?

Are the black characters given minor roles, or solely negative characteristics?

Are black cultures portrayed as exotic and/or unusual?

Is a realistic portrayal of countries and lifestyles given?

Are the names of characters from ethnic minorities realistic?

Is racist language used?

Does your stock contain books which encourage a discussion of racism and prejudice?

Gender

Are boys and men given the more prominent, active roles?

Are jobs and tasks stereotyped as 'masculine' or 'feminine'?

Is sexist language used?

Do you have books which encourage a discussion of sexism?

Do you stock a range of books which will appeal to both boys and girls, given the reluctance many boys have to read?

Class

Are working class people portrayed as stupid or subservient?

Do books contain a range of lifestyles which include the working class, e.g. stories set in flats/terraced housing, people with a range of jobs, e.g. cleaner, shop assistant, unemployed?

Are such lifestyles portrayed realistically?

Are people's dialects and accents ridiculed?

Disabilities

Do books contain stories/information about disabled people?

Are disabled people given positive roles or are they always portrayed as victims to be pitied?

Are the real problems which disabled people face discussed in texts, e.g. access issues?

Figure 12.1   Evaluating books using an equal opportunities checklist

pictures or text, then they need to be discarded. There are a number of checklists which can be used. It would be a valuable task for a group of school staff to devise their own. In Figure 12.1, we present a short checklist of key questions to consider.

Most schools are now aware of the need to provide a range of dual-text books, particularly if the school has children who speak English as an additional language. However, this is not as straightforward as it seems. In order to make the book easy to read in terms of comparing text, often the writing system of a particular language is distorted. For example, Chinese writing starts at the top of a page and runs down the page vertically. However, in many dual-language books, the text is placed horizontally, to match the English. Similarly, Urdu text starts on the right-hand side of the page. This means that the first page of a book written in Urdu is at the opposite end to the first page of a book written in English. In dual-text books, both English and Urdu start at the same place. This appears to readers of Urdu as if the book is starting on the last page. This needs pointing out to children.

The English subject leader needs to keep up herself to date with the latest fiction and non-fiction texts aimed at children. There are a number of ways to do this. The magazine *Books for Keeps* provides a regular source of information and as it often contains useful material such as interviews with authors, the library would benefit from subscribing to it. There are also many annotated booklists which provide details of books people have found to be good or useful. *Letterbox Library* is a particularly good source of books which consider equal opportunities issues. We provide a list of other useful resources in the annotated bibliography at the end of this book. There are also some very useful sites on the World Wide Web, although, of course, you need access to the Internet in order to use these. Again, we list some of these sites at the end of this book. It is always useful to have a 'Suggestions board' in the library. On this board, children and staff can recommend books they have read or heard of, as well as making suggestions about other aspects of the library.

The language co-ordinator also needs to ensure that she keeps the library looking attractive. The intention is to promote reading and make the library a place where all children want to go. Posters can be obtained from most publishers of children's literature. Displays can be organised by particular classes in turn. You may want to organise displays based around a particular theme or genre, with activities for children to do which enhance their understanding of and appreciation of a particular theme. One co-ordinator describes such a project in her infant school:

The Year 1s were doing work on 'Houses and Homes'. I collected all the relevant information books and put them on a display. There was also a collection of interesting objects such as pottery houses, models of flats, cardboard castles and so on. The children added their models as the topic went on. I also set up a display of fiction books about houses such as *Miss Brick the Builder*. Children put stories they'd written there. I made a range of activities related to the books for the library. I had 'Fact File' sheets, which asked children to find out particular facts about houses using the reference books. I had charts relating to particular books and the children filled them in when they'd read those books. There were lots of activities relating to the fiction books like making a wall where each brick had the name of one of their favourite authors. It was a great success and I now try to make sure that each year group has this kind of activity at least once during the year. The teachers are welcome to set one up for themselves at other times, mind you.

Again, there are books which provide ideas of a range of interesting activities to set up in a library and we list these in the annotated bibliography.

The last point concerns the use of the library. The co-ordinator needs to monitor how and when the library is used if it is to provide maximum benefit to teachers. All teachers need to have a voice in what happens in the library if it is to be used enthusiastically by them all. You also need to ensure that they are all clear about how to train children in library and information retrieval skills. If they are not, you will have to organise relevant staff development training. In some schools, the language co-ordinator or specially trained classroom assistants are given the role of working with each class on developing information retrieval skills in library sessions. We would argue that this is deskilling teachers, and as information retrieval skills should be an integral part of classroom life, all teachers should be confident and able in this area.

Many schools use public libraries as well as their own and for those schools that do not have their own library, they are a valuable resource. However, the use of the public library needs to be carefully organised by the English co-ordinator. Classes need to be timetabled to use the library, a time-consuming activity in itself. Class teachers are usually responsible for ensuring that all the children in the class have library tickets and return books they borrow. The role of the subject leader should be limited to having overall responsibility for liaison with the children's librarian. This may include inviting the librarian into school to talk to children and parents. As one co-ordinator has noted:

> We regularly invite the children's librarian in when we have an open evening that is focusing on literacy. They set up a stall with a range of books and tapes on display and get parents to join if they've never been down there. They're more than happy to be involved in this way.

The English subject leader can also provide the librarian with children's work to display in the children's library. The work should be related to texts and include drawings, paintings, models and 3D work as well as writing. Most children's librarians would welcome this level of liaison and the co-ordinator has much to gain from cultivating such a relationship.

Promoting the use of public libraries and making the school library into an attractive and exciting environment which promotes reading is the task of any enthusiastic English subject leader. The co-ordinator should also monitor the way in which books are displayed throughout the school and encourage each teacher to have an attractive and well-kept book corner. As Chambers (1991) points out:

> Reading areas signify...value. You don't devote a place solely to one special activity unless you believe it to be enormously important. Just by being there, used in a certain way and protected by simple, reasonable rules, a reading area announces to children, without the teacher having to say anything about it, that

in this classroom, this school, this community, reading is understood to be an essential occupation.

(Chambers, 1991, p. 30)

There are also other ways of promoting reading and literature to children. In the next section, we consider how this can be done through the introduction of special themes into the school, such as 'Book Week' or 'Poetry Week'.

Organising 'theme' weeks

Organising whole-school events which focus on an aspect of English can be exciting and invigorating. They can also be time consuming and exhausting, so if you are considering this, do make sure that you allocate the time to undertake what will be a major commitment. In this section, we provide you with a range of practical advice on setting up such weeks and provide you with further details about useful publications which give more detailed help.

Having a whole-school event can be a way of promoting a particular aspect of English in a way which unites children and teachers. This can generate incredible energy and enthusiasm and parents quite often become swept up by the tide of excitement. The effect of such an event can be long-lasting and have benefits in a wide range of areas. The most popular of these theme weeks is a 'Book Week'. This is a week in which, as its name implies, the whole school focuses on different aspects of books. Such events can include:

- book displays
- visits by authors/illustrators/publishers
- book-making workshops
- book sales
- book trails
- raffles of books
- storytelling sessions
- book games/competitions/quizzes/crosswords
- curriculum activities related to books
- taped/videoed book reviews
- drama based on texts
- visits by local celebrities, e.g. football teams, in which they promote books
- story prop-making sessions for parents
- dressing up as characters from books.

Poetry weeks may involve:

- visits by poets
- poetry writing workshops

- poetry quizzes/competitions/games
- poetry trails
- drama activities linked to poems
- a range of activities linked to poems – sequencing, cloze, etc.
- creating music/models/paintings which reflect the moods of poems
- assemblies in which classes share favourite poems.

The possibilities are endless! However, such events need careful preparation. You would be well advised to set up a working party which will help you to plan it. This could include parents and non-teaching staff, e.g. lunchtime supervisors. Because of the possible costs involved, it is a good idea if you can persuade your headteacher to join in. Well before the event, you need to hold a staff meeting which will inform the staff of your plans and progress. This is a chance for all the staff to contribute their ideas and feel involved in the week.

Authors and local celebrities need a lot of notice if they are to be booked. You will need to contact publishers – they are often willing to send free posters and materials which promote their books. Games and activities need to be prepared in advance. You will want to publicise your event and so you need to contact the local press in plenty of time. Local bookshops may be willing to donate prizes for a raffle in return for free publicity. If you are having a book shop/club during the week, this needs organising well in advance. If you work in a school in a poor socio-economic area, it will probably not be viable to hold a book shop or club. You would not want to put parents under pressure to buy books when they have little money. One co-ordinator describes how they got around this:

> We decided to have a secondhand book stall every morning during book week. We advertised locally for secondhand children's books and got an enormous response. We then sold the books for very small sums of money, from 1p to 10p. It was incredible. Every morning, we had a crush of children and parents. Children who had never owned books of their own before were going home with two or three every day.

School library services and local libraries will often be willing to lend extra books for activities or displays. Some libraries may even want to get involved in other ways; for example, coming into school to talk to children about the librarian's role. Libraries may also have other resources which you could borrow. One public library in Sheffield, for example, has a box of puppets and stuffed toys which are related to particular books. They are happy to lend this to schools for a nominal fee.

There are a number of ways in which other people may be asked to help out during the week. If your school is situated near an Initial Teacher Education institute, you could contact them to see if any students would be willing to help out during the week. This provides you with extra pairs of hands and also gives the students some very valuable experience. Similarly, secondary schools within your pyramid may be happy to send children to your school to engage in activities related to the week. Parents are usually willing to join in such weeks with enthusiasm. They may be invited in to talk about their favourite books or poems, or to help out in workshops. A particularly successful way of involving parents in activities related to books has been to encourage them to make story packs/bags. These are outlined in Chapter 11.

There are a number of useful publications which will provide more detailed help in organising book and poetry weeks. Among these is a publication from the Reading and Language Information centre: *Good Ideas for Planning a Book Week.*

Once you have organised the week, you need to provide a full programme of events for the staff in your school. It is useful if you provide them with a 'Book Week Pack' which collects together a range of information and resources. This could contain:

- a timetable of the week's events across the school

- a list of resources you have collected and will keep centrally for the week, but which they can borrow

- a list of activities which could be undertaken in the classroom relating to the theme

- photocopiable sheets which contain activities related to the theme

- a list of books they may find useful.

It will also be useful to send a letter to parents, informing them of the aims and objectives of the week and what they can do to get involved. During the week, make sure to collect photographs of as many different events as you can. This can be made into books about the week by the children, and also inform any future request for money from businesses and trusts. If they can see that you have been successful in organising such events in the past, they may be more inclined to offer you a donation in the future. Once the week has finished, you can evaluate it carefully in order to inform any future events of its kind. The evaluation should include staff, children and parents. The whole process is time consuming but very worthwhile, as one co-ordinator has made clear:

> It took months of preparation. I was exhausted by the end of the week. It didn't help that I'd made the book trail too complicated and had to get to work by 7.45 a.m. every morning in order to have enough time to set it up! Still, it was absolutely brilliant. The children produced some amazing work and they still talk about how one teacher dressed up as Spot the dog to draw the raffle prize! The parents got really involved too. There was such an atmosphere of celebration of literature. I definitely would do it again, but once a year is enough for me!

Resourcing a multilingual school

Dual-text books and multilingual resources should be a regular feature of all schools. If children are familiar with a range of languages and scripts, they will be more aware of the multilingual nature of our society. However, there are particular issues to think about when resourcing classrooms for children who speak English as an additional language. Merchant (1992) outlines the ways in which the reading curriculum for bilingual children should be resourced. As well as dual-text books, you should also try to find dual-language 'Talking Books' for the computer. There are many good quality story-tapes which are produced in a number of languages and you should find a wide selection in the multicultural resource suppliers in the same list. Books which include plenty of rhyme and repetition, which promote prediction skills and with which children can join in are extremely useful for reading to/with young bilingual children. Story props also help the children to grasp key elements of the story and so stuffed toys, puppets, cut-outs and magnet board figures are all useful to have handy when reading a story. The children can then play with them afterwards, retelling the story in their first language if they wish.

Parents could be encouraged to come into school to make story-tapes in their first language, as well as other resources such as dual-text books, story props and games. Parents could be encouraged to share rhymes and songs in their first language and if the parents do not feel able to transcribe them there may be bilingual teachers in school who could help. However, you must beware of always relying on bilingual colleagues to translate, whatever the occasion. They have many other jobs to do and you will be placing an additional burden upon them. Some LEAs have translation services which you can use. If you are bilingual yourself and share the first language of many of the children in school, you will no doubt be more than aware of the difficulties involved in being a co-ordinator for the language curriculum and having such a valuable skill. Resisting demands to provide a translation service 'on tap' is no easy task! Your school may be able to find extra funding for activities with parents, funding which could pay for additional bilingual assistance. One school managed to fund a tutor for workshops aimed at Bengali parents through their local WEA (Workers' Educational Association). The parents made some wonderful resources and also gained much confidence through attending the sessions. Another school attracted funding from the local TEC in order to develop story packs for the children. You need to be enterprising as well as keeping an ear to the ground for local developments.

Alphabet charts from different scripts are also useful to have on display in the classroom, as are labels and notices in different languages. They can promote much discussion as well as sending a message to the children that their language is valued. This is equally true whether or not the children can read and write using the script of their first language. Many suppliers also provide other resources which contain letters and words from a variety of scripts, such as dominoes, alphabet books and lotto games. You may not always need to buy resources. If, for example, you set up a Health Centre in the structured role-play area, you may obtain free multilingual leaflets and posters from a local health clinic. You could ask parents for old copies of multilingual newspapers and magazines to place in a home corner or a 'newsagents'.

There are many other resources which could also contribute to the development of language skills as well as promote confidence and self-esteem for young bilingual children. These include dolls, toys, games and jigsaws which reflect their everyday life and contain positive images, as well as dressing up clothes and props for the home corner. And in providing such an inclusive curriculum, you will be ensuring that all children benefit from such an affirming environment:

> Bilingual pupils come to school with knowledge and experiences that are valuable and important. Schools and teachers that create learning environments which celebrate cultural diversity, recognize prior learning and provide for the full participation of bilingual learners in the English curriculum will be helping all pupils to grow in competence in all aspects of English.
>
> (Browne, 1996, p. 166)

Keeping up to date

New resources for English are appearing all the time. There are numerous schemes and books appearing every week as well as a range of computer software. How can the language co-ordinator keep up with such a rate of change?

Journals are one way of keeping in touch with new developments. We provide a list of current journals at the end of the book. The educational media are also a useful resource and the *Times Educational Supplement* and the education section of the *Guardian* often contain reviews and advertisements for new resources. Internet sites which are maintained by particular publishers and educational suppliers are also worth having a look at occasionally. However, it is not always possible to get a clear picture of what new schemes and resources offer. Some companies will send representatives with samples or others may offer to send you goods on inspection. You local LEA English adviser will be able to provide you with some advice if he or she has seen in action the materials you are interested in. They may even point you towards schools which have purchased the resources so that you can get first-hand information. Some LEAs have resource centres which contain a range of materials which you can go and have a look at before purchasing. It seems self-evident to say that you should look at resources carefully before making a major purchase, but in the heat of the moment we may make mistakes:

> We had a rep in from the publishing company. She was really nice and helpful

and, well, before I knew it I'd agreed to buy a new reading scheme. She didn't put pressure on me at all and in fact told me to think about it but I felt pressurised by an upcoming inspection and thought that we needed new reading schemes in otherwise they would complain about the state of our books. Anyway, the children haven't taken to the scheme and ... well, neither have the teachers actually. The head wasn't too pleased with me, as you can imagine. I'll never do anything like that again. It should have been a whole-staff thing and we should have looked at a number of schemes over time ... well, you learn by your mistakes.

Chapter summary

This chapter has looked at the ways in which an English subject leader can organise and manage the resourcing of the English curriculum. It has provided the co-ordinator with a range of practical suggestions and raised a number of issues which need further consideration. We have suggested that the task of managing resources is not an insignificant one and needs careful organisation if it is to be done successfully. We have also indicated that the English subject leader needs to ensure that she keeps up to date with new developments in order to ensure that the English curriculum reflects current theory and research. This need not be a daunting task. Indeed, we hope that many language co-ordinators would want to contribute to the dynamic process of developing the English curriculum by contributing to the very journals we have suggested they consult. Keeping up to date with new developments may also mean creating them.

13

Managing the Inspection Process

The experience of undergoing an OFSTED inspection can be a most stressful experience for teachers. From their interviews with a wide range of teachers, Ouston, Earley and Fidler (1996) concluded that 'trauma would not be an inappropriate word' to describe the experience of being inspected. Nevertheless, they also stress that once schools had gone through the process and had time to reflect upon it, 'there could be a regeneration of energy in the school, and the necessary internal pressure for change' (p. 100).

It is important, therefore, to view the inspection process as a positive tool for curriculum development rather than as a stick to be beaten with. This is much easier said than done, of course. There are key questions that need to be asked, and answered, before we can be totally convinced that the inspection model we have is the most effective one. How positive an experience has it been for all those schools who have been classified as being in need of special measures? Are staff in those schools helped to improve the situation or blamed and demoralised further in a rather simplistic approach to school improvement? Why have almost all the schools deemed as 'failing' been located in areas of low socio-economic status? This chapter cannot even begin to explore these important questions about the inspection process. Rather, we want to provide the English subject leader with specific advice about key issues in order to ensure that they get the best from that process.

We begin by considering some of the issues that the subject leader needs to think about in the months preceding an inspection. We move on to examine the inspection week: the interview, dealing with being observed, and organising children's work. The final part of the chapter looks at action planning as a result of feedback given by the inspection team and suggests that co-ordinators should use the inspection process as a checking device for assessing the efficiency of their management of the English curriculum.

Before the inspection

OFSTED place a great emphasis on the inspection of English. It is a key area in the school and needs the closest attention if the school is to convince inspectors that it has the English curriculum under control. It is also a major area of concern for parents, and as one co-ordinator has said:

> I know that the standards in English are the first place that parents will turn to in the inspection summary. Most of them won't care what it says about geography or design and technology, for instance, but I do know that they will care if it says our standards in the teaching of reading are not up to scratch. I'm sure it won't say that, but it does make me feel nervous.

It is therefore important that the English subject leader is thoroughly prepared as this can increase confidence and contribute to the well-being of the whole staff. Headteachers and other members of the senior management team need to ensure that they provide full support for the English subject leader throughout the inspection because of the particular demands of that role. It may be worth having a meeting with the senior management team before the inspection to discuss how you can be supported in the weeks preceding the inspection. For example, it may be possible to provide you with some extra non-contact time in order to ensure that everything is in order. In some schools, particularly small ones, the English subject leader may also have management responsibilities as well as having other subject areas to co-ordinate. For these individuals, inspection may prove to be even more stressful, but it is worth remembering that the more organised you are about the process, the easier it will be to manage.

Some co-ordinators find themselves in the position of taking over the area of English shortly before an inspection when there is much to do in terms of putting policies in place. There would be little point in devising hurried policies simply for the sake of the inspection. These would be very unlikely to reflect practice in school. Rather, the co-ordinator should take a deep breath, make an immediate action plan and impress the inspection team with the clear-headed vision with which she has approached the task of reviewing the English curriculum! In the weeks leading up to the inspection, the co-ordinator should make an immediate start on the action plan and do what she can before the inspection team arrives. Once the inspectors are apprised of the situation, they may make judgements about the overall management of the curriculum co-ordination by the senior management team rather than criticise the new English subject leader for the lack of development in the English curriculum.

An essential point to bear in mind is that the inspection team will not be expecting perfection – it doesn't exist! There is always room for improvement in any situation. It is more important to convince them that there is a definite plan for the development of the English curriculum and you are absolutely clear about where the school is in relation to that plan. It doesn't matter how far along that plan you are as long as the inspectors can see evidence of the school actively working towards it.

It is advisable to scrutinise the curriculum vitaes of the inspection team well in advance in order to ensure that you are satisfied with the range of expertise offered. One co-ordinator has stated that she was very unhappy because English in their nursery and infant school was being inspected by an inspector whose background had been in secondary science. There are obvious implications regarding an inspector's subject knowledge here. The expertise of inspectors is particularly important if you work in a school with a large number of bilingual pupils. Teaching bilingual pupils in the early years is a specialised skill and if you are being inspected by someone who does not have an understanding of the development of English as an additional language you could be seriously misrepresented in the final report. If you are very unhappy about the experience and expertise of some members of the team you could ring up OFSTED and make a complaint.

The English co-ordinator can also seek support and advice from other quarters. If you have contacts with a school who has undergone an inspection, it might be worth asking the language co-ordinator if they would talk with you about their experience so that you can be prepared for the process. Obviously no two inspection processes are exactly the same but there may be some pointers or advice that may prove useful. Similarly, it is advisable to contact the LEA link inspector for the school in order that he or she may provide specific advice and guidance which meets the needs of your school. The LEA advisory team for English may also be able to offer some help if it proves necessary, although it is worth noting that LEA teams are often stretched supporting the link schools that they themselves are allocated.

So what are the inspectors looking for with regard to English? It will be necessary for you to acquaint yourself with the most recent edition of the *Framework for Inspection*. Examine each of the statements relating to English in the framework in order to assess how well the school is performing against each one. If the school is under-performing in a particular area of English, be clear about why and what you are doing to improve the situation. If you have been fulfilling your role as subject leader as outlined in this book so far, you will not need to worry. Much of the paperwork will be in place and you will be absolutely clear about what needs to be done to improve the teaching and learning of English in the school and how you plan to address the areas of weakness.

Before the inspectors arrive, you will be asked to send various documents to them in order to provide them with a range of information about the subject. You should send:

- *Policies and schemes of work.* If these are not completed, you need to indicate that they are still in progress and what needs to be done in order to complete them.

- *Information for parents.* If you do provide booklets for parents which give information about reading and writing in school, send these to the inspection team. They will indicate the quality of school–parent liaison.

- *Evidence from tests.* You will need to send any results of tests such as baseline assessments, SATs and reading tests. These can be accompanied by any 'value added' information that you or your LEA can provide. Quantitative data, such as test results, should always be contextualised by more qualitative data in order for them to be interpreted as accurately as possible.

You may wish to send other relevant information, such as examples of recording formats for English, reports of events in school such as Book Week, photographs of parent workshops, audio and video tapes of drama events – the possibilities are many! Send off anything that you think will provide information about the school's achievements in English. One co-ordinator relates how he deliberately sent off additional information:

> There isn't enough time to tell the Inspector doing English everything that you want to. You keep on thinking, 'I must tell him that.' So, for example, the thing that the two of us had worked on for EAL, we sent a copy of the scheme we produced. Now they didn't ask for that, but it was the thing we had that we thought would impress them.

Any information in relation to the identification of and provision for children with Special Educational Needs in literacy and oracy is important to submit. Other information sent to the inspectors by the head will include the School Development Plan and the School Prospectus. These will include sections relating to English. The inspector for English will make himself or herself familiar with the place of English within the SDP. They will also be keen to ascertain how resources are managed and how money for English has been spent. You may keep an account of the English budget yourself. If so, send that off as well.

Finally, if you have any information relating to a review you have carried out of the quality of the teaching of English throughout the school, or material which demonstrates how you have used information gained from a scrutiny of children's work to make judgements about continuity and progression in English, send that off also.

In the weeks preceding the inspection, you will need to ensure that everything is in as good an order as it can possibly be. Here is a checklist:

- Are all the documents in order? Are staff familiar with all of them?

- Do the resources for English look well presented and ordered?

- Have all the staff got their planning and assessment for English in order?

- Are the portfolios of children's English work, collected for moderation processes, organised?

The last point is one that needs thinking about well before the inspectors arrive. The English inspector will ask to see a range of work for each year group in school. Usually, this will be looked at on the evening of the first day. The class teachers need to choose three children from each year group from across the ability range and then collect together samples of their work in English. This should be done in conjunction with the English subject leader. You need to ensure that the portfolios present the full range of work included in the English curriculum; for example, include non-narrative as well as narrative and writing. Place first drafts and subsequent drafts in alongside finalised pieces also. Include work that relates to the areas of speaking and listening and reading, not just writing. Ensure that you provide evidence of English work in ICT. The inspector will be looking for progression and continuity across the year groups as well as evidence of attainment. The portfolios should also demonstrate evidence of the good quality feedback the teachers give to children, with a range of constructive comments that help children to improve their work.

It is inevitable that the process of devising policies and schemes of work will have generated lots of paperwork along the way. There may also be other bits and pieces of paperwork around that may be useful to keep together; for example, notes on INSET sessions attended, particularly extended LEA or university-based courses. Outlines of staff meetings you have run on English could be included and any notes or inputs made by external contributors to the English curriculum such as advisers or advisory teachers. It may be useful to put these together in a folder so that you have them handy for inspection week. A co-ordinator outlined the file he put together:

> I prepared a file for the inspection that contained policies, schemes of work, drafts of every stage of everything...I took a photocopy of the piece of paper that we had compiled when we looked at our range of reading schemes and we made judgements as to what we were going to adopt. It is not an official document. It's not in anybody's policy folder or anything like that, I am the only one with a copy of it so I put it in my folder. When the inspector asked, 'How do you use the Oxford Reading Tree?', my answer was supported by the paper in the file. I made the file with a view to the inspector coming through the door at 12 o'clock and saying 'Have you got anything from the time the staff made the policy on...?' In a sense it contained the best bits of paper that I thought showed that we had worked hard and met their criteria...

In some schools, a member of the governing body has the responsibility for liaising with the English subject leader in order to oversee the

English curriculum. As one governor who fulfils this role has said:

> It keeps at least one of the governors in touch with what is happening in the school with regard to the literacy curriculum. I go in about once every half term and have a chat with Sue, the English co-ordinator. She tells me what has been happening and I ask her about various aspects of the curriculum. Other governors are linked with other curriculum areas. This liaison means that one governor has detailed knowledge about one area of the curriculum, standards and so on.

The recent report of the Literacy Task Force (1997) mentions 'dedicated literacy governors' (p. 6) and asks LEAs to include governors on any training conferences which outline new initiatives in the teaching of literacy. Once you have identified a specific governor for English, you will need to keep her or him informed of issues relating to the teaching and learning of the subject in school. You should invite the governor into the school in order to see what happens with regard to English. And, of course, he or she could be invited to any major events relating to the English curriculum such as book weeks and parents' evenings.

If you have everything prepared and in place in the weeks before inspection, it will lessen the stress on you and your colleagues. Of course, there would be no need at all to spend hours preparing for inspection if you had achieved that level of organisation normally. But the reality is, as we have stressed, that the English curriculum is constantly developing and therefore it would be impossible to have everything neatly and tidily packaged ready for inspection at any minute. We would want to advise against, however, a model which leads to hours of intense preparation for an inspection and then a complete relaxation after it, with little curriculum development occurring for some time. The ideal process is one which builds upon the continuing work of the co-ordinator so that there is not a last minute rush, but a steady gathering together of material which documents the hard work and progress which has occurred over time. You will, in this case, be more than ready to meet the inspector for English.

The week of the inspection

Very early on in the inspection process, usually on the first evening, the inspector for English will examine a range of work. The previous section indicated the sorts of things you should include. This is an opportunity to impress the inspector with the range and quality of your school's work in English.

During the inspection, the inspector who has the responsibility for English will interview you. As Anwyll (1995) points out, the interview:

> is not a major interrogation but an opportunity for the inspectors to clear up anything that they weren't sure about in the pre-inspection documents, to

explore further issues on which there was little information and to give co-ordinators a chance to explain or point out other relevant matters.

(Anwyll, 1995, p. 5)

They will probably ask you the types of questions listed below. We would like to point out that these are not questions derived from any official document produced by OFSTED, they are simply questions which we feel they are likely to ask, albeit phrased differently. They are included in order to provide you with a rough guide to the issues which may arise in your interview. Of course, there will be questions specific to your school which we cannot pre-empt here. However, you may find it useful to prepare answers to some of these questions beforehand so that you feel more confident about the interview. You can always refer to your notes during the interview if you need to remind yourself of particular details.

Standards of achievement in the subject

These questions are intended to ascertain whether or not you have a clear grasp of the levels of attainment in English across the school, and how this level of attainment compares both locally and nationally. You need to be clear about how any 'value added' formula is worked out. Have teacher assessments, test and SATs results in front of you as you answer these questions.

- What is your perception of the standards being achieved in English?

- How does it compare with local/national standards?

- What evidence do you have for your assessment of the attainment of children?

Monitoring and evaluation

Your answers to these questions can be supported with evidence, e.g. assessment and recording evidence, notes of peer observations (which should be anonymous), notes from relevant staff meetings, portfolios of work, language audits, etc.

- How do you monitor the English curriculum? How do you know if the policies and schemes of work are being adhered to?

- What methods do you have for evaluating how well the school's aims in English are being achieved?

- How is this evaluation fed back to the whole school?

Policies and schemes of work

The 'inspection' file we mentioned earlier may come in useful here. It could contain any drafts and 'work in progress' as well as other relevant documents.

- When were your policies and schemes of work devised?
- How were they devised?
- What processes are there for their review and development?
- How do you and your colleagues approach English work across the curriculum?

Planning

Again, you need to provide evidence of the process you use to ensure progression and continuity across the English curriculum. For example, if you collect in colleagues' medium-term English planning in order to check it over, demonstrate how this is done and how you give feedback.

- What is the system for the long-term, medium-term and short-term planning of English? (This question will be relevant whatever system of planning you use, including the National Literacy Project.)
- What is your role in the planning of English by individual teachers?

Assessment

There is a variety of types of evidence you can present here: assessment formats and any drafts, examples of completed ones, examples of written reports to parents on attainment in English, children's self-assessment in English.

- How is assessment undertaken in each of the ATs?
- How does this relate to the planning process?
- When, and how, did you develop the current recording formats?
- What support is given for teachers in the reporting of English to parents?
- What is the process of self-assessment in English for children?
- What use is made of test results, e.g. SATs, reading tests?

Teaching and learning strategies

The inspector may want to find out what role you have played in supporting staff in the adoption of relevant teaching and learning strategies for children. For example, have you provided opportunities to explore and discuss ways of organising classes to support work on group discussions, or sustaining independent work? Have you explored the issue of when to use ability and mixed ability groups in English work? Have you discussed ways of sustaining and supporting a number of simultaneous activities, and indeed agreed on the optimum number of sustainable activities occurring at any one time? These are key issues which you will need to have addressed.

- Have you led any initiatives on the development of teaching and learning strategies for English in the school?
- How do you monitor the use and effectiveness of various teaching and learning strategies for English?

English as an additional language

If children in your school speak English as an additional language, the inspector will want to ensure that, as far as possible, the school is meeting their needs. They will want to clarify your role in this process also.

- How are the needs of children who speak English as an additional language identified and met?
- How do you liaise with bilingual support staff and class teachers on this matter?

Special Educational Needs

You will need to co-ordinate with the SENCO in your school in order to ensure that you have all the relevant information which will help you to answer any such questions.

- How are the needs of children with SEN in relation to English identified and met?
- How do you liaise with the SENCO, class teachers and any SEN support staff on this matter?

Staff development

Evidence of staff meetings and internal and external INSET will be useful here. You could also present any relevant information from language audits completed in the past.

- How are the needs of staff in relation to the English curriculum identified?

- How are these needs met?
- How is staff development monitored?
- How do you use external agencies?

Resources

An outline of how you have managed the budget will be useful. The inspector may also be interested in how English is allocated money – a set amount every year, or specific amounts for areas of priority?

- How do you manage resources for English?
- How are the resourcing needs for English identified?
- How do you organise use of the library?

Your role

Because the English subject leadership is such a central role in school, you need to ensure that you are able to impress upon the inspector that you have a secure grasp of the subject and that you are confident in helping other members of staff to develop their subject knowledge in English. This does not mean that you need to have a degree in English, although of course you have an advantage if that is the case. Nevertheless, you should be able to demonstrate that you are up to date with recent developments in the subject, e.g. through INSET, reading of professional journals or award-bearing courses.

- How long have you been the English subject leader?
- What training have you had for the role?
- What relevant qualifications or experience have you got in the subject?
- How do you ensure that you keep up to date with the subject?

External liaison

Evidence here could consist of reports and materials used in parent workshops, booklets to parents, relevant press cuttings, the school booklet, etc.

- How do you communicate issues relating to English to:
  - parents
  - governors
  - LEA
  - any other relevant agencies?

It is always the best policy to be open and honest in the interview. If you do try to present an overly rosy picture that does not reflect reality, inspectors will pick up on the areas of discrepancy between your answers and what they have observed. They may also ask other members of staff about things that you have mentioned and will take note of any inconsistencies. If there are areas of the English curriculum that need to be developed, then be honest about it. Let the inspector know that you are well aware of it too, and inform him or her of your strategies for improving it. If there are areas to be developed, these should already have been identified in the School Development Plan. All you need to do is remind the inspector that they are specified there and that everything is under control.

The final report

Towards the end of the week in school, the English inspector will have a brief meeting with you to report back his or her main findings. This may take the form of a very informal chat after school one day. If you have been undertaking your role as subject leader in a conscientious and careful way, you will be well aware of the issues relating to the teaching and learning of English in your school. There should, therefore, be no surprises for you in this feedback or the final report that the school receives. The inspectors may have placed a different emphasis on certain areas than you yourself have, or may have been more incisive in their analysis of weaknesses, but basically their report should reflect your own analysis of the situation. If the inspector does make a judgement that you disagree with, it would be important to inform the senior management team of this straight away. You need to make clear to the head why you disagree with a particular judgement so that the head can be well prepared in order to raise it with the Registered Inspector at the appropriate time. This will be in the verbal report given to the senior management team at the end of the inspection period. A school cannot challenge the validity of an inspection team's judgement but they can challenge the evidence upon which that judgement was based. You will need to prepare material concerning the evidence base in question so that the head can present this to the Registered Inspector.

You need to evaluate the comments made in the feedback in the light of your experience and wider knowledge. For example, if you work in a school with a large number of bilingual pupils, the report may state that the children are not achieving the national norms in English. There is no need to panic at this statement. It does not mean that you are necessarily underestimating the abilities of the children and not pushing them far enough. Of course, that could be the case, but it is unlikely that every school which teaches bilingual pupils is under-achieving in this way. You may have been inspected by someone who does not understand the issues involved in teaching bilingual pupils, or even someone who is not clear about the principles and processes of acquiring an additional language.

Do not focus solely on the negative aspects of the report! It is easy to say that, when in fact those particular paragraphs seem to leap off the page to you. But amongst the areas identified for further development, there will be areas which the inspectors have identified as working successfully. Ensure that these are pointed out to staff, parents and governors.

We include below a **fictitious report** based on our extensive reading of the English sections of OFSTED reports. It is not intended to bear any resemblance to any actual school, but is provided simply to indicate the types of comments that are generally made.

English

Standards of achievement in English are in line with national averages throughout the school. At Key Stage 2, there is evidence of under-achievement in speaking and listening, relative to prior attainment, in a small number of pupils. Lessons observed were satisfactory or good in more than 90 per cent of lessons observed in Key Stage 1 and satisfactory or good in 75 per cent of lessons observed in Key Stage 2.

Teachers' planning is generally of a good standard, with the English subject leader taking an effective role in ensuring continuity and progression across the school. Although planning for speaking and listening is well developed at Key Stage 1, this is not so at Key Stage 2. Although there were examples of effective use of structured group discussions and debates in one class, generally pupils have insufficient opportunities to make use of talk to extend their learning. Drama is integrated well into the curriculum at Key Stage 1 but is not extended to ensure progression throughout Key Stage 2.

Reading is given appropriate emphasis with well-resourced areas in each classroom, stocking a wide range of fiction and non-fiction texts. Children are allowed to make constructive use of these areas in Key Stage 1. At Key Stage 2, there is not enough emphasis on structuring children's work with information texts in order to further develop their information-retrieval skills. A strong emphasis is placed on the development of a basic sight vocabulary and a knowledge of phonics at the same time as encouraging children to use a range of cues when reading. Reading records do not at present reflect the range of children's reading skills and need to be developed further. Scheme and non-scheme materials are integrated well. A home–school reading scheme is well developed with supplementary reading materials and regular seminars for parents.

Writing is generally satisfactory, with evidence of a common approach to the process of writing. The planning, drafting and editing process is well established although in some classes at Key Stage 1 this could be developed further. Teachers plan a range of forms, purposes and audiences for writing although these are not always communicated satisfactorily to pupils. An effective spelling policy is evident throughout the school and is an area of strength. Handwriting is not approached consistently throughout the school.

The English subject leader is highly committed and has worked hard to develop policies and schemes of work that reflect the work of all the staff. They have managed the successful introduction, monitoring and evaluation of a literacy hour. The moderation of written work amongst staff is helping to establish consistent standards in compositional aspects and spelling, but needs extending to handwriting and punctuation. The subject leader has started a programme of curriculum evaluation but is hampered by limited non-contact time.

Reporting findings

The senior management team will feed back the draft report to staff as soon as they receive it. Staff will need some time to absorb the findings before becoming involved in major debates about the implications. After a few days the staff may feel ready to begin to respond to the report and devise action plans in order to address areas that need improvement. The parents will need to be informed. The Registered Inspector provides a summary of the inspection report for the school which is based on the 'Main Findings and Key Issues' section. When this is given out to parents, there should also be some information provided by the school which explains how they will be addressing some of the issues raised. For example, the school might want to say:

> You will see that the inspection report has said that the standards in spelling are not as high as they should be. We are working hard to make sure that we improve the standards in this area. We know that you will join us in wanting to raise the children's achievements and we know that many of you have already started by joining in the spelling workshops we started last year. These went very well and all the parents who came said that they enjoyed them. We want to carry on with these and extend them to Thursday morning as well. We also want to invite you to a special parents' evening we are having on how to help your child with spelling on....

It is useful to have a meeting in which the inspection report is presented to parents verbally. This will enable them to ask questions and ask for clarification. The school may want to provide a hard copy for each parent although many schools would find the cost of doing so prohibitive. It would also be important to provide translators for bilingual parents and the written report translated into parents' first languages if possible. Even if parents are not literate in their first language, there may be someone in the family who is.

Action plan

From the report, the school will be expected to devise an action plan. This should clearly demonstrate how the school is going to address issues which have arisen from the inspection and needs to be completed within forty days of the inspection. You will need to devise the action plan for English. As we have stated, if you have been fulfilling the role of subject leader for some time, the report should not contain any surprises. The action plan you will need to devise should look very much like the one you had before the inspection. An action plan will need to be made for every issue raised as a key concern in the report. Figure 13.1 gives an example, based on the inspection report devised above.

In the final comment from a co-ordinator, we find that the action planning stage is a time to take a cool, calm look at what is needed and not rush headlong into making rash decisions:

> We made full use of the link inspector to advise us on our action plan. The other thing I would do if I was doing it again would be asking if anybody could put me in touch with another school that had a similar 'verdict' so that I could go and see what they did. You need to not panic and have a calm look at it....If there is something along the lines of 'The school must ensure that there's continuity and progression in the teaching of spelling at Key Stage 2', that is the point at which you just get in a few sales reps and have a look at the stuff they are offering, you don't go buying too many schemes. Because at the end of the day you want something that is workable...you want something that everyone can live with for 4–6 years so to overdo it would be as bad as doing nothing at all.

The final point we wish to make is that you need to ensure that you don't get the inspection process out of proportion. If you focus on developing the English curriculum in school to its fullest potential in order to achieve the highest possible standards of work, and ensuring that you have plenty of evidence to demonstrate this work, then you will have nothing to worry about. You can then use the inspection itself as a checking device for your own monitoring and evaluation. If the inspection report presents a wildly different picture from your analysis, you will need to re-evaluate your monitoring and evaluation procedures. If, however, the inspection reflects your own feelings and ideas then you can congratulate yourself on the effectiveness of your role!

If the inspection report finds that there are serious weaknesses in the teaching and learning of English in the school then you will need to take immediate action. It would be advisable to contact the LEA English adviser as soon as you know that this is the case (which will be at the end of the week of inspection), as well as your link inspector/adviser. They can then provide you with appropriate help in devising an action plan within the required forty-day period. In the long term, you will need to carry out a major reassessment of the English curriculum, using the model outlined in this book. And don't forget that there will be a whole range of other English specialists who will be able to help in the process of rebuilding the curriculum – literacy consultants, HE institutions and other English co-ordinators in the area.

It would be important, in these circumstances, to remain calm and reassess the whole picture with the help of others. If you have been the English co-ordinator in the school for some time, you will obviously feel a strong sense of responsibility. There would be little point in entering a

Aims	Success criteria	Tasks	Timescale	Action by	Cost
To review the speaking and listening policy at Key Stage 2	• Revised speaking and listening policy at Key Stage 2	• Staff meetings • Working party address the issue immediately	November '97 – January '98	Subject leader Working party Report to all staff	
To review the planning process for speaking and listening at KS2	• Improved planning of speaking and listening at KS2	• Staff meeting on planning oracy • Follow-up meeting to check progress	November/ December 1997	All staff, follow up meeting KS2 staff	
To develop use of oracy across the curriculum at KS2	• Improved standards in S&L across the curriculum at KS2	• INSET sessions • Subject leader/ demonstrations • Meeting of subject co-ordinators – look at recent SCAA documents	January to Feb. 1998	Subject leader KS2 staff Subject co-ordinators	Buying in trainer – £300
To extend use of debates and structured group discussions across KS2	• Improved standards in S&L at KS2	• Staff released to observe sessions in some classrooms where structured discussions and debates are used well	February 1998	Head to organise rota of staff release	£200 for supply costs to release staff
To develop staff expertise and confidence in the teaching of drama	• Staff feel more confident and equipped to teach drama • Drama work more consistently included in the planning of year teams	• INSET session • Drama files developed which contains a range of activities and lesson plans for staff	March 1998	Subject leader	LEA adviser – £140 for day.

Figure 13.1. Action plan for raising standards in speaking and listening at Key Stage 2

round of self-recrimination and blame – you must move forward. It may be that you have not been supported sufficiently in the role. If this is the case, then discuss with senior management the possibility of having more non-contact time in which to carry out your duties. You may need further training in some aspects of the role. There may be some relevant training in the area, such as the national training for subject leaders which is in the planning stage at the moment. Ask your LEA English adviser for details. It would be useful to find a 'mentor' – an English co-ordinator in another school who has had much experience and can provide you with support and guidance. This would also provide you with an opportunity to see how English is being taught successfully elsewhere. Any or all of these options would be better than simply giving up the role and moving to another subject. You would still need guidance in the generic skills necessary as a co-ordinator and you would also have to cope with the demands of developing sufficient subject knowledge for that area.

Chapter summary

This chapter has outlined the processes involved in preparing for and undergoing an inspection. We have stressed that the inspection process should be managed in such a way that it becomes a useful tool for checking self-evaluation. We have not dealt with issues relating to the worst possible scenario, that is, the school being assessed as being in need of special measures. We feel that that is beyond the scope of this book and would refer subject leaders to their LEA for appropriate advice and support. We would hope that some of the processes described in this book would be an integral part of the recovery process.

Whatever the outcome of the inspection, it is clear that the English subject leader has a major role to play and should ensure that she has as much support as possible. Inspection is a difficult time for all staff involved in it. Make sure that you have support mechanisms in place, both in school and outside. If you are calm and organised, you will have a positive effect on other staff who may feel more nervous than you. And once it is all over, you can get on with the business of developing the English curriculum and continuing to improve your skills as subject leader. Surviving the inspection process is one more step along this road!

Conclusion

For many who read this book, the role of the English subject leader may appear to be overwhelming. There are so many responsibilities and so little time, how can the role be made more manageable? In this conclusion, we discuss some ways in which the co-ordinator might begin to address this very real concern. We look at the issue of time management and the support that can be gained from the head. We conclude by suggesting that, for most of us, having a perfect grasp of the role is impossible.

Managing the role

Many co-ordinators get very little, if any, non-contact time. How can they possibly achieve the level of work that is suggested by this book? We would like to stress that a co-ordinator cannot achieve levels of very good practice across every area at once. That would not be feasible. Rather, we would expect most colleagues to focus on areas of priority and work to bring those up to a satisfactory level rather than tackling everything all at once. For example, if schemes and policies are in place in your school but there has been little work done on monitoring and evaluation, then that is the place where you need to start. Therefore part of this book should be referred to when necessary rather than worked through in a sequential manner. You will need to set yourself a personal long-term action plan (see Figure 3.3 in Chapter 3). Be realistic about this. Part of this action plan will concern work in school and some aspects will be related to your own needs as a co-ordinator. Both are important.

Part of deciding on priorities for the action plan will involve assessing what the major needs of the school are. If the development of the English curriculum is a priority area in your school, you need to negotiate with the head for some non-contact time. If this is not forthcoming then you need to make it clear to the senior management team that your action plan will be realistic. If you haven't got the time, your action will be limited. Be careful of committing yourself to so much work that you cannot possibly successfully complete it. This will lead only to feelings of inadequacy. The balance between striving for the highest possible standards and overstretching yourself is difficult to achieve, but achieve it you must if your work as a co-ordinator is to be an exciting challenge, rather than a difficult burden. If subject leaders are to develop their roles effectively, the issue of non-contact time needs to be recognised as a need nationally. Subject leadership is such a key issue in terms of school development that this review of the role is long overdue.

There has been some interesting work on the types of headteachers you may work with and the support they may give co-ordinators (Stow, 1989). Whiteside (1996) suggests that it is critical for the co-ordinator to identify the views that senior management hold of their role and their part within the school management culture (p. 35). We suggested in Chapter 1 that this is discussed in the initial interview for the post of co-ordinator. We also feel that every co-ordinator should have a yearly review of their role with the head or member of the senior management team. In this yearly review, the definitions and parameters of the role should be discussed, evaluated and if necessary renegotiated. This would be an opportunity to state your needs in terms of non-contact time. If you work in a school which appears to give little acknowledgement to the role of subject leader, we suggest that it is actually raised as an item at a staff meeting. The staff could be asked to brainstorm the different aspects of the role of the co-ordinator. Once colleagues (including the head) were aware of the scale of the role, it could be suggested that the school had an overall policy relating to subject leadership so that the issue becomes depersonalised. If the policy states that there should be non-contact time according to the priority the subject is given in the School Development Plan, then it is much easier to ask for this on an individual level.

Apart from the issue of negotiating non-contact time, how can an English subject leader manage her time effectively? There are no easy answers to this problem. There is too much to do and not enough time to do it in. Setting short-term as well as long-term priorities helps. Your long-term action plan will help you to get things into a broader perspective. However, we also feel that time in the short term needs to be allocated to tasks according to immediate priority levels. Having a list of 'Must do this week/should do this week/would like to do if possible this week' helps. You are most unlikely to get around to the last category! That will no doubt rise to the top of the list as an essential before long. Having a particular day of the week in which you try to get jobs done relating to your role as English subject leader might also help. For example, you might decide that every Wednesday for an hour and a half after school, you are going to get through your list of priorities. Of course, life is not that simple and there are weeks when you will be interrupted or unable to devote the time to the role of co-ordinator. However, simply having this as a regular slot helps. It is useful to let other members of staff know that this is your day to carry out co-ordination tasks so that they either leave you alone or save their queries concerning the English curriculum until then.

One co-ordinator who adopts a similar approach has a small noticeboard in her classroom where she lists the tasks she is working on. The head and other colleagues can, at a glance, see her workload. If she is asked to do more, the co-ordinator refers colleagues to the noticeboard where the new task is added to the bottom of the list!

Apart from the task of allocating non-contact time, there are also a number of other ways in which a headteacher can prove to be helpful or otherwise to the English subject leader. It is not possible to deal with all of the possibilities here (for a more thorough discussion, see Stow, 1989). Instead, we outline a few of the key issues that have occurred frequently in our work with co-ordinators.

Inability to delegate

Some co-ordinators have described how they are working with a head who actually wants to do most of the development work in English themselves. This can lead to much frustration, as the co-ordinator wants to get on with the job but is not left alone to do it. The head wants to see everything the co-ordinator produces before it is acted upon or insists on changing things agreed by a working party. What can the subject leader do to manage this situation? We suggest that one way forward would be to negotiate with the headteacher to share parts of the role of the English subject leader. The head would be asked to take responsibility for a particular area; for example, that of assessment, recording and reporting in English. The tasks each had to do could be negotiated and written down – this could be a mechanism for ensuring that you were left to do the jobs you had been allocated.

Too high expectations

Some headteachers are so good at delegating tasks to the subject leader that in fact the subject leader feels overwhelmed by the amount of work that needs to be done. If this is the case, you need to be assertive and outline just how much you feel you can get done within the time you have. Insist on having a yearly review. If you have been keeping a journal, you can provide this as evidence of the workload your role involves. If you don't keep a journal, a long list will do! This is likely to be a school-wide problem and so you may need to talk with the rest of the staff about the issue and approach the head as a team to discuss realistic expectations.

Uninterested in your work

Some co-ordinators feel undervalued because the head appears to take little interest in their work and provides very little feedback. If this is the case for you, you need to ensure that you get support from other quarters: other members of staff or co-ordinators from other schools. But the problem is not going to go away unless you discuss your feelings with the head. This is obviously difficult to do but may be productive in the long run. Heads may not even realise that they are failing to boost the morale of their staff. Often we can prompt reflection in someone else by providing a good role model, so praising staff for their work in English in a staff meeting (in the presence of the head, of course!) may prompt your headteacher to do something similar. Everyone needs feedback and positive support in order to raise their self-esteem and feel better about their work. Adults are no different from children in this respect!

Further professional development

You will develop many skills in your role as a co-ordinator. It is important that these are acknowledged and utilised to full advantage. There are now many opportunities for accredited professional development courses that have work-based elements in them. You may be able to gain some credits for a Masters degree, for example, by carrying out tasks related to your role as subject leader. This work will no doubt involve reflecting on your role and relating your practice to relevant research and theory.

You may want to begin the work of reflecting on your role before enrolling on a professional development programme. This work could then be put forward on application and may receive some prior accreditation. This could reduce the actual work needed to be undertaken as part of the course. It would also prove very beneficial to your role in the meantime.

Keeping a journal in which you note down the activities you are undertaking and your reflections on them would be a start. These entries should not be descriptive. You need to demonstrate that you are able to synthesise and evaluate events in order to improve practice. You could develop a portfolio which provides a range of evidence of the work you have undertaken as a co-ordinator and demonstrates that you can reflect carefully upon this work. The portfolio could include such evidence as:

- examples of schemes, policies, records, booklets devised
- action plans
- minutes of working party meetings
- journal extracts detailing events, reflections on processes
- photographs of displays, children's work
- evaluations of staff meetings you have planned and delivered
- comments on reading you have undertaken relating to the role of subject leader.

At the present time, it is not clear how the National Professional Qualification for Subject Leaders will develop. However, when such a qualification is available, if you have already started the work of reflecting upon and evaluating your role you will be more than ready to undertake such a course.

We would also like to encourage co-ordinators to develop the reflective aspect of their roles by undertaking research and writing. Again, there may be a course run by a higher education institute which would be useful to undertake. Research is a vital aspect of the process of finding out about what is happening in order to find ways of improving it. And if you have carried out a small research project, or developed curriculum materials, or planned a successful event relating to the English curriculum, why not write about it for a professional journal? Journals welcome articles from practising teachers. In this way you will be able to disseminate your excellent work as well as build up the portfolio of skills developed in your role as English subject leader.

Ultimately, it is entirely up to you how far your role of English co-ordinator is developed. As we have said earlier, there should be no expectation that you achieve perfection in every area outlined in this book, rather the expectation should be that you are constantly reflecting upon and evaluating your achievements as subject leader. The process of developing our skills as co-ordinators is a dynamic one and the role should be constantly evolving and responding to changes. In this sense, the co-ordinator's role runs parallel to the curriculum development which she leads in that both are concerned with a continuing process of change.

References

Abbot, C. (1994) *Reading IT.* Reading: Reading Language and Information Centre.

Alexander, R. (1992) *Policy and Practice in Primary Education.* London: Routledge.

Alexander, R., Rose, J. and Woodhead, C. (1992) *Curriculum Organisation and Classroom Practice in Primary Schools: A Discussion Paper.* London: Department of Education and Science.

Anwyll, S. (1995) Every step you take, *Language and Learning*, Jan/Feb, pp. 3–7.

Ashworth, E. (1988) *Language Policy in the Primary School: Content and Management* Kent: Croom Helm.

Barnes, D., Britton, J. and Rosen, H. (1976) *Language, the Learner and the School*, Harmondsworth: Penguin.

Barrs, M., Ellis, S. and Thomas, A. (1990) *Patterns of Learning: The Primary Language Record and the National Curriculum.* London: CLPE.

Barth, R. (1990) *Improving Schools from Within: Teachers, Parents and Principals Can Make the Difference.* San Francisco: Jossey-Bass.

Barton, R. (1994) *Literacy: An Introduction to the Ecology of Written Language* .Oxford: Blackwell.

Bell, L., and Rhodes, C. (1996) *The Skills of Primary School Management.* London: Routledge.

Bennett, N. and Carre, C. (eds.) (1993) *Learning to Teach.* London: Routledge.

Bolton, E. (1985) Assessment: putting the horse before the cart, *Times Educational Supplement*, 22 November.

Brice-Heath, S. (1983) *Ways with Words.* Cambridge: Cambridge University Press.

Bromley, H. (1997) Reading schemes for beginners, *Primary English*, Vol. 2., no. 5, pp. 28–31.

Browne, A. (1996) *Developing Language and Literacy 3–8.* London: Paul Chapman.

Brownjohn, S. (1994) *To Rhyme or Not to Rhyme?* London: Hodder Fawcett.

Campbell, R. J. *Breadth and Balance in the Primary Curriculum.* London: Falmer Press.

Campbell, R. J. (1985) *Developing the Primary School Curriculum.* Eastbourne: Holt, Rinehart and Winston.

Chambers, A. (1991) *The Reading Environment.* Stroud: The Thimble Press.

Clay, M. M. (1979) *The Early Detection of Reading Difficulties.* London: Heinemann.

Clemson, D. and Clemson, W. (1989) *A Really Practical Guide to the National Curriculum 5–11.* London: Thornes.

Coles, M. and Banks, H. (1990) *Primary INSET English: Organising and Planning In-Service Training.* Leamington Spa: Scholastic.

Corson, D. (1990) *Language Policy Across the Curriculum.* Clevedon: Multilingual Matters.

Cox, B. (1991) *Cox on Cox*, Sevenoaks: Hodder & Stoughton.

Day, C., Whitaker, P. and Wren, D. (1987) *Appraisal and Professional Development in Primary Schools*. Milton Keynes: Open University Press.

Day, C., Whitaker, P. and Johnston, D. (1990) *Managing Primary Schools in the 1990s*. London: Paul Chapman.

Day, C., Hall, C., Gammage, P. and Coles, M. (1993) *Leadership and the Curriculum in the Primary School*. London: Paul Chapman.

Dean, J. (1995) *Managing the Primary School*. (2nd edn.) London: Routledge.

Dearing, R. (1994) *The National Curriculum and its Assessment: The Final Report* London: School Curriculum and Assessment Authority.

DES (1975) *A Language for Life* (The Bullock Report) London: HMSO.

DES (1985) *Education for All* (The Swan Report) London: HMSO.

DES (1989) *Planning for School Development*. London: HMSO.

Dougill, P. (1993) *The Primary Language Book*. (2nd edn.) Buckingham: Open University Press.

Fullan, M. (1982) *The Meaning of Educational Change*. Toronto, OISE Press.

Garratt, B. (1987) *The Learning Organisation*. Glasgow: William Collins.

Hannon, P. (1995) *Literacy, Home and School: Research and Practice in Teaching Literacy with Parents*. London: Falmer.

Hannon, P. and Jackson, A. (1987) *The Belfield Reading Project Final Report*. Rochdale: Belfield Community Council.

Hargreaves, D. and Hopkins, D. (1991) *The Empowered School: the Management and Practice of Development Planning*. London: Cassell.

Hester, H. (1990) Stages of English, in M. Barrs, S. Ellis, and A. Thomas (1990) *Patterns of Learning: The Primary Language Record and the National Curriculum*. London: CLPE.

HMI (1987) *Quality in Schools: The Initial Training of Teachers*. London: HMSO.

HMI (1988) *The New Teacher in School*. London: HMSO.

HMSO (1991) *The Professional Training of Primary School Teachers*. London: HMSO.

Houlton, D. (1985) *All Our Languages: a Handbook for Teachers*. London: Edward Arnold.

Karavais, S. and Davies, P. (1995) *Progress in English: Assessment and Record-Keeping at KS1 & 2*. Reading: Reading and Language Information Centre.

Keating, I., Roberts I., Robertson and Shenton, L. (1996) Policy documents on the wall or in the waste bin? *Reading*, vol. 30, no. 3, pp. 35–7.

Lankshear, C. with Gee, J. P., Knobel, M. and Searle, C. (1997) *Changing Literacies*. Buckingham: Open University Press.

Lawley, P. (1997) Hit your targets, *Managing Schools Today*, February.

Lewis, J. (1997) IT and literacy: it's not a toy, *Primary English*, Vol. 2, no. 5, pp. 16–19.

Literacy Task Force (1997) *The Implementation of the National Literacy Strategy*. London: DFEE.

Louden, W. (1991) *Understanding Teaching*. London: Cassell.

Lunzer, E. A. and Gardner, K. (Eds.) (1978) *The Effective Use of Reading*. London: Heinemann.

Marsh, J., Payne, L. and Atkinson, S. (1997) Batman and Batwoman go to school: the role of popular culture in the literacy curriculum, *Primary English*, Vol. 3, no. 2.

Merchant G. (1992) Supporting readers for whom English is a second language, in M. Harrison, and C. Coles *The Reading for Real Handbook*. London: Routledge.

Merchant, G. and Monteith, M. (1997) Laptop as messenger, *Reading*, Vol. 31, no. 2.

National Curriculum Council (1989) *NCC Consultative Report (English)* NCC: London.

National Literacy Project (1997) *The National Literacy Project Framework for Teaching* (draft). Reading: NLP.

Neate, B. (1992) *Finding Out About Finding Out*. London: Hodder & Stoughton.

Nixon, J. (1992) *Evaluating the Whole Curriculum*. Buckingham: Open University Press.

Nutbrown, C. E. and Hannon, P. (eds.) (1997) *Preparing for Early Literacy with Parents: A Professional Development Manual*. Nottingham: Real Project/NES Arnold.

OFSTED (1994) *English – A Review of Inspection Findings 1993–94*. London: HMSO.

OFSTED (1995) *Guidance on the Inspection of Nursery and Primary Schools*. London: HMSO.

OFSTED (1997) *Standards in Quality in Education 1995–96: the Annual Report of HMCI of Schools*. London: The Stationery Office.

Ouston, J., Earley, P. and Fidler, B. (1996) *OFSTED Inspections: The Early Experience* London: David Fulton.

Pollard, A. and Tann, S. (1993) *Reflective Teaching in the Primary School: A Handbook for the Classroom*. London: Cassell.

Rosen, H. (1969) Introduction, in Douglas Barnes, *Language, the Learner and the School: a Research Report*. Harmondsworth: Penguin.

Russell, S. (1996) *Collaborative School Self-Review*. London: Lemos and Crane.

Sallis, E. (1996) *Total Quality Management in Education*. (2nd edn.). London: Kogan Page.

School Curriculum and Assessment Authority (1995) *Planning the Curriculum at Key Stages 1 and 2*. London: SCAA.

School Curriculum and Assessment Authority (1996a) *Boys and English*. London: SCAA.

School Curriculum and Assessment Authority (1996b) *Standardised Literacy Tests in Primary Schools: Their Use and Usefulness*. London: SCAA.

Shorrocks, D. (1993) *Implementing National Curriculum Assessment in the Primary School*. London: Hodder & Stoughton.

Shulman, L. S. (1987) Knowledge and Teaching: Foundations of the New Reform, *Harvard Educational Review*, Vol. 57, no. 1, pp. 1–22.

Shreeve, A. (1997) *IT in English: Resources for Learning*. Coventry: NCET.

Stevenson, R. J. and Palmer J. A. (1994) *Learning: Principles, Processes and Practices*. London: Cassell.

Stoll, L. and Fink, D. (1996) *Changing our Schools*. Buckingham: Open University Press.

Stow, M. (1989) *Managing Mathematics in the Primary School: A Practical Resource for the Co-ordinator*. Wiltshire: NFER-Nelson.

Street, B. (1997) The implications of the 'New Literacy Studies' for literacy education, *English in Education*, Vol. 31, no. 3, Autumn, p. 45–59.

Teacher Training Agency (1997a) *Standards for the Award of Qualified Teacher Status*. London: TTA.

Teacher Training Agency (1997b) *National Standards for Subject Leaders* (revised draft). London: TTA.

Webb, R. and Vulliamy, G. (1996) *Roles and Responsibilities in the Primary School: Changing Demands, Changing Practices*. London: Taylor and Francis.

Whiteside, T. (1996) The role of the co-ordinator auditing for development, in J. O'Neill and N. Kitson *Effective Curriculum Management*. London: Routledge.

Wray, D. and Lewis, M. (1997) *Extending Literacy: Children Reading and Writing Non-Fiction*. London: Routledge.

Wray, D. and Medwell, J. (1997) *QTS English for Primary Teachers: An Adult and Self-Study Guide*. London: Letts.

Annotated Bibliography

This bibliography is divided into sections in order to facilitate ease of reference. However, we realise that some books belong in a number of categories. We have placed texts in the section which we feel most strongly represents the content. It is not a complete list; we realise that there are many excellent books which are not here. This is intended to be a brief guide to texts which may be useful to the English co-ordinator.

General

Browne, A. (1996) *Developing Language and Literacy 3–8*. London: Paul Chapman.

This is a comprehensive overview of the teaching of literacy in the early years and throughout Key Stage 1. Browne provides some useful practical advice as well as discussing key issues in the teaching and learning of literacy in a thorough and thoughtful way.

Neate, B. (1992) *Finding Out About Finding Out*. London: Hodder & Stoughton.

A very useful book which examines the structures and registers of children's information texts and provides a range of practical ideas for using the texts in the classroom.

Wray, D. and Medwell, J. (1994) *Teaching Primary English: The State of the Art*. London: Routledge.

This is an excellent collection of individual chapters, each dealing with particular aspects of the English curriculum. There is some very useful material on assessment and the section on developing and assessing children's oral skills is most welcome.

Wray, D. and Lewis, M. (1997) *Extending Literacy: Children Reading and Writing Non-Fiction*. London: Routledge.

This book is based on work undertaken in the Exeter Extending Literacy (EXEL) project. It contains a range of useful ideas for using non-fiction to develop reading skills and demonstrates how writing frames can help children to structure non-narrative writing. There are some lovely examples of children's work.

Reading

Adams, M. J. (1990) *Beginning to Read: The New Phonics in Context*. Oxford: Heinemann Educational.
 A review of research into reading development with advice and guidance on the teaching of phonics.

Barrs, M. and Thomas, A. (1991) *The Reading Book*. London: CLPE.
 A useful overview of many areas of reading with some useful advice on working with bilingual pupils and fostering liaison with families.

Bielby, N. (1994) *Making Sense of Reading: The New Phonics and its Practical Implications*. Leamington Spa: Scholastic.
 A useful and readable look at how children learn to read which carefully integrates recent research and practice in phonological awareness. The book provides a good starting point for colleagues who need to update their knowledge about reading.

Clay, M. M. (1979) *The Early Detection of Reading Difficulties*. London: Heinemann.
 Now in its fourth edition, this book provides a detailed account of the philosophy and practice of Reading Recovery. The emphasis given to techniques for the systematic observation of young readers and writers is useful for all teachers. Colleagues working with pupils with reading difficulties will find this particularly useful.

Goswami, U. and Bryant, P. (1990) *Phonological Skills and Learning to Read*. London: Lawrence Erlbaum.
 Although the style of this book is quite academic, it is well-written and particularly worth reading. It plots the research background that informs our current knowledge of phonological awareness and the teaching of letter-sound correspondence. This text will strengthen the co-ordinator's subject knowledge and provides plenty of food for thought.

Harrison, C. and Coles, M. (1992) *The Reading for Real Handbook*. London: Routledge.
 This book contains a range of excellent chapters including work on the theory of reading, assessment and record-keeping and supporting bilingual readers.

Millard, E. (1996) *Developing Readers in the Middle Years*. Buckingham: Open University Press.
 A thoughtful discussion of key issues with regard to reading in the middle years. Millard challenges many assumptions made about the reading habits of children in the upper primary school and explores topics such as the different text choices girls and boys make.

Millard, E. (1997) *Differently Literate*. London: Falmer Press.
An excellent overview of research on reading and gender and an outline of Elaine's own research in the area. Examines the issues surrounding the underachievement of boys in literacy.

Reid, D. and Bentley, D. (1996) *Reading On! Developing Reading at Key Stage 2*. Leamington: Scholastic.
Lots of practical ideas for extending beginning reading. Contains a useful section on group reading.

Riley, J. (1997) *The Teaching of Reading*. London: Paul Chapman.
A very useful book which includes a summary of the debates over the approaches to the development of reading skills. Riley includes work from her own research which throws further light onto the reading process.

Writing

Browne, A. (1993) *Helping Children to Write*. London: Paul Chapman.
A comprehensive look at children's writing development. Contains useful advice on providing a stimulating writing environment, assessment and biliteracy.

Clay, M. (1975) *What Did I Write?* London: Heinemann Educational.
A classic introduction to children's early writing development. Some lovely examples of children's writing.

Hall, N. (ed.) (1989) *Writing With Reason*. London: Hodder & Stoughton.
A lovely collection of essays which capture the energy and excitement involved in encouraging young authors. Some good examples of children's writing.

Littlefair, A. (1991) *Reading all Types of Writing*. Milton Keynes: Open University Press.
This book provides a clear assessment of the reading demands made by different kinds of texts. It looks at the educational implications of genre and register and provides important theoretical perspectives that will inform classroom work.

Mudd, N. (1994) *Effective Spelling: A Practical Guide for Teachers*. London: Hodder & Stoughton.
A clear and comprehensive guide to the teaching of spelling. Contains some useful advice for classroom activities.

National Writing Project (1989) *Becoming a Writer*. London: Nelson.
Useful overview of the stages of early writing development. It provides clear guidelines for creating a stimulating writing environment and fostering the development of the emergent writer.

National Writing Project (1990) *A Rich Resource: Writing and Language Diversity*. London: Nelson.

An excellent introduction to the issues related to bilingual writers. Richly illustrated with examples of children's writing.

National Writing Project (1990) *What are Writers Made of? Issues of Gender and Writing*. London: Nelson.
Another excellent publication resulting from this important national project. Clear and comprehensive look at the influence of gender on attitudes to writing and writing content and style.

Peters, M. (1984) *Spelling: Caught or Taught?* London: Blackwell.
Now a classic overview of the development of spelling with some sound practical advice.

Oracy

Coldwell, E. (1991) *Storytelling*. Stroud: Thimble Press
First published in 1980, this small book emphasises the importance of storytelling in children's language development. Full of practical advice, this book will not only help to convince colleagues of the benefits of story but turn them into enthusiastic storytellers!

Grainger, T. (1997) *Traditional Storytelling in the Primary Classroom*. Warwickshire: Scholastic.
A very useful book which contains practical guidance on storytelling as well as including eight traditional tales which can be retold in the classroom.

Howe, A. (1992 *Making Talk Work*. London: Hodder & Stoughton.
Some excellent ideas for promoting talk across pairs, small and large groups. Includes a useful section on equal opportunities issues.

Norman, K. (1990) *Teaching, Talking and Learning in KS1*. London: NATE/ NOP.
Lots of practical ideas on the organisation of talk in the early years classroom.

Norman, K. (1990) *Teaching, Talking and Learning in KS2*. London: NATE/ NOP.
Another very useful book in this series on promoting oracy in the classroom. Looks at cross-curricular issues.

Wells, G. (1986) *The Meaning Makers: Children Learning Language and Using Language to Learn*. London: Hodder & Stoughton.
A classic text. Reports on the Bristol Home–School Language Project. Excellent on language acquisition, the transition from home to school, classroom talk and the importance of early experiences of literature.

Wilkinson, J. (1995) *Introducing Standard English*. London: Penguin.
A clear and accessible guide to Standard English. It looks at the relationship between spoken and written English, explores the nature of Standard English and relates it to primary and secondary teaching.

Children's Literature

Meek, M. (1988) *How Texts Teach What Readers Learn*. Bath: The Thimble Press.

Demonstrates the lessons in reading to be found in the work of significant children's authors such as Allan Ahlberg, John Burningham and Pat Hutchins.

Styles, M., Bearne, E. and Watson, V. (1992) *After Alice: Exploring Children's Literature*. London: Cassell.

Some fascinating essays on many aspects of children's literature.

Styles, M., Bearne, E. and Watson, V. (1994) *The Prose and the Passion*. London: Cassell.

More essays on children's literature with an exploration of the role of popular fiction in enticing children into reading.

Styles, M., Bearne, E. and Watson, V. (1996) *Voices Off: Texts, Contexts and Readers*. London: Cassell.

A third volume in this series containing a range of rich essays on children's literature. Includes contributions from children's writers, illustrators and publishers.

Thomas, H. (forthcoming – due in Spring 1998) *Reading and Responding to Fiction: Classroom Strategies for Developing Literacy*. Leamington Spa: Scholastic.

Lots of practical ideas for applying narrative theory to the classroom.

Media

Buckingham, D. (1993) *Children Talking Television: The Making of Television Literacy*. London: Falmer Press.

Buckingham conducted research with young children on how they interacted with and analysed television. It reveals a greater sophistication and level of analysis of the media than many teachers give children credit for.

Craggs, C. E. (1992) *Media Education in the Primary School*. London: Routledge.

Contains a useful introduction to the subject along with some good practical ideas.

Robinson, M. (1997) *Children Reading Print and Television*. London: Falmer Press.

An excellent book which compares the acts of reading televison and printed narratives and suggests that there are many links which can be made between the ways in which children interact with both.

Knowledge about language

Bain, R. (1991) *Reflections: Talking About Language.* London: Hodder & Stoughton.
> Lots of practical ideas on how to get children to reflect on language and its use. Includes a useful reflection on the teaching of grammar.

Bunting, R. (1997) *Teaching About Language in the Primary Years.* London: David Fulton.
> Contains useful summaries of key concepts and terminology in linguistics and presents a range of ideas for working with children on aspects of language at text, sentence and word level.

Carter, R. (ed.) (1990) *Knowledge about Language and the National Curriculum: The LINC Reader.* London: Hodder & Stoughton.
> A collection of interesting essays which explore a range of important issues including knowledge about language, gender differences in writing and bilingualism.

Sealey, A. (1996) *Learning about Language.* Buckingham: Open University Press.
> Contains a range of useful suggestions on using texts to work with children on various aspects of language.

Subject knowledge

Crystal, D. (1988) *Rediscover Grammar!* London: Longman.
> A comprehensive and accessible guide to the basics in English grammar.

Hudson, R. (1992) *Teaching Grammar: a Guide for the National Curriculum.* Oxford: Blackwell.
> By taking a close look at the Standard English and grammar strand in the National Curriculum, this book is useful on building up the subject knowledge of primary colleagues. There are clear explanations of what sorts of grammatical understanding are expected at each level. A few examples are used which teachers could build upon.

Wray, D. and Medwell, J. (1997) *QTS English for Primary Teachers: An Audit and Self-Study Guide.* London: Letts.
> A useful starter for auditing your own subject knowledge of English. Provides suggestions for further reading.

Assessement and record-keeping

Barrs, M., Ellis, S., Hester, H. and Thomas, A. (1988) *The Primary Language Record.* London: CLPE.
> Although you may not use the record upon which this book is based, The Primary Language Record developed by ILEA, there is still much

useful information and advice about the assessment of English.

Karavais, S. and Davies, P. (1995) *Progress in English: Assessment and Record-Keeping at KS1 & 2*. Reading: Reading and Language Information Centre.

A useful and practical guide to assessment and record-keeping in English. Underpinned by sound principles of language development and informed by current thinking in assessment, this book will be very useful to subject leaders who need to update school practices in this important area. Recording formats can be photocopied or adapted to suit the needs of your school.

Poetry

Balaam, J. and Merrick, B. (1987) *Exploring Poetry 3–8*. Sheffield: NATE.

A useful book which focuses on a few poems and provides a sequence of related activities. Includes ideas for developing response to poems through drama and art.

Brownjohn, S. (1994) *To Rhyme or Not to Rhyme? Teaching Children to Write Poetry*. London: Hodder & Stoughton.

A collection of activities which will develop children's skills in poetry writing. Will ensure a move away from acrostics!

Ellis, S. (ed.) (1995) *Hands on Poetry: Using Poetry in the Classroom*. London: CLPE.

This book provides tried and tested approaches to teaching poetry and will be important for the staff reference library. It provides good starting points for discussion and will help you to build staff enthusiasm for enjoying and writing poetry.

Merrick, B. (1991) *Exploring Poetry 8–13*. Sheffield: NATE.

Like the companion 5–8 volume (see Balaam and Merrick, above), contains ideas for work related to a number of poems.

Drama

Fleming, M. (1994) *Starting Drama Teaching*. London: David Fulton.

A useful introduction to the theory and practice of drama teaching. It is a useful overview for those new to teaching drama and contextualises teaching examples.

Readman, G. and Lamont, G. (1994) *Drama: A Handbook for Primary Teachers*. London: BBC Education.

Lots of practical suggestions and lesson plans which work beautifully in the primary classroom.

Bilingualism

There is a series of three excellent books which contain a review of relevant theory/research and practical advice:

Edwards, V. (1995) *Reading in Multilingual Classrooms*. Reading: Reading and Language Information Centre.

Edwards, V. (1995) *Speaking and Listening in Multilingual Classrooms*. Reading: Reading and Language Information Centre.

Edwards, V. (1995) *Writing in Multilingual Classrooms*. Reading: Reading and Language Information Centre.

Gregory, E. (1997) *Making Sense of a New World*. London: Paul Chapman.
Very good overview of the development of reading skills in bilingual children with some practical guidance for the classroom.

Houlton, D. (1985) *All Our Languages: a Handbook for Teachers*. London: Edward Arnold.
A practical guide for classroom practitioners with plenty of ideas on how to recognise and use the first languages of bilingual children. Also includes ideas for valuing and using the experiences of children who are learning to read and write in community languages is also included. The book draws on the work of teachers who have established a multilingual ethos in their schools.

Special Needs

Martin, T. (1989) *The Strugglers: Working with Children Who Fail to Learn to Read*. Buckingham: Open University Press.
A sensitive discussion of the issues relating to children with reading difficulties. Contains case study material which underlines the lack of self-confidence and self-esteem many children who struggle with reading feel.

Reason, R. and Boote, R. (1994) *Helping Children with Reading and Spelling*. London: Routledge.
A manual of materials for work with children who have literacy difficulties. Contains a range of useful advice and information. Valuable for informing Individual Education Plans.

Partnership with parents

Brice-Heath, S. (1983) *Ways with Words*. London: Cambridge University Press.
A classic account of literacy practices in white working class, white middle class and black communities. Suggests that schools need to value literacy experiences of all children rather than validating only the experiences of the 'mainstream' children.

Hannon, P. (1995) *Literacy, Home and School: Research and Practice in Teaching Literacy with Parents.* London: Falmer Press.
    Very useful overview of key research in the field with much practical advice and reflection on important issues in the area.

Nutbrown, C. and Hannon, P. (eds.) (1997) *Preparing for Early Literacy with Parents: A Professional Development Manual.* Nottingham: REAL Project/NES Arnold.
    This is an excellent manual for developing work on early literacy with parents. It is packed full of ideas, useful OHTs, handouts, etc., including contributions from a variety of people working in nurseries, schools and family centres.

ICT

The NCET, in association with NATE, have published a series of very useful and clearly written handbooks:

Shreeve, A. (ed.) (1997) *IT in English: Case Studies and Materials.* Coventry: NCET.

Shreeve, A. (ed.) (1997) *IT in English: Literature Review.* Coventry: NCET.

Shreeve, A. (ed.) (1997) *IT in English: Planning and Management.* Coventry: NCET.

Shreeve, A. (ed.) (1997) *IT in English: Resources for Learning.* Coventry: NCET.

Role of the language co-ordinator

Dougill, P. (1993) *The Primary Language Book.* (2nd edn.) Buckingham: Open University Press.
    Looks at various aspects of the English curriculum rather than how to manage it but does contain some useful advice and good ideas. Contains a quiz to find out how effective a co-ordinator you are!

Peel, R. and Bell, M. (1994) *The Primary Language Leaders' Book.* London: David Fulton.
    Like Dougill, is primarily concerned with working with co-ordinators on the content of the English curriculum. Its strength lies in the questions posed and tasks set which develop the co-ordinator as a reflective practitioner.

WWW

Sites on the Internet regularly change addresses (URLs) and new ones come on line all the time. At the time of going to press, these URLs are correct. Our own web site will keep up to date with many of these links, so visit there first to be on the safe side! If you have difficulty connecting to sites, you may also use the word search facility on a search engine, entering the title of the site between speech marks, e.g. 'IT and English'.

Sheffield Hallam University: The Centre for English in Education
http://www.shu.ac.uk/schools/ed/english
We provide links to a number of useful sites.

English and Media Centre
http://www.rmplc.co.uk/orgs/emedia/index.html
Contains a range of useful information and links but is focused towards upper end of primary and secondary.

Norman Crawford's English and IT Home Page
http://dspace.dial.pipex.com/town/estate/Kap38
News, resources and links – a very useful site.

English Teaching in the United Kingdom
http://www.gosford-hill.oxon.sch.uk/etuk/etuk.htm
Links to a range of interesting sites.

Centre for Language in Primary Education
Http://www.rmplc.co.uk/orgs/clpe/index.html#ContentsCatalogue
Information, news and a useful list of their excellent publications.

Reading and Language Information Centre
http://www.reading.ac.uk/AcaDepts/en/ReadLang/home.html
Based at Reading, this centre provides a range of excellent publications. Search the catalogue on-line!

National Literacy Trust
http://www.literacytrust.org.uk/
Useful addresses and contacts as well as information about current national literacy initiatives.

IT in English
http://www.ncet.org.uk/cits/english/index.html
NCET site. Extremely useful links and information on ICT.

First For Education: Subject links – English
http://www.repp.com/support/register/subject/subeng.htm
Links to a range of sites including material on language and electronic books.

Children's Literature Web Site
http://www.acs.ucalgary.cal/~dkbrown/index.html
One of the best sites on children's literature on the WWW.

Media Education Resources
http://www.oise.on/ca/~nandersen/mediaed.html
A very useful site for those of you interested in media literacy.

Professional Associations

NATE
50 Broadfield Road, Broadfield Business Centre, Sheffield S8 OXY.

UKRA
School of Education, University of Exeter, Exeter, Devon EX1 2LU.

Journals

Books for Keeps
English in Education (a NATE publication)
Journal of Research in Reading
Language and Learning
Primary English (a NATE publication)
Reading (a UKRA publication)

Other useful contacts/resources

Letterbox Library
2nd Floor
Leroy House
436 Essex Road
London
N1 3QP
Sells a range of excellent anti-racist, anti-sexist and multicultural books. Mail order only.

National Literacy Trust
Swire House
59 Buckingham Gate
London
SW1E 6AJ
Publishes annually a very useful annotated bibliography, *Guide to Books on Literacy*.

Index